BEYOND REGRET

LIVING
YOUR LIFE
PURPOSE
IN SPITE
OF
PAST
CHOICES

LAURIE DRIESEN

© 2015 Laurie Driesen

All rights reserved. No part of this book may be reproduced, stored in a retrieval system, or transmitted in any form or by any means, electronic, mechanical, photocopying, recording, or otherwise without prior written permission from the publisher.

Published by Silver Path Resources LLC
www.silverpathresources.com

ISBN 9780996203005
ISBN-10 099620301X
ISBN 9780996203012 (pbk)

Cover Design by Thauer Art Direction

Scripture taken from the HOLY BIBLE, NEW INTERNATIONAL VERSION. Copyright © 1973, 1978, 1984 International Bible Society. Used by permission of Zondervan Bible Publishers.

www.silverpathresources.com

Dedications

This book is dedicated to my mother, Polly Porter. Without her faithful Christian teaching when I was a child and her diligent intercessory prayer when I was in college, I would not have found my road to a vibrant relationship with the Lord.

I also dedicate this book to Bette Lu Schwarz. Her wise and patient counsel and her unwavering belief in me as I grew spiritually helped me to continue to press forward and get past regret.   I will always be grateful for her friendship.

Acknowledgements

As I began writing on the topic of regret, it soon turned into a bigger project than I had expected as I sensed God leading me to incorporate difficult subjects relating to regret, such as pain, suffering, free will, and God's sovereignty. God used my personal experiences and challenges to give me insight into what would be included in this book. There were many times that I woke up in the middle of the night and wrote as God impressed on my heart important concepts that are laid out in *Beyond Regret*. I attribute everything that is worthwhile and helpful in this book to the work of the Holy Spirit in my heart and mind as I wrote the chapters. I am thankful for God's personal guidance in taking *Beyond Regret* from a burden on my heart into printed pages that may help to further His mission in the world.

I would also like to thank the following people:

My sister, Linda Lijewski, for her faithfulness and diligence in carefully examining every word on each page of the book, checking flow of ideas, proofing, and editing. Her encouragement and support helped me to persevere in this project.

My husband, Neil, for his patience, understanding, and support as God has taken me through the challenging road of writing *Beyond Regret*. His sense of humor kept me smiling as I delved into writing about difficult subjects.

My daughter, Jessie, for her insights about adding information that may help young people as they deal with choices and desire to prevent future regret. I am thankful for the blessing of having her in my life, especially during years of pain, growth, and beyond.

Table of Contents

Introduction.................................... ix

Part 1 Understanding Regret.................. 1
Chapter 1   One Small Degree........................... 3
Chapter 2   The World is Full of Regret................ 8
Chapter 3   Why Me?................................... 14
Chapter 4   Anatomy of a Bad Choice................... 26
Chapter 5   Anger – The Fallout of Regret............. 35
Chapter 6   Beyond the Guilt and Shame................ 42
Chapter 7   Volcano of Regret......................... 48
Chapter 8   Those Stubborn Consequences............... 52
Chapter 9   If Only................................... 59

Part 2 Moving Beyond Regret.................. 65
Chapter 10   Repentance............................... 67
Chapter 11   Forgiveness.............................. 84
Chapter 12   The Power of the Past.................... 92
Chapter 13   The Battlefield of Choices............... 98
Chapter 14   The Process of Healing.................. 103
Chapter 15   Dealing with Ourselves.................. 109
Chapter 16   Following God........................... 114
Chapter 17   Blessings in the Midst of Pain.......... 126
Chapter 18   Prayer – Answered and Unanswered........ 134

Chapter 19 The Sovereignty of God. 145
Chapter 20 God's Gift of Grace 151

Part 3   Preventing Future Regret 163
Chapter 21 God Turns Regret Upside Down 165
Chapter 22 Sacrificing Our Future 170
Chapter 23 Busyness – The Business of Being Busy. 181
Chapter 24 Working on Our Words 193
Chapter 25 Anatomy of a Good Choice. 202
Chapter 26 The Best Answer for Regret. 216

Part 4   Living Your Life Purpose 227
Chapter 27 God's Purpose 229
Chapter 28 God's Will. 237
Chapter 29 Raw Material Crafted into Instruments 245
Chapter 30 The God of Second Chances. 248
Chapter 31 Destiny. 251
Chapter 32 Conclusion – This Very Thing. 259

Author's Note: What's next?. 265

Introduction

REGRET. THE MOMENT IN TIME *that steered me in a new direction. The decision that I wish I had never made. The path that I should never have taken. The choice seemed right at the time but later deceived me. It didn't cause pain until the consequences starting popping up on the landscape of my life. My steps followed the path, while my unfulfilled heart longed for something different. Here I am, in the life I have constructed with hundreds of bricks. Choice upon choice, brick upon brick, circumstance upon circumstance. I am living the consequences of my choices.*

Regret encompasses that sense of loss, hopelessness, and dissatisfaction that we feel today when we look back at yesterday. This book is intended to provide a path through and a way out of the mire of regret that bogs us down and keeps our heart and mind stuck in the past. In simple words, this book will provide drops of hope in the ocean of regret. This will be good news to those of you who are convinced that deep in the unchangeable record of the past, there is no hope, only painful memories and even more painful consequences that form the circumstances of the life you are living. My hope is that each page of what you are about to read will help you move beyond regret, that persistent dark cloud of the past.

Not only can you and I be free from regret but we can live out the purpose of our lives in spite of the mistakes of our past. This book will help you set out to do just that. Rather than give you steps to follow, platitudes to live by, or positive thinking skills as ways to get past the past, my intent is to take you deeper into the truths that reveal the heart of the matter of regret. Answers to the following questions are woven throughout these pages: What is regret, how do our choices lead to regret, why do we do things we'll later regret, and how do we avoid future regret? Most importantly, we'll examine how we can we live out our true purpose in life, regardless of where we are today.

We all have a desire deep within to be fulfilled and satisfied that we have accomplished the purpose for which we were born. Ephesians 2:10 says, "For we are God's workmanship, created in Christ Jesus to do good works, which God prepared in advance for us to do." Of all God's creation, we are His masterpiece! Let's face it, we will not be truly fulfilled unless and until we live out what we are created to be and do.

If you are young, you may be carrying the weight of regret from bad choices. You don't know the steps forward to ensure a better future. If you are older and living a life that has resulted from many poor choices, you want to know you haven't missed your chance to accomplish God's will for you. Wherever you are in life, whether young or old, there is still hope for you to fulfill the purpose for which God created you.

You doubt. Your mind tells you it is not possible. It's too late. So much has gone wrong in your life that you aren't able to find the sense of purpose that you seem to have missed.

But you have hope! That may be why you are reading this book. You want to know what this author might have to say about regret, God's Word, and fulfilling your purpose in life.

Whether you have doubt or hope, this book is for you. In the following pages, you will find reasons to let go of regret and press forward into a better future. You will learn what God has to say about His true purpose for your life. I pray that you are open to God's truth and willing to move beyond regret, finally!

PART 1

Understanding Regret

CHAPTER 1

One Small Degree

It doesn't take much to get off a healthy path. Imagine yourself driving a car a long distance from point A to point B. If you deviate even one degree from the straight line to your destination, you will end up in a totally different place. In fact, the longer you drive, the farther you will be from your original destination. In other words, the longer you live, the more one degree of deviation directs you further and further from your original goal.

One small degree. One seemingly insignificant decision can alter our path by one small degree. New crossroads and turns begin emerging. We make new choices from an array of fresh options. Decisions based on that one small degree of deviation can eventually take us miles away from where we hoped to be.

The circumstances of our lives are built upon sequences of decisions. Where we end up is actually the result of many choices that surfaced from the twists and turns created by other decisions. At times, it may be difficult to pinpoint one choice that caused regret. So much has happened and life has taken countless turns. Many people look back on their lives and ask the question, "How did I end up here?"

Today's pain from yesterday's choices

Circumstances today remind us that what we are experiencing is a result of something that happened in the past. Questions fill our minds about why we chose that, why we did that, why we let that thing happen. The pain is overwhelming because it's done; there is no way to change it and hope is gone. It's in the past, "c'est fini." There is finality to it – no way of going back to change what has been done. Reality tells us that it's all over and guess what? We could have done it differently. We could have made another choice, handled it differently, resolved it and changed the outcome. We could have, we should have, and we would have… if only we could do it again!

If there were just a glimmer of hope, it would keep our hearts from feeling the cold, hard blackness that comes with finality. But regret doesn't offer that sliver of hope. It doesn't offer a means of change. It doesn't offer a "do-over." Cold, hard facts can bring hopelessness and despair to a heart.

How can I define regret so accurately? Because I have made mistakes in almost every area of my life. Today I am experiencing the results of choices I made years ago. I am living through the consequences of those choices. I have felt the overwhelming pain of regret fill my mind and heart many times.

I committed my life to the Lord at age 25 and experienced a dramatic life change. I was so excited about my flourishing faith and was sure that my life would be great. I believed God would provide a husband (soon) and I would work a little bit and have a few children. I even entertained the idea that because I was so on fire with faith, God might even match me up with a pastor and I would become a pastor's wife! I thought I'd be a good wife for a pastor because I love people and I'm a nice person. My "plan" went beyond that. I imagined that at age 35, when my kids would leave in the morning for school, I'd sit down (in my beautiful home, of course) with my computer (back then, a typewriter) and write books (bestsellers).

That's not exactly what happened. At age 25, while I was so earnestly studying the Bible, seeking the Lord and waiting on His wonderful plan (rather, *my* wonderful plan), I was invited by my sister to take a vacation to Mexico. With my heart unguarded, ready to go to the ends of the earth for the Lord, I fell in love with someone I met during that trip and my whole life changed.

One degree that continued branching out until my great pre-planned life story was greatly rewritten by that one simple choice.

When I returned home, my new boyfriend and I communicated through phone calls, letters, and visits. The following year, I decided to pack my bags and move to Mexico. I spoke only a little Spanish at the time and my boyfriend didn't speak any English. My family members watched me pursue a path they considered to be impulsive, hasty, and short-sighted. In spite of the opposition, I traveled 2,500 miles away, learned another language, and married a man from a foreign country, nearly rupturing several family relationships.

If I could put 25 years into a nutshell, it would read something like this: I married three times, divorced twice, and moved across the country multiple times. I spent 20 years as a single mom dealing with the challenges of running my own business and managing a house. At one point, I suffered financially, nearly losing much of what I had worked for. During those long years of singleness I dated several men who were not right for me, resulting in years of emotional depletion while having no choice but to be the captain, maintain my ship afloat, and tread to keep my mouth above the water line.

Looking back at my life path, I am ashamed to list all of the regrettable things that have filled my road with mud, boulders, and potholes. It is fair to note that although a portion of the rocky road was caused by my choices, some of the stones were definitely tossed onto my path by choices made by others.

Now, at age 55, I'm writing a book about a very different topic than I would have chosen had I sat at my typewriter at age 35, as I had so aptly planned.

Because I am so conscious of regret in my life, my eyes have been opened to noticing many other people living with regret. Life seems to get tougher as time goes on. Mistakes get bigger. Crimes get worse. Divorces are more prevalent. Debt grows out of control. Houses are lost. Jobs are eliminated. Parents are overloaded. Choices have become countless – increasing bad choices tenfold. I believe that because of these general statistics I've just mentioned, regret has been pushed to the forefront of the minds and hearts of many people.

In your own life, you may be experiencing many regrets or one big regret. You may want to learn the best way to deal with the regret that you have. Is there a way to find a drop of hope in the ocean of regret? Is there anything good that can come from regret? Is there any way to prevent future regret? Is there any hope for this thing called "regret" that everyone claims they have at some point in their lives?

God – let's have a talk

The Bible has a lot to say about each of these areas. God has made promises that relate to our past, present, and future. Someone may ask, "Why do you have to bring God into this? Can't I just forget the past and learn positive thinking skills or follow a ten-step plan to eliminate regret?"

Regret, by definition, is painful. Any meaningful conversation about regret usually develops into a spiritual discussion about pain and suffering. We begin to ask questions that sound something like, "What is the purpose?" And more specifically, "Why did God allow this to happen in *my* life?" When people attempt to answer the hard questions relating to pain and suffering, God is usually invited (or demanded) to participate in the discussion.

God wants to be involved in our quest to move beyond regret. He created us and wants an intimate relationship with us. He is not waiting for us to "fix" ourselves and then enter into relationship with Him. On the contrary, we need to come to Him first – He will take us through the "fixing" process.

The Bible contains a rich history of imperfect people who made many mistakes. God has faithfully allowed the history of His people to be recorded in His Word so that we can come to know Him better and find hope for our lives. Apart from God's Word, we would probably stay stuck in the mire of regret. We would continue to seek out the five, seven, or ten-step plan to get rid of our regret.   Or, we can go deeper! Do you want to know what God has to say about our lives, our past, our mistakes, our pain, and our future? By digging into the Bible, we will uncover the treasure of hope that God offers us!

CHAPTER 2

The World is Full of Regret

We live in a broken world

Don't be surprised if you look back and feel a deep sense of regret over the consequences of your choices. The realization that you are on a totally different road than you hoped or planned can envelop your heart with a gnawing pain that grows into deep regret as time goes on.

How can we work so hard to live a happy, successful life and still end up with regret?

You and I are trying our best to find happiness and success within the framework of a broken world system. We are affected by our choices, the choices of others, natural disasters, sickness, disease, accidents, and a host of other factors that make up this world system in which we live. Knowing that, if we believe that we can make it through a nice, long life unscathed and with no regrets, we are definitely wrong!

The fact is that God's originally perfect creation became a fallen and sinful world. Even those who don't believe the Biblical account agree that we live in a broken world system. The evidence is too great to ignore. People and nature are not perfect. Nature is awesome and amazes us with its beauty. But at times, it seems out of control and the wrath of its storms and earthquakes creates paths of destruction. Men and women have learned and discovered ways to accomplish incredible things. Yet with his intelligence and abilities, man has also carried out unimaginable, evil acts against humanity.

How God's perfect world became broken

Most of us are familiar with the story of the fall of man in Genesis chapters 1-3. God created Adam and Eve and placed them in the perfect, beautiful Garden of Eden. God instructed that they would have freedom to eat of any tree in the garden except the Tree of Life. This is exactly the tree they were drawn to and they disobeyed the command of God. Satan convinced them to question God's Word and tempted them to eat the forbidden fruit in spite of God's command. Genesis chapter 3 explains the depth of consequences of this one choice that introduced sin into the world. The consequences impacted Adam, Eve, Satan, animals, nature, and all future mankind. Sin and death entered God's perfect creation.

Some may ask, "Why was God so severe in His punishment for eating one little piece of fruit?" Adam and Eve did more than simply eat of the forbidden fruit. They placed their wills above God's Word and broke their intimacy with God. What was the first thing Adam and Eve did after realizing they disobeyed God? They hid from God, breaking the intimate fellowship they had known with Him.

Why must we suffer today for the choice Adam and Eve made thousands of years ago in a distant land? That is a valid question. Let's consider this from a more simplified standpoint. Let's just say that Adam and Eve never sinned at all. What about the next generation? Consider their sons, Cain and Abel. Cain sinned against Abel, killing him because of jealousy and anger. Subsequent generations committed all sorts of sin that affected the lives of others. What if you would have lived in one of those early generations? What choices would you have made with the wonderful gift of free will that God gave you? Would you have been completely obedient to God and resisted all efforts of Satan to get you to disobey God's Word?

Innocent (?) little children

I find it fascinating that little children do not have to be taught how to be naughty. They just naturally are naughty. In fact, if a child is in a room filled with toys (Garden of Eden) and you say, "you may play with all of these toys, except the one in the corner (fruit of the Tree of Life)…," which toy does that child immediately head off toward to grab? The forbidden toy in the corner. Yes, with the wonderful gift of free will, we all naturally want what we think we want, want what we can't have, and think we want what we shouldn't have, even at the price of being disobedient to get it.

Does that same child need to be taught how to be good? Yes! The child tells a little white lie and his parents teach him that he should always tell the truth. The child hits another child and his parents teach him that he must not hit others.

During a recent visit with my daughter-in-law and my baby granddaughter, we spread out the baby's cute, colorful toys on the living room floor. The baby didn't want to be bothered with her toys and went straight for the items on the coffee table. Her mother redirected her and we tried again to get my granddaughter to focus her attention on the playthings that were made just for babies like her. But no, she crawled right back to the coffee table. My daughter-in-law sighed, commenting that her baby always seems to want the one thing she knows she can't have.

Someone might say, "Well, children can be naughty, but that doesn't mean they are sinners!" I would argue that man's sinful nature is inherent even in cute, innocent little babies. From the moment a baby is born, he exhibits selfishness. He cries until he gets what he wants. His needs "rule" his behavior. We were all born thinking about ourselves. Oh yes, those adorable, precious little babies that we love so much are born selfish!

PRIDE – THE SIN THAT RESIDES IN ALL OF US
In the Garden of Eden, Eve had access to all the fruit she wanted, yet she desired what was forbidden because of *pride*. She wanted to determine for herself whether the forbidden fruit was good or bad for her. God's Word wasn't good enough. She felt she was missing out on something.

Doubting God's Word is the beginning of sin and failure. It places us on a path of thinking we know better than God. If you or I were one of the first human beings on this earth, we would most likely have made the same choice that Adam and Eve did. We are enticed to sin with the same argument: God is unfair and He is holding something back from us. We don't trust that God knows best and He has given His Word for our good. No, we want to test for ourselves what life has to offer. We want to rule ourselves.

God told Adam and Eve, "On the day you eat of the fruit of the tree of knowledge of good and evil, you will die."   When Adam and Eve ate of the forbidden tree, they didn't die physically that same day, but they did die spiritually. They broke the spiritual fellowship they had with God by their disobedience. Since we are born of Adam and Eve, we inherited their sinful human nature.

Consider the child I previously described who was told not to touch the one toy in the corner. Why does the child want that one toy? Because of the sinful nature he inherited. He *naturally* wants to be his own boss, rebelling against authority.

Consider our own lives… who has been ruling our decisions and actions? If I am honest with myself, I realize that many times I rule my own life. Even as a Christian, how many times have I gone my own way out of ignorance, rebellion, or simply thinking I knew best?

God's Ten Commandments

Most people are very familiar with the Ten Commandments, even if they don't know God's Word. The Bible tells us that these commandments are "written on the hearts of men." We know this is true because throughout the history of the world, cultures have similar unspoken rules that people accept as basic truth. Stealing, murder, lying, adultery, etc. are just plain wrong in every society. Deep inside we know that it's wrong to take something that belongs to someone else and we know it is wrong to sleep with another man's wife. Men have certainly done these things, but if you ask them whether they are right or wrong, they agree that those things are wrong.

When people ask why there is so much suffering in the world, my question back would be, "If all people obeyed the Ten Commandments, how much suffering do you think would be eliminated from this world?" The reality is, when men and women are given the freedom to choose good or evil, they will do just that. They will choose good at times and evil at times. Both exist in the world because men and women are free to choose.

FREE WILL – A GIFT FROM GOD

Actually, it's our experience with the bad that shows us just how good "good" is. It's the sin in our lives that shows us clearly that we need a Savior. The bad causes us to seek the good. The good shines its light on the bad.

Free will is influenced by both good and evil. We aren't truly free unless we have choices. It is free will, the ability to choose that exposes what is inside of us. Our choices are a clear reflection of what is in our heart. Freedom of choice allows us to be our true selves. Could that be why God created free will?

I remember when my daughter was very young, yet old enough to express her own feelings and thoughts. She threw her arms around me and said, "Mommy, I love you!" My heart was warmed to the core. The feeling I had in receiving her love was so much more valuable to me than if I would have said to her, "You must love me, tell me that you love me. Now do what I say!" It's free will that makes love so precious. The person receiving love is aware that the person giving love chooses to do so. He is not coerced or forced. His love is from the heart. The giver is free to choose to give and the recipient receives a true, flawless gift that is free of coercion. A relationship is born out of freedom, not forced out of bondage. Man, God's highest creation, is free to *choose* to love and obey God.

How hard it must be for God to give mankind the gift of free will, fully knowing that some of His precious creation will reject Him. God will lose some of those He loves. But He doesn't want puppets. He won't force us to love and obey Him. He knows we won't be happy and fulfilled as puppets. We won't reach our full potential if we are limited by the strings of a puppeteer. No, God's plan for us is much higher. We are created in His image; therefore, we have much more potential than a puppet. God knows us personally and we are each created as unique individuals with gifts, talents, and abilities. When we choose to walk with God, we enjoy the blessings that He has designed for us. We can be who God created us to be. We can be in relationship with God! This is the precious treasure that God seeks in His masterpiece of creation and is the reason He has allowed both good and evil to coexist together for a time on earth.

So, before you continue reading, just allow yourself to come to the deep realization that we were given the gift of free will and are influenced by both the good and the bad that exist in this world. We are personally affected by many factors, some of which are out of our control, within the world's broken system. We are bound for mistakes, suffering, and regret just by virtue of our sinful human nature and being born into this fallen world. When we accept the fact that our choices can lead to regret, then we can get started figuring out the best way onto a healthier path. We can get on with learning about and participating in God's plan and living out the purpose for which He created each of us.

CHAPTER 3

Why Me?

*Even without all the answers to my questions,
He is the answer to my life.*

LAURIE DRIESEN

YEARS AGO, ONE MORNING I was filled with regret about where I was in my life. I spent time reflecting on my first divorce, several failed dating relationships, and my brief second marriage. I began wondering why God allowed this to happen in my life. Why didn't God intervene? Why did He allow me to get involved in situations that He knew would fail? Not only was I confused about why but it counteracted everything I believed about God. It seemed that God had fallen short of my expectations. To be honest, it made me feel that God was a stranger, no longer a familiar friend, because what He allowed absolutely made no sense to me. It didn't go along with what I perceived to be His character and it certainly was not similar to how He had worked in my life in the past. Since it was too hard for me to figure out, it was holding me on the wayside of my Christian road. I felt stuck and couldn't seem to make any progress.

Finally, I decided to take a different approach. I began to pray that God would give me *His* truth about my situation, whatever He wanted me to know or understand about it so that I could move on. I prayed that

He would guide me into knowing how to process something that I felt I would never completely understand.

Then, that same day, God gave me a revelation that drove its truth right into the depths of my heart. *Even without all the answers to my questions, He is the answer to my life.*

Do you feel like you are stuck in your Christian walk? Maybe you've had a disappointment or God did not seem to come through for you in an area of your life. You have reached the limit of your understanding of your circumstances. You don't see the way forward and your heart is not ready to say, "Even without all of the answers to my questions, He is the answer to my life."

We don't need all of the answers in order to completely trust in the Lord. We can continue to seek the answers but we don't need to wait until they come before we rely on God. Submission and trust in spite of turbulent storms show God that we know that He is in control. Questioning is our way of striving to be in control. We may be personally offended that God would allow pain in our lives. Why can't suffering and trouble stay far away, on the other side of the world, on the TV screen or in the newspaper? Why won't God keep hardship and pain from personally invading our lives?

MAN'S QUEST FOR ANSWERS

Throughout history, man has tried to answer the question, why do bad things happen to good people? Why all the suffering? We might be able to remotely understand things like war and sickness, but we can't understand the seemingly coincidental things that happen to people, causing much suffering and even death. A driver turns right instead of left and has an accident. Someone chooses the restaurant on the corner rather than the one down the street and gets held up at gunpoint. A mother believes her toddler is inside the house and answers a phone call and the child drowns in the backyard swimming pool. A motorist hits a patch of ice on the freeway and is killed by another vehicle. These are true incidents that have caused families to ask, why? People are filled with anguish and regret. For years a person may ask, "Why did I make that choice?" "Why didn't God cause the circumstances to go the other way?" "Why?"

With bigger life choices and mistakes, we may be able to trace the dotted line back to the beginning and figure out where we went wrong. One degree off the path and we kept moving, laying new decisions over the old ones, until we were off track by miles. But these small, seemingly insignificant choices that seemed harmless in the moment caused life-changing, devastating events. Regret can be almost unbearable during these times of realization that if a person would have made a different choice, life would be different altogether.

When we ask why, what we are really asking is, "Why did God allow it?" "Why did God *allow* me to take that road and experience that life-changing accident?" When terrorists crashed planes into the World Trade Center on 9/11, the question wasn't, "Why did the terrorists do such a thing?" We can answer that question, they were filled with hate and wanted to kill people, plain and simple. But the question that surfaced on that day was actually, "Why did God *allow* this to happen?" When multiple tsunamis in the Indian Ocean rose over shorelines in 2004, killing over 230,000 people, we wanted to know why! Then the scientists told us why; an undersea earthquake, which turned out to be the largest earthquake ever recorded, caused the tragedies. But their explanation was not good enough. That answer does not satiate our desperate desire to understand. Our question is spiritual, and again we cry out to the Creator of the universe and ask the futile question, "How could you let this happen?"

NOWHERE ELSE TO TURN
We attempt to rely on our own understanding of situations and events in our lives. But when we reach the end of our ability to understand, we cry out for God to answer. In effect, many times we are seeking

to pull God into our world of pain and operate on our terms. We want Him to answer our questions, fix our problem, and make life better again. When God doesn't do what we want, how do we respond? Are we willing to cling to the Lord in spite of unanswered questions? Or will we be offended when He doesn't give us what we need? Are unanswered questions a way for God to test our motives in following Him?

In John 6:41-66, Jesus' followers began to grumble and argue about His teaching. His listeners began to realize that in order to follow Jesus, they would have to give up many of their wrong beliefs and accept His teaching. When Jesus miraculously multiplied the bread and fish and fed the crowds, they wanted to crown Him as their king. But when Jesus taught them hard truths, many rejected Him. They decided to turn away and no longer follow Jesus. Aren't people much like that today? If they can't have Jesus on their own terms, they don't want Him! When Jesus starts laying out what the cost will be as a follower, people reject Him. When people are satisfied and everything is going well, they like Jesus. When they have to give up their own understanding or suffer, then they may abandon their faith.

In John 6:68-69, after many of Jesus' followers had turned away and left, Jesus turned to Peter and asked, "You do not want to leave too, do you?" Peter summed up the bottom line of Christianity when he answered, "Lord, to whom shall we go? You have the words of eternal life. We believe and know that you are the Holy One of God." That statement is the crux of the truth. Even if we don't understand or things are hard for us, we have nowhere else to turn but to the Lord.

ASKING THE RIGHT QUESTIONS

James chapter 1 tells us that we should consider it "pure joy" when we face trials because the testing of our faith produces perseverance, and perseverance produces character. James goes on to encourage us to pray for wisdom. When we are confused by our trials, God promises to give us wisdom if we ask Him for it. We are also admonished not to be double-minded as we seek wisdom. Suffering is prime soil to nourish questions and doubt that cause us to begin to disbelieve what we know to be true about God. James warns us against doubting God. He says in James 1:7 that the man who is double-minded will not receive anything from the Lord because he is unstable and doubts God. Faith keeps our feet planted in firm soil, ready and able to receive help from the Lord.

We know that God's ultimate goal is to make us more like His Son. He can use all of the bad things that happen to accomplish this goal. But why does God allow the suffering that He can "use" in our lives? Isn't there another way to make me more like Christ? And why would God use a bad choice or a senseless coincidence to do a wondrous work in me? Many of us would rather not be "wondrous," just happy! I might say to myself, "Let someone else be wondrous, and leave me alone!"

Although we can understand to some extent where suffering comes from and how God can use it for our good, much of the question of suffering is still too big for us to comprehend. "Why me?" "Why her?" "Why my child?" "Why my husband?" "Why this?" In order to give a complete answer to the question of suffering, one would have be on the same intellectual level as God and possibly even be equal to God. Unfortunately, our God is just too big and His wisdom is too lofty for us to comprehend. We come to the realization that God Himself has chosen not to provide explanations for every question we demand of Him.

And so, we are left with unanswered questions and the choice to either continue to cling to the Lord or to abandon Him altogether in disappointment. I have chosen to follow Jesus, even with my limited understanding and unanswered questions. What I have learned over the years is to change my questions. I have begun to practice asking questions that I know the Lord is pleased to answer, such as:

1. "How will you use this in my life to accomplish your purpose?"
2. "What is it that you are trying to teach me?"
3. "What would you have me do?"

"How will you use this in my life to accomplish your purpose?"
It may take time to realize the answer to this question. It may take years to experience the blessing that God promises. Whether it takes days or years, we will come to recognize God's hand working things out for good in our circumstances.

"What is it that you are trying to teach me?"
I have consistently found that I don't have to do a lot of digging to find the answer of what God is trying to teach me. Usually, I know what the Master Gardener is targeting to prune out of my life, using painful circumstances to reach those useless weeds. When we get squeezed, our true nature is revealed. All of our imperfections, impatience, selfishness, and anger find their way right up to the surface where the pruning can occur. We may also be surprised to find that deep inside, our faith also surfaces as the Holy Spirit comforts us and fills our hearts with the peace that passes all understanding. Then our faith is purified as the ugliness is pruned away.

"What would you have me do?"
In light of what I understand about what God is trying to teach me, I have no choice but to seek what God would have me do about it. How does He want me to change? Is there a decision I've been avoiding that I know must be made? Spending quiet time with the Lord, reading His Word, and praying are essential in determining what my next steps will be.

God is in control
God has the ultimate victory over sin, pain, evil, and suffering while allowing the precious gift of free will on earth. Peter tells us in 1 Peter 5:8, "…

Your enemy the devil prowls around like a roaring lion looking for someone to devour." When we are in pain, we think Satan is in charge and suffering is in control. We may not even be sure who is in control but we doubt that God is the one in the driver's seat. We know that He is a good God, so why would He be so mean to us?

Pain gets our attention

It is a shame that some people don't pursue God until the pain starts. I have often thought that it is out of God's mercy that He allows pain. When we gather in Heaven, we will meet many people who would not be there if they had not experienced pain in their lives. The pain was the thing that got their attention, causing them to seek the Lord and submit to the changes He was after in their lives. Yet we disdain the very thing that God uses to transform us. Many changes in my life were a direct result of mistakes and suffering. Where would I be if God would not have stopped me in my tracks with the loud voice of pain? I hate suffering but oh, how valuable is the gleaming gold that God lifts out of the pain when all of the dross pours off!

So, in one simple sentence I will state a profound truth regarding suffering. God takes what Satan inflicts upon God's people and turns it upside down, actually using that suffering and pain as a tool in His mighty hand to crush Satan's purposes and make us more like Jesus.

The cleft of the rock

You say, "But I don't feel like I'm becoming more like Jesus, I only feel pain and I want it to stop!" Yes, we feel immediate pain and discomfort and cry out for relief. But let this principle, this truth of Scripture overturn your perspective and understanding. The principle is this: Many times we do not see God's hand until after He has done His work. That sounds simple, doesn't it? But this is a very deep truth of Scripture that many of us just don't believe or take seriously until we are past middle age and see proof of it for ourselves. Then we are convinced that this principle actually is Scriptural and true.

In Exodus 33:18 Moses asked the Lord to show him His glory. In verse 22 God said that He would place Moses in the cleft of the rock on the side of a mountain. God said that Moses could not see Him directly but that He would cover him with His hand until after He passed by. So God passed by the mountain and after He passed, He removed His hand and Moses saw the glory of God. This sounds insignificant and simple. But this is something that we need to hold on to in our times of despair. We may not see the glory of God and recognize His hand in our circumstances until after He has done His work. Moses was asking to see God – now! And God answered with, "You'll see Me but not now, you have to wait until after I have moved and passed by." Isn't that how we feel many times? We want God to show Himself, prove Himself now, then maybe we'll believe and trust. God asks us to stick with Him through the process, through the suffering, through the pain. Then, on the other side of all of that, we will look back and see the proof of God's handiwork.

This principle is further defined in Exodus 3:12. God instructed Moses to go before Pharaoh and bring the Israelites out of Egypt. When Moses questioned God about this assignment, God said, "And this will be the sign to you that it is I who have sent you. When you have brought the people out of Egypt, you will worship God on this mountain." Wait a minute, Moses would not see the "sign" until after the children of Israel arrived on the mountain of Horeb? Moses wanted proof that it would all take place as God said *before* he went to Pharaoh. But God explained that Moses would understand and receive confirmation of the plan *after* it all took place. As parents, we do this with our children when we instruct them. They can't understand the big picture as we tell them what to do. But we comfort them by saying that it will all turn out alright and they will later see why it was good to follow our directions.

How many times have we said, "Oh, now I understand! Now I see why things had to work out the way they did. Now I am thankful that the Lord allowed this to happen in my life." You see, we are like the little boy peering through the knothole of the fence watching a parade go by. He sees only what is in front of him at the moment it passes by the knothole. But God is above the fence watching the entire parade, what is behind and what is up ahead. He only allows us the small knothole of understanding. Our perspective is so very limited!

A GLIMPSE OF PAIN FROM A HIGHER VIEW

If we were to take a bird's eye view over the very broad picture of Satan, God, and man, in other words, the dynamics of good and evil, we might be afforded a glimpse of understanding of why things are the way they are. Satan tempted Adam and Eve, bringing sin into the world and severing their intimacy with God. This caused a permanent divide between God and man that man is simply not able to fix. Then Satan continues to tempt man with destruction as his goal. Man is filled with pride, doubts God's Word, disobeys and falls into sin, continuously causing separation in his relationship with God.

If we imagine for a moment that God could be in a dilemma, we might call this a God-sized dilemma. God wanted man to have free will, the most beautiful gift He could give the crowning masterpiece of His creation. God created man in His own image, gave man a soul that never dies, and free will to choose between good and evil. These gifts are what make humans unique from the animals of God's creation. But Satan, God's adversary, wants to cause pain and destroy the crowning masterpiece of God's creation. He takes advantage of man's ability to choose and causes many people to make hurtful and harmful choices. What can God do with this God-sized dilemma?

BUT GOD...

Much of what God does is simply incomprehensible to our sense of reason. As God chooses not to remove our gift of free will, Satan is free to roam the earth and wreak havoc.

But God... don't you love those two words that we see often in Scripture? These two words mean... "Hold on, things are about to turn around" or "wait until you see what God is going to do about this!" But God does what only He can do in light of this great dilemma. He uses the very pain and suffering that Satan intends for destruction of God's people and causes it to be worked out for the good of His people. He uses suffering to change His people to be more like Jesus. He uses pain as a refining tool to bring us forth as gold out of suffering, just as the goldsmith surfaces the gleaming gold from the fire, freeing the gold of impurities. God uses the fire to free us from the impurities of our sinful human nature. He brings us through the mess of our problems just as the silversmith diligently works with the temperature of the heat as he seeks to burn off all of the dross and pour out the glimmery, shiny silver that can only be purified through the boiling substance.

Those of us who have experienced how God accomplishes this firsthand know exactly to what I refer. This is a Biblical principle that permeates both the Old and New Testaments. God will not allow our mistakes and suffering to go to waste. He uses it for His glory. He uses it to refine us. He uses it to debilitate evil and overturn the effects of Satan's attempt to destroy us.

The only way our suffering can seem useless is when we are ignorant of this principle, turn away from God, and do not submit to the refining process. Instead we complain and ask the unanswerable question of "Why?" Submitting to the refining process means that we trust that God is in control and He will use our pain ultimately for good in our lives. We then can look for ways to learn and grow during the process. When God accomplishes His work in us, our suffering is not wasted. God is glorified and we are refined in the process!

Should we seek to suffer in light of this principle? Certainly not! I believe that God has instilled this principle into His creation in order to exhibit His victory and power over evil. As Believers, we pursue a life of obedience and victory. No, we do not seek pain and suffering nor do we desire it for our families. But God (there it is again…) uses the *inevitable* pain and suffering that permeate our lives for His glory. In our deepest pain, God manifests Himself to those who seek Him. His Word comes alive and His promises give us hope. God becomes real to us and our relationship with Him deepens as we experience His love and compassion. No, we don't seek pain although we are encouraged in Scripture not to disdain it when it comes. When inevitable suffering invades our path, we understand it more clearly in light of God's Word and we experience God's power through it. In this way, we obtain the victory that God wants for us, in spite of troubles and regrets.

AND THE VICTORY GOES ON

But God (there it is again) doesn't even stop there! When we are humbled, healed, and strengthened and have become more like Christ, we are admonished to go and do likewise – serve others who are suffering. We are directed to give to them the compassion and healing touch that we received in our dark times. Thus God's healing power is multiplied and ministers to others who may also come to know Him and trust His Word.

What if the pain and suffering causes death – that ultimate enemy over which we have no control? What if the end of the road of our pain or the suffering of a loved one is death? What if there is war and death is all around? The age-old enemy of death surfaces in each of our lives at some point. That is a guarantee.

But God (again!) has the ultimate victory over this ultimate Enemy of life. Jesus crushed and debilitated this Enemy at the cross. Jesus exhibited His power over death by raising people from the dead during His earthly life. We think this is marvelous and wish we could have seen Him actually call Lazarus out of the grave. Do you know what is even more wonderful and more powerful than Jesus raising someone from the dead? After having been beaten, crucified, and buried in a tomb, Jesus walked out of the grave! Jesus' power over sin and death is confirmed completely and proven undeniably when He fulfilled what He told His disciples in Mark 8:31… that He would be killed and would **rise again** after three days. That, of course, would be impossible. But God (yes… again!) does the impossible, the unthinkable, the incomprehensible, and turns Satan's ultimate weapon of death into God's ultimate gift of life… **eternal life**!

CHAPTER 4

Anatomy of a Bad Choice

"Sow a thought, and you reap an act; sow an act, and you reap a habit; sow a habit, and you reap a character; sow a character, and you reap a destiny."

CHARLES READE

WRONG THOUGHTS LEAD TO WRONG ACTIONS

After I broke off a wrong relationship, several friends commented that they knew all along that it wasn't going to work out. They saw the dynamics clearly and could make an unclouded assessment. Of course, when I was deep inside the situation, I couldn't see what they saw. It's always clearer from the outside looking in.

When others witness the choices we have made, their judgments can be harsh. Quite possibly they judge what they see without understanding what led up to the point of choosing. We know that we didn't purposely make a bad choice. We did it because it actually made sense at the time of choosing. We could not foresee the inevitable consequences. We didn't go directly from seeing everything clearly to being stuck in a big mess. No, somehow we gradually went from good to not-so-good to bad and then to worse, until what once *appeared* to be good became unbearable. Finally, when we were on the outside of the situation and it became part of our past, we looked back and said, "What was I thinking?"

Thoughts determine actions. The thought comes first, then the deed. What we choose and things we do flourish directly from the way we think and believe. I chose a wrong relationship because I did not *believe* that God had a plan for me. I *thought* that there was not a better person for me. I *believed* that I missed out on God's ideal plan for me. I *thought* I had missed my chance in life to find the right person. I *thought* that I had to simply make it work rather than find a relationship that was better suited to me. Based on my thoughts and beliefs, I made a wrong choice.

Because Satan seeks to deceive us, he works first on our minds and thought life. Satan would rather have us *believe* wrong than to *do* wrong. If our beliefs are wrong, soon our actions will mirror what we believe. It all begins with the thought life.

The first area of our thought life that Satan attacks is what we think about God. Our view of God is the root of all other beliefs. If our view of God is distorted, it affects how we think and what we choose to do. Satan wants to distort our view of a good and loving God. He wants us to think of God as cruel, harsh, and unfair. Satan led Eve to think negatively about God by asking her why God would prohibit the fruit. If we think God is mean and unjust, we lose our desire to be in relationship with Him.

If we doubt what God says in His Word, the protective fences around our choices are torn down and we fall into sin. We take control of our lives and when we are in charge, we make mistakes. We may learn from our wrong steps; nevertheless, we are forced to experience the ramifications of our choices.

When God tells us not to do something, it's because He doesn't want us to get hurt. When He places limits it's because there are consequences outside of those limits. Much regret would be avoided if we simply believed God's Word rather than experiment with choices that later become infested with consequences. We think that God is unfair when He doesn't give us everything we want. Truthfully, if God had given me everything I wanted at different points in my life, I would not be in a good place today. I'd be married to someone else, I'd be doing something else, and I would have missed out on what I am enjoying in life today. The choices I made that threw stones of regret onto my life path can be directly traced to a lack of trust in God and/or doubting that He had a good plan for my life.

TWISTING THE TRUTH

Mistakes and bad choices usually fall into one of the following categories:

1. The choice seemed good at the time.
2. We knew it was a bad decision but chose it anyway because of the perceived benefit at the time.

I spoke to a woman recently who told me that she was considering becoming involved in an extramarital affair. She said, "I know I'm going to regret this later but I'm going to do it anyway." I explained to her that she would experience regret and now is the time to prevent it. Why purposely head in the direction of more pain? Eventually, she decided against making this wrong choice.

Sometimes we just can't resist doing something that feels good even though warning lights are going off and we know that pain will result. The benefit of the situation seems to veil the inevitable consequences that we know will come our way. Why is it that we are not convinced that a choice is bad as long as there are elements of "good" woven throughout, like tempting, gleaming strands of gold, too pleasant to resist? We believe it's a good choice and later the ugly reality proves that we have fallen prey to a lie.

We must be very discerning and wise. Satan's lies resemble the truth. In fact, his lies, which are woven throughout the world's system, consistently contain an element of truth in them. I've heard it said that all good lies have truth in them. The more clever the lie, the more like the truth it will sound. Why is that? Because Satan knows that we will immediately recognize a blatant lie and reject it. But when we are faced with something that closely resembles the truth, we'll be more apt to buy into it.

I heard Pastor Adrian Rogers give this example: Which is more dangerous, a clock that is five minutes wrong or a clock that is five hours wrong? You might say that the clock that is five hours wrong is more dangerous but that's not the case. If it is five hours off, you know it is way off and you ask for the correct time. But a clock that is five minutes wrong can cause you to miss your airplane. The lie that is closest to the truth is much more dangerous because it is much more deceptive and we are more likely to accept it as truth.

The dictionary definition of "twist" is to "entwine one thing with another" or "to combine or intertwine by winding together." Satan's method of deceit is to twist God's truth with a lie. Something inside may cause us to question it but then we see the little glimmers of truth shining through and we say, "Oh, that must be true!" Yet those little bits of truth are intertwined with lies and if we aren't very discerning, we'll easily fall into deceit. If we stand back far enough, those gleaming threads of truth woven into the tapestry of a belief system can make the whole thing appear to look good. Only when you get up close and examine each thread with discernment and the truth of God's Word can you begin to recognize and sift through the lies.

When this system of twisting the good with the bad seeps into our choices, we end up in an overall bad situation that has enough good threads to make us believe we are doing the right thing. For example, I was in a relationship that was not healthy or good for me yet there were enough good strands woven in with the bad to justify it. This is the classic scenario for many situations we experience. Our inner voice shouts, "This is not right. Something is wrong here!" Then another small voice whispers, "But there's a part that is so good. If you give this up, you'll lose out on all these good things!" We are blinded to the truth that has been twisted with deceptive lies.

When selfishness is one of the threads

When we are deceived into believing lies, there is one common thread that is inevitably woven into the intricacies of the anatomy of our choices. That thread is called "selfishness." If we weren't selfish, we would be much more inclined to set aside our desires and accept the truth of God's Word. Yet we long to please ourselves first and foremost and that gives us the incentive to twist a few lies into God's truth in order to accommodate our desires.

This selfishness is prevalent and is at the root of the discord that exists among people. When we hear people discussing their differences in beliefs, what we would really hear, if selfishness had a voice, would be, "I believe this way because it suits me. I don't believe what God's Word says because I don't agree with it. I don't like what God says. It isn't fair! God isn't nice if He doesn't allow this. I can't believe God wouldn't want me to be happy – and this would make me happy!" Once again it's that age old argument, "Did God really say........?"

Those unfaithful feelings

Feelings can run our lives. Feelings may be the first consideration for many people as they contemplate a decision. The truth is that Christians will never experience victory in their lives if they consistently base their decisions on feelings and emotions. Feelings can be nice and it is very helpful if our feelings support what we know we should do. But many times our feelings don't support the right decision. Having feelings is not a sin, it's following them that is wrong. We must become mature enough to do what is right in spite of feelings that try to lead us otherwise. Our feelings can keep us out of God's will and purpose for our lives if we rely on what we feel rather than what we know to be true. We are depending on our feelings rather than the Word of God to determine our path.

If our lives are a mess, the dotted line of personal examination can most likely be traced to relying on, depending on, and following those unfaithful feelings. We need to keep our feelings and emotions under control rather than allowing them to direct our life path. Truth is our faithful and trustworthy guide!

Years ago I watched a special on TV about a team of researchers who were studying crocodiles. They were out on a boat filming the reptiles and recording their behavior. During the activity one of the team members somehow fell into the water. I couldn't believe it! I began to get very tense, half expecting to watch a documentary on how a crocodile eats its prey. The commentator explained how important it was for the woman to remain calm and stay still until the boat could reach her and pull her to safety. He said that if she followed her urge to thrash about or swim to the boat, she would only draw attention to herself. The crocodile would then attack her as prey. But if she didn't move at all, the crocodile wouldn't see her as a threat or pay any attention to her and she would be safe.

It was so frustrating to watch her in the water knowing that hungry crocodiles were nearby and she was in danger. I found myself asking… *Why doesn't she just take her chances and get out of there?* As if he could read my mind, the commentator said, "Even though everything inside of her is screaming to escape as quickly as possible, she is going to have to ignore her urge to swim away. She is safe only if she doesn't move." I watched as she obeyed the truth rather than her fleshly instincts and reasoning and remained perfectly still. Finally, the boat made its way to her and she was lifted aboard. I breathed a sigh of relief and wondered if I had been the one in the water, would I now be safely in the boat or would I have been a delicious dinner for some crocodile?

Feelings are so strong that many of us fall into this trap of deciding what is right and true based on how we feel about it. We think if something feels good then it must be right and true. If something feels bad then it must be wrong. For example, a young person goes out on the town one night, meets a nice person, has sex that night and says, "This was a good decision; this feels right." They start dating and inevitably, soon have their first big argument. They feel bad and may come to the conclusion, "This is a bad decision, this feels wrong." Their beliefs about the relationship may be based soley on feelings, not on any other criteria. When our criteria for right thinking is based on feelings, we can very easily be led into wrong decisions.

God's truth never changes

We think truth changes! If we don't feel something is true, then we determine that it must not be true. Or we fall into the people-pleasing trap and refuse to disagree with those who are caught up in lies. We think that what is true for someone else isn't necessarily true for us. Or we rationalize. We decide for ourselves what is true. And finally, we can be pragmatic; we don't ask is it true – we ask, does it work? And if it doesn't work for us, we reason that it can't be true. On the other hand, if it works for someone else, then it is true for that person. When we make up our own mind about what is wrong and right, we become our own god. And there we are, right back at the beginning again (Adam and Eve). We are faced with the question, "Is God's Word true or do I know better?"

One of the first things I learned as a young Christian back in my mid-twenties was this: My faith should be based on fact, not feeling. God has graciously given us His Word. His Word never changes. His Word is our anchor when the waves of emotions and feelings toss us about. He knows how fickle we can be and how our emotions can steer us in different directions. Yet God is faithful and His Word is true.

What if following the truth of God's Word is hard and painful? Although deep joy and better choices come from a walk with the Lord, self-discipline can be painful. Living by the truth of God's Word may not make life easy or fun all the time, but it will keep our feet from falling into the quicksand of regret. We need to be disciplined to do what's right, even when we feel like doing what we know is wrong. Discipline means choosing now what we'll be happy with later on.

Sifting our experience through the truth of God's Word

There is another voice that shouts even louder than our feelings: the voice of experience. One of the biggest contributors to our filter of truth is the reality of something we have experienced. No one can argue with my personal experience and my interpretation of situations that I have lived through. My experience tells me that if I made a certain choice and the circumstance worked out well, then it must have been right for me to make that decision. Makes sense, doesn't it? On the other hand, if I made a choice and things turned out wrong, then I must have made a mistake. However, this may not necessarily be true.

I have been guilty of filtering my viewpoint through the sieve of my experience and ending up on the other side of the situation with a wrong assessment. In fact, most of my life-changing mistakes have contained elements of this dynamic woven through the anatomy of the wrong choice.

We need to place our experiences *under* the Word of God. What does this mean? It is very simple. Since the beginning of time people have formulated doctrines and belief systems based on their experiences. They let their experiences override what the Bible says. As Christians, we must submit our experiences to the scrutiny of Scripture and if they don't line up, we accept what God says rather than "re-write" what He has already said. For example, a woman may have had a positive sexual experience with a man she has just met, feeling that it has enhanced the relationship. Because of the positive results, she disregards what the Bible teaches about sex outside of marriage. She places her experience above the Word of God and believes she is doing the right thing. Placing her experience *under* the Word of God should cause her to say, "Even though my experience tells me this is the right thing to do, it doesn't pass the test of Scripture and I believe God's Word has authority over my choices."

THE UNDERLYING CAUSE OF BAD CHOICES

We choose wrong and sin because we are sinners! All of our sin is ultimately against God, the One who set the standards. As long as we believe that we simply "made the wrong choice," we risk continuing to make new mistakes that will cause regret. Below you will see the difference between attitudes that can result from considering our bad choices as wrong versus sinful.

Wrong Choice	**Sin**
I will not make that same choice again	Recognize that I am a sinner
I'll do better next time	Repent of my sin
I can change myself	Allow God to change me
"I can"	"God, forgive me, make me who you want me to be!"

Although we may be able to change some of the things that we do, we can't change our nature. But God can! God wants to change more than our behavior, He wants to work on who we are, what we think, and ultimately what we choose. God desires that our motives and actions be in line with His Word. Rather than say, "I can make better choices," we can turn to God and say, "Please change me so that I will make better choices!"

CHAPTER 5

Anger – The Fallout of Regret

"In your anger do not sin…."

Psalm 4:4

Regret's potential

Regret is powerful. It has the potential to change people. One cannot examine the subject of regret without addressing the issues of anger, resentment, and revenge. For some people, regret seems to breathe life into one or more of these aspects. A man who has never been an angry individual might develop into a person who not only feels angry but handles his anger in an unhealthy way. A woman who has never been vengeful might begin to retaliate against another person, even though this trait had never surfaced before in her personality. Regret can bring out the worst in us. If we aren't careful, we become resentful, angry, vengeful people.

Which is worse, to anger another person or to be angry that the other person angered you?

Who is worse, the person who inflicts the pain or the person who exacts revenge?

Don't they both have similar qualities? Are not both of them developing and exhibiting similar character traits as they inflict pain or retaliate against pain inflicted?

We must watch how we respond to regret and pain in our lives. We can either become kinder and more patient or we can become hard and hateful.

Anger – the fallout of regret

Being a Christian doesn't mean that we will never be angry. In fact, the Bible doesn't say, "do not get angry." What it does teach is that when we get angry, we are not to sin. God's Word teaches us principles that will help us deal with inevitable anger as we try to thrive and survive in a world full of sinners.

James 1:19-20 tells us, "...Everyone should be quick to listen, slow to speak, and slow to become angry, for man's anger does not bring about the righteous life that God desires." Being slow to anger means not allowing anger to be our first response to people and situations that bother us. Some people have anger consistently resting right below the surface of their emotions. Then something small happens and they blow up with an angry response that far outweighs the small thing that angered them. Being slow to anger means being quick to forgive as we try to understand others and give them the benefit of the doubt.

We are not to hold on to the anger and keep it inside of our hearts. Ephesians 4:26 instructs us, "In your anger, do not sin. Do not let the sun go down while you are still angry and do not give the devil a foothold." We must learn to deal with issues quickly rather than keep the anger in our hearts where it can fester and grow. When we guard our anger, we are placing a protective fence around it, essentially saying, "This is mine, I have a right to feel angry." We are nurturing our anger and training ourselves to become angry much more quickly. We nourish anger by thinking about the situation, talking about it with others, being critical of people, and thinking too highly of ourselves. Nourishing anger means feeding it, making it stronger, eventually developing it into a character trait.

Proverbs 29:11 tells us, "A fool gives full vent to his anger, but a wise man keeps himself under control."

There is such a thing as "righteous" anger. When we witness or experience sin or injustice, anger will rise up in our hearts. Feeling anger is one thing; responding to it in a sinful way is another.

As regret grows over time, the problem is that anger may grow with it. It can happen slowly, over the course of years, until we realize that we have become very angry over a choice or a situation. At times, professional counseling is necessary to go through the process of surfacing the root cause of the anger and then dealing with it in a healthy way.

It is much easier to deal with anger at its onset. If we understand that anger itself may not be the issue, rather how we handle our anger, we have a better chance of overcoming this potentially volatile and damaging emotion.

The "Re's" to watch out for

Resentment. When we are injured by someone's words or actions, we are filled with feelings of hurt. Resentment is simply continuing to feel the hurt. The word comes from the French word "ressentiment." So it's clear that if we feel something over and over or keep on feeling the hurt, we are now in the realm of *re-sentiment:* re-feeling the pain, reviewing the incident, rehashing the past and resenting the person. For those of us who do not consider ourselves angry people, we need to re-think this thing called resentment. Even though we may not exhibit anger outwardly, resentment is hidden anger within us. It is actually anger turned inward.

Isn't that exactly what we're experiencing when we rehash something in our minds? We tap into our memories and review every detail, stirring up the pain all over again. Resentment is fueled and makes the pain feel as fresh as the day it happened.

One problem with resentment is that if we don't deal with it and get rid of it in our lives, it can turn to bitterness. It can make us bitter people. I looked up the word "bitter" in the dictionary and none of the definitions relates to people. It is an adjective that relates to food or an adverb that means "extreme." It means to have a "harsh, acrid taste" or intensity such as "bitter cold." In the true sense of the dictionary term, it is not a word that describes people. It is a word that was never invented to apply to people! But it does, doesn't it? We know many bitter people. They have lost their sweetness. A sour, bitter flavor permeates their words, attitude, and treatment of others.

I've heard it said that resentment is like drinking poison and waiting for your enemies to die. In other words, the only person resentment hurts is You. It's true, resentment changes us, poisons us, and makes us bitter.

So where does that leave us? We still feel the pain of the incident. Some of us may still be living out the consequences of what someone did to us. Is there anything we can do about this inward killer called resentment?

Revenge. Revenge is in God's hands. I used to think vengeance and retaliation were extreme cases of anger reserved for criminals or crime movies. But with deeper consideration about this subject, I began to notice things that I hadn't given much thought to previously. Lately I've noticed various forms of retaliation all around me. Here are some examples:

- A driver cut someone off and the other driver sped up to cut the first driver off
- A woman spoke rudely to someone, explaining that the other person spoke rudely first and she was responding the way she thought he deserved

- A customer was put on hold for too long when calling his bank and decided to retaliate by closing his account
- A woman was rude to a salesclerk because a clerk in another store had been rude to her earlier in the day
- An individual was not nominated for a prestigious award because the behind-the-scenes decision makers were angry about his political views

My eyes and ears have been open to these subtle forms of retaliation and I am honestly surprised at the extent of this issue in the lives of many people. In talking with others, I've heard hints of revenge in comments and complaints. Maybe it's not overt and outright revenge, but even simple, hateful comments come from the same source – a desire to retaliate. Maybe that is why Jesus answered the following when asked in Mark 12:28 which of all the commandments was the most important: Jesus answered in verses 29-31, "…Love the Lord with all your heart and with all your soul and with all your mind and with all your strength. The second is this: Love your neighbor as yourself. There is no commandment greater than these."

People who retaliate are not treating others as they would want to be treated. Instead, they are choosing to treat others in the same way they have been treated. When others inflict pain into our lives, our first reaction to pain might be one of the following:

"It's not fair! Where is the justice?"
"I'm going to make sure this never happens again."
"I'm going to get back at the person who did this to me."
"I'm going to make sure the person gets what he deserves."

We long for justice. We desire for hurtful situations to be made right again. If we don't trust God, we may believe we should be the ones to bring justice. We may feel that if we forgive or let it go that the person will go unpunished. What they did will be forgotten and justice will never be done. Things will never be right. The Bible teaches us differently. It is not up to us to make sure that every person who has hurt us receives what is "due" to him or her.

I'm not referring to setting boundaries or doing what is healthy for us. Healthy boundaries may feel like revenge to the person who has hurt us because consequences can feel like retaliation. But this is not the same as paying back, gaining satisfaction, inflicting pain, or injuring someone in order to balance the scales of justice again. There is a big difference between setting boundaries, making healthier choices relating to people and situations, and devising ways to pay them back for what they did.

Many people make retaliation a lifestyle. They talk rudely or harshly to people or withhold kindness or actually inflict pain as a way to feel "satisfied" that justice has been accomplished. Romans 12:19-21 says, "Do not take revenge, my friends, but leave room for God's wrath, for it is written, 'It is Mine to avenge, I will repay' says the Lord. On the contrary, 'if your enemy is hungry, feed him; if he is thirsty, give him something to drink. In doing this, you will heap burning coals on his head.' Do not be overcome by evil, but overcome evil with good."

When we choose not to retaliate against others, we help prevent ourselves from becoming angry and vengeful. In other words, taking revenge changes us! If we retaliate, even in small ways, we are essentially training ourselves to be vengeful. Why do you want to develop into being an angry, vengeful person? You may say, "I would never take revenge against anyone, I'm not a vengeful person." But we all must ask ourselves, "Are there threads of revenge in our response to others who hurt us?"

When we resist the temptation to retaliate against others for hurting us, we become more forgiving, tolerant, patient, and kind. If we really love God, we will allow Him to take care of people and situations that have caused us regret. We will allow Him to be God of our problems and work them out in His perfect way. We need to trust that God will take care of the repayment for wrong done to us. God promises to vindicate us. Psalm 17:2 says, "May my vindication come from you; may your eyes see what is right." We can forgive more easily and be peaceful with our circumstances when we know deep inside that God will deal with those who have hurt us, in the way that He knows is best.

Replacing anger with God's peace

There have been times when I have felt anger over something in my past. Sometimes I am angry with myself for not choosing differently. Turning my anger over to God is the only way I can experience peace.

We can pray the following:

Lord, help me to trust you with this situation that makes me so angry. It's in my past and there is nothing I can do about it. Please forgive me for holding on to my anger. I ask you to change my perspective and bring something good out of this. I trust that you are in control and will work it out for the best. Please fill my heart with your peace. Enable me to forgive and put this issue behind me. Help me to keep looking forward and not dwell on things that make me angry. Thank you for your peace. In Jesus' Name, Amen

CHAPTER 6

Beyond the Guilt and Shame

REGRET. WE TEND TO HIDE the shame of our bad choice in the deep recesses of our hearts. Yes, that's a good place for the pain and humiliation. Even when we bury the shame and move on with life, it rises to the surface – fresh as ever – when our past is exposed. Time numbs us as our lives become busy and filled with distractions. But someone asks a question that drives a knife right to the pain.

Your fiancé asks you if you ever had an abortion, and he reads the shame on your face.

You complete an application for a job and are asked on the application, "Have you ever been convicted of a crime?" Shame and regret fill your heart all over again.

It never seems to go away, rising from deep inside your heart to the outside edge where you feel it the strongest. How do you push it back down, into the deepest corner, and lock the door so that it can't get out?

Shame can be extremely unhealthy and damaging. When left to simmer unattended, shame can become one of the biggest stumbling blocks to moving past the past. Not only do we wallow in the mire of regret, but the painful feeling that we've done something wrong or dishonorable looms over us like a dark cloud. If we don't deal with shame, whatever its source, it will grow like a weed within us, threatening to tie us down in regret and choke life out of our future.

The fruit of shame
Shame has the ability to create a myriad of problems for us, such as shyness, sense of inferiority, low self-esteem, self-condemnation, and even self-hate. These seeds, when well watered and nourished, grow into bad choices, bad relationships, loneliness, negative self-talk, and self-sabotaging behavior. I call this the "fruit" of shame. Sometimes, there is so much bad fruit that we can't even see or identify the root from where it came. It's just there, and has been for many years, growing, flourishing, and feeding off of the root of something that was planted years earlier. The seeds of a wrong choice, negative influence, failure, or rejection are buried deep within us.

The difference between guilt and shame
Guilt and shame can be confused. Guilt is a tool that helps us recognize that what we did was wrong. Destructive shame, on the other hand, gives us the sense that *who we are* is wrong. Guilt says, "What you did was bad." Shame says, "You are bad."

Shame goes beyond the action, motive, and result. Shame digs into the deepest part of our self-esteem and self-worth. It speaks into the deepest part of us and tells us that because of what we did, we are not valuable. Our inner self feels wounded. Shame is a very damaging emotion because it makes us feel inferior or unworthy.

True guilt inspires us to act differently and begin to make changes in our lives. (In the next section we will see the difference between true and false guilt.) Shame leads us to isolation and disconnection from others. Guilt leads us to take responsibility for our choices and admit what we did wrong. Shame leads us to evaluate ourselves negatively and determine that we are not as good as others. Guilt motivates us to move forward; shame threatens to hold us back. Guilt is seeing clearly what we've done; shame is seeing ourselves as a failure.

Guilt	Shame
Prompts me to act differently	Leads to isolation and disconnection
Encourages me to take responsibility	Causes me to evaluate myself negatively
Moves me forward	Holds me back
"What I have done is bad"	"I am a bad person"
Activates my conscience	Increases low self-esteem
Pinpoints the problem	Cloudy – can't identify the root
My Heavenly Father disciplines me	"God doesn't love me"

The feeling of guilt ideally helps us identify the wrong we have done. We feel guilty because we *are* guilty. Even if we are able to forgive ourselves and forget what we did, our status before God is GUILTY. When we sin, we are guilty in God's eyes whether or not we *feel* guilty. The guilty feeling we have is just that – a feeling! The feelings are warning signs that we need to repent and be forgiven.

We should be careful of friends, counselors, or professionals that encourage us to simply "forgive ourselves" and omit the fact that we need to be forgiven by God. The Bible tells us that our sin needs to be forgiven by God because ultimately He is the one against whom we sin. We should be thankful for the guilty feeling that warns us that there is something deeper going on that needs to be forgiven by God. In this regard, guilt is used by God as a tool, prompting us to seek forgiveness from Him.

True guilt and false guilt

It seems that all guilt feels the same. We feel remorseful and wish we had not done the thing we regret. But if we continue to separate the good from the bad, we find that although true guilt and false guilt may feel the same, the difference between them is significant. One is a road that leads to hope and healing and the other is the quicksand to discouragement and death.

True guilt prompts us to take responsibility for what we have done. It leads us to repentance and a change of behavior. We are willing to turn and change. We are ready to give up whatever it was that caused us to make the selfish choice. True guilt inspires us to seek a remedy for the situation created by our choice. It will encourage us to reconcile with an injured person where possible. It leads us to become right with others to the best of our ability. True guilt forces us to humbly ask God for forgiveness. We receive the forgiveness that God promises and we lean on Him for guidance in moving forward in our lives.

On the other hand, false guilt makes us feel remorse, but we are not willing to take the action needed to turn and change. False guilt causes us to be sorry for what we did, but only because we got caught or the consequences were painful. We may feel remorse but not seek forgiveness. If we have sought forgiveness from God, false guilt stays with us even after we have been forgiven. We still feel guilty and cling to our past. **This is the essence of regret!** Living in regret means we hold on to our past, wallow in the consequences of our choices, and don't move forward through forgiveness and newness of life in our Christian walk.

During the night before Jesus' crucifixion, two of His disciples sinned greatly against Him. Judas betrayed Jesus for 30 pieces of silver and led those who wanted to kill Jesus straight to Him. Peter fled and denied Jesus adamantly three times, just as Jesus had said that he would. Both Judas and Peter felt remorse and anguish over what they had done. After Judas realized what he had done and learned that Jesus was going to be executed, he threw the silver coins at the Pharisees and went out and committed suicide. He was remorseful but not repentant. He was sorry for what he did but he did not seek forgiveness and reconciliation with Jesus. Peter, on the other hand, was not only remorseful when the rooster crowed three times as Jesus had predicted, his heart was repentant and he received Jesus' forgiveness.

After Jesus' resurrection, Jesus spent time alone with Peter by the campfire and asked him three times if he loved Jesus. Peter answered "yes" three times, symbolizing the complete forgiveness Jesus offered Peter for each denial. Then He commissioned Peter to "feed His sheep," moving Peter past his failure and on to God's will for his path for the future.

Two men who sinned against Jesus and had the same opportunity to be forgiven, yet each chose different paths based on remorse for what they had done. Which path will you choose when guilt, shame, and regret fill your heart as a result of failure and mistakes?

What is the answer?

When a person requires surgery, the doctor performs an operation, essentially cutting the person open, working on the sick part, then sewing up the wound. The same doctor who inflicts the pain of surgery stitches up the hurt area and provides medicine for healing. The Bible works in a similar way. When we hold our failures and regrets up against the light of Scripture, we feel guilt and shame and we know we need "surgery." Oh, how it hurts to have the light turned on to our sin and shame! Many times, we don't even know how wrong we are until someone shines the light of God's Word on our actions. So the shame is exposed, with all of its ugliness. God uses His Word to open the wound, exposing all of the pain and dysfunction, and then, miraculously, He provides the precious balm needed for healing.

Isn't that just like our God? He shines the light on our mistakes, exposing them to the truth of His Word. Then He helps us past the shame and the deep realization that we blew it. He heals us of the natural consequences of regret and shame. In the very same pages that convict us, God provides the promise that takes us past shame and into freedom and right standing with God. Romans 8:1 states, "Therefore, there is now no condemnation for those who are in Christ Jesus, because through Christ Jesus the law of the Spirit of life set me free from the law of sin and death."

WILLING TO BE WILLING

We know that we have a role to play in our healing of guilt and shame. Rather than flounder in the quicksand of shame that threatens to sink us beyond the point of hope, we need to be willing to turn and seek the path of healing and restoration. Our part in the process is to seek God's help and place our faith in Him. Sometimes, we can be so bogged down with guilt and shame that we don't have the faith or strength to recognize what we should do to begin the path to healing.

If you struggle with lack of faith and disbelief that God will forgive you and heal you, are you willing to ask God for more faith? Are you willing to ask God to give you the faith that you need to keep your hope in Him? I love the verse in Mark 9:24 where the man seeking healing for his son exclaimed to Jesus, "…I do believe, help me overcome my unbelief!" Many times over the course of my Christian walk I have felt doubt or inability to do my part in moving forward. I have cried out to God, "Help my unbelief!" and "Make me willing to do what I need to do!"

CHAPTER 7

Volcano of Regret

People may have regret buried deep in their hearts that stays dormant unless something triggers it. You are fine and not dwelling on regret, but it is there, buried deep in the busyness of life. You're distracted, you don't think too much about it, but then something happens. You apply for a loan and realize that you aren't eligible because of the financial choices you made years earlier. You go to the doctor and learn that your cholesterol is too high because of the food choices you have made. Your adult son is living an irresponsible life and you blame yourself for choices you made as a parent. You apply for a job and have to explain why you were fired from your last job. The pain of the past becomes as fresh as yesterday. And then you feel the pain of the consequences that threaten to spew old poison into your new life.

On the road of our present lives, signs begin popping up everywhere saying things like, "Consequences," "Remember, you deserve this," and "What were you thinking?"

Climbing the wrong mountain
The consequences may not be the result of one choice we made, but may be a direct result of the *road* we chose to travel *after* taking a wrong turn. The problem is that the wrong road can look so much like the right road while we are traveling on it and the scenery doesn't look so bad from up close. Certain elements of the path are nice, so the incentive to get

completely off that road and find a new course just doesn't exist. There is a pretty tree or plant that creates a distraction from the craggy rocks lining the road. We keep going, further and further until we find at the end of the road there is a massive volcano, ready to erupt and spew out all of the poison that has been stored up.

How were we to know that the beautiful mountain we were climbing was actually a treacherous volcano? It looked like any other mountain, fine on the outside, offering many aspects of goodness. So we hiked up the mountain along the side with the trees and the winding path. Soon we were all the way up to the peak. The view looked good from that vantage point, even though it might not be quite what we had hoped for out of life.

Once at the top, we looked down into the opening and began to see what was inside of the mountain. Not quite what we expected. And why was the mountain rumbling and churning beneath our feet? Soon we realized that this wasn't a mountain after all; this was what most hikers would avoid when mountain climbing. In fact, most wise nature lovers who have studied well before hiking would have recognized this volcano while contemplating it from the bottom perimeter. A volcano might have some aspects of beauty, it might even look like any other mountain from afar, but there is nothing that can change a volcano into a harmless mountain. No, a volcano has a hidden element that is not visible to the naked eye from miles away. A magma chamber filled with molten rock that, when given the right combination of elements in nature, has no choice but to erupt.

If you have ever seen a video of a volcano eruption, you have probably wondered who actually took the video. Did he get away safely? How close did he have to get to the disaster before he said, "This is close enough!" I don't know. What I do know is that I never fail to say to myself, "I sure hope the cameraman got out before the lava flowed down the side of the volcano!" The cameramen get out unscathed. I have also gotten out unscathed, but not without feeling a few effects of simmering, smoky aftermaths. Yes, life has gone on and I am certainly a much wiser mountain climber.

The question is, why does the cameraman get so close to danger? Doesn't he realize that getting too close increases his chance of being burned by the molten lava festering beneath the surface of the earth? He obviously ignores the caution signs as he proceeds to take his photographs. I also have ignored the yellow flags along my path that whisper "caution, be careful, think it through." Actually, at times there were flashes the color of bright red shouting, "Stop, turn around, danger!" Yet I still went forward. This reminds me of a lighter version of the same dynamic. I was in third grade and on stage during a production at church. I was about six inches from the edge of the stage and my eyes wandered over the large audience of parents. I asked myself how far I could inch my toes over the edge of the stage without falling. So I inched, inch by inch, until I fell the three feet off of the stage onto the hard cement, right on my knees. I quickly ran around to the side door, up the flight of stairs and back into my place on stage, hoping not too many parents even noticed.

Back at school that following week, one of my friends graciously and eagerly recounted to others the story of how my knees got so black and blue. The trauma had disappeared for me, buried deep in the corner of my heart called "forget it and move on," until she announced it to my world of school. It hurt to experience the inevitable aftermath of a stupid mistake.

Since it is clear that there is nothing we can do to change the past, what choices will lead us forward? Will we trust God? Will we forgive others? What about forgiving ourselves? Are we able to do that? New signs begin appearing on the road of life. There is a fork in the road that says "resentment" on one path and "forgiveness" on the other. Another fork in the road displays a street sign that says "regret" and the other says "thankful." There is another intersection with two signs. One says "the past" and the other says "the future."

I am thankful that I'm not living on the volcano of the past, where the lava spews the strongest and burns the hottest. At times, I am tempted to go down the road of the familiar past, the road called "despair and hopelessness." The familiar is comfortable, those feelings that come naturally from regret. But I know what awaits me should I try to run the race of life facing backwards; it's filled with molten rock. I know I'll get burned. I choose the right road, straining forward toward the unknown, the unpredictable, exercising faith on the road called: **"Hope for my future."**

CHAPTER 8

Those Stubborn Consequences

THOSE STUBBORN CONSEQUENCES

SIN AND DISOBEDIENCE ARE LIKE seeds planted deep in the soil of our lives which, when fertilized with bad choices and watered by time, flourish into bitter consequences. The residual effects seem unequal to the seeds that were sown years before. Hosea 8:7 states, "They sow the wind and reap the whirlwind…." We sow a few seeds of bad choices and the harvest far outweighs the little seeds that were planted. We feel that we don't deserve the magnitude of the consequences. Yet this is a principle that we cannot ignore when examining the subject of regret. The rules of natural consequences apply to all of us. The results from our choices are bigger than the seemingly small amount of time and effort it took to make the decision. We reap more than we sow, worse than we sow, and longer than we sowed!

One of the most difficult aspects of regret is the pain that goes on and on, in spite of the fact that what is causing the pain is buried deep in the past. It's over, the relationship has ended, the job is eliminated, the house is lost, the money is gone, the death is unchangeable. How do we get past the past when the pain continues in the present?

Today's pain from yesterday's choices
Most of the pain we experience is likely due to consequences of our own choices. Our lives are a direct result of the maze of choices that we have made. If we are honest with ourselves, had we made better choices, we would not be suffering pain from the past. Some of our suffering may be caused by other people or circumstances that were out of our control. But for the moment, let's focus on pain caused by my own worst enemy – ME! There are principles that help us navigate those stubborn consequences, the inevitable lava that continues to spew into our lives.

God disciplines us through consequences
God has put in place the law of natural consequences. Everything we do has a cause and effect. If we plant good seeds, we will see a good harvest. If we plant the seeds of bad choices, we experience consequences. We will reap what we sow. What was planted will grow! If we identify an area of our pain that was caused by our own choices, we must face responsibility for our actions.

God uses natural consequences to discipline, change, and teach us. He provokes us to make different choices. Scripture tells us in Hebrews 12:7, "Endure hardship as discipline, God is treating you as sons. For what son is not disciplined by his father?" Verse 11 says, "No discipline seems pleasant at the time, but painful. Later on, however, it produces a harvest of righteousness and peace for those who have been trained by it."

God corrects us because He loves us
I was in a store and overheard two women having a heated discussion. One woman was apparently relaying to the other what she thought about something the woman did. The other woman said, "Stop correcting me,

you are always correcting me." The first woman replied, "I don't love you enough to correct you!"

Thank God that He loves us enough to correct us! We get offended when God corrects us or when we suffer the natural consequences of our choices. This is another area where the temptation to be offended looms overhead, waiting to sink into our hearts every time we experience the results of our past choices.

Recently my husband attempted to correct my thinking on an issue that we were discussing. I resisted but knew that he was right. In our church service that following Sunday, the pastor asked flat out if God was using other people to get us to see something we need to change. I laughed to myself that God would not only use my husband to correct me on an issue but then use the pastor to tell me that He was using my husband to correct me! (Did anyone ever say that God has a sense of humor?)

Correction or discipline is not fun. The more we resist correction in our lives, the more apt we are to stray away from our relationship with the Lord. If we recognize God's ways in the matter of regret, we will be more likely to submit to Him rather than continue to seek ways of escape from the pain. Here are some principles regarding how God uses consequences to discipline us:

God humbles us

When we recognize where we went wrong in the past, there are some things we can do in the present that may soften many of the consequences. One of the things we can do is seek out those we have hurt and ask for forgiveness. This is our part in making the wrongs of the past as right as possible through taking responsibility for our actions. We seek out those we have offended and say, "I know I was wrong and what I did hurt you. Please forgive me."

We are not responsible for the other person's response to our effort to make things right. We are only responsible for being obedient to the call of God to do our part. We trust God to handle the rest.

God teaches us

The Psalmist said in 119:71, "It was good for me to be afflicted so that I might learn your decrees." God's goodness sometimes must include pain in order to teach us to learn from God and follow Him. If we are successful on our own and God removes the consequences of our choices, what is our incentive to follow Him? Unfortunately, we have none. We are inclined to run our own lives, apart from God, unless He teaches us how to desire and follow Him.

God gives us hope for the future

We may not have control over the past, but we do have control over the present and the future. Today is the day to plant seeds that will produce a better harvest for our future. Regret for the past is not a good seed to plant. It's like a weed that will grow out of control in and around the good seeds we are trying to plant. Identifying every weed, taking responsibility, and enduring the consequences as discipline from the Lord will allow the new seeds to flourish without getting choked by regret.

God promises to restore us

When we endure discipline, learn from God, and humble ourselves during the pain of those stubborn consequences of our choices, the Bible has good news for us! Whether we have regret because of self-inflicted pain, suffering at the hands of others, or pain from the years that we didn't follow the Lord, God promises to lift us up and restore us.

> "Humble yourselves before the Lord, and he will lift you up." James 4:10
> "Though you have made me see troubles, many and bitter, you will restore my life again." Psalm 71:20
> "I will repay you for the years the locust has eaten…." Joel 2:25

> "…to bestow on them a crown of beauty instead of ashes, the oil of gladness instead of mourning and a garment of praise instead of a spirit of despair.…" Isaiah 61:3

Many people living in regret may be trying to figure out how they can make it up to God and get back into His favor after all they have done. But this principle in Scripture says the opposite. God says He will make it up to us! God views the mistakes from our past and our separation from Him as directly related to sin in our lives. Whether or not you knew the Lord during your past, God knows you cannot make it up to Him. Instead, God wants you to live righteously before Him and *let Him* bring restoration to your life.

Restoration in the midst of stubborn consequences

When we have faith, God will bring restoration to us even as we live daily with the physical results of our past choices. Some physical consequences of our choices will never go away. Whether we made mistakes or were the victim of others' poor choices, some consequences have become permanent. A child is aborted, money is wasted, a house is foreclosed, a job is lost, a relationship is broken, a crime is committed, and many other choices create permanent aftereffects. God doesn't always remove the consequences of sin and disobedience. Instead, He calls us to place our faith in Him in order to experience restoration and healing.

In Numbers chapter 21, the Israelites experienced God's discipline for their sin when venomous serpents appeared in their camp. In verse 7 the people went to Moses and said, "…We sinned when we spoke against the Lord and against you. Pray that the Lord will take the snakes away from us.…" Moses prayed for the people but the Lord did not remove the snakes. Instead, God instructed Moses to create a snake and place it high on a pole so that the people could look at it and live. Moses created a bronze snake, placed it up on a pole and anyone who looked up at it after being bitten by a snake was healed.

It seems like a strange story but it is a vivid picture of lifting our eyes out of our circumstances and placing our faith in God. There was absolutely no physical reason for the bronze snake on the pole to actually cure a person from a snake bite. But looking up at the snake on the pole reminded the Israelites of their sin and taught them to look up and trust God. If they looked up in faith, God healed them from the snake bites. In John 3:14, Jesus actually referred to this incident as a foreshadowing of Himself. The bronze serpent was a symbol of sin and judgment, just as Jesus was lifted high on the cross for our sin and judgment.

If we look around at our circumstances, we will be constantly "bitten" and hurt by them until we are discouraged and give up. But if we look up and place our faith in Jesus, we will experience miraculous healing and restoration even in the midst of the painful circumstances.

Years ago I was listening to a radio talk show and the host was interviewing a man who was born as a result of the rape of his mother. His mother was brutally raped, became pregnant, and chose to have the baby rather than get an abortion. Daily she lived with the physical reminder of that crime, that painful incident in her life as she raised her little boy. But she chose to press forward and make the best life she could for her child. I listened as the man relayed how God had worked in his life to help him feel loved in spite of how he was conceived and brought into this world. He became a very strong Christian and was thankful that his mother had chosen to keep him, raise him, and give him a good life. God blessed both mother and son because of their faithfulness in spite of regretful circumstances. They looked up to God in faith and, therefore, experienced restoration and blessing in spite of the unfortunate circumstances.

HOPE FOR PERMANENT CONSEQUENCES

Are you experiencing permanent consequences for the choices you made in the past? Rather than wish that the consequences would disappear, place your faith in the One who can heal and restore, even in the midst of the pain. Instead of looking around and complaining about the circumstances of your life, lift your eyes up! Place your faith in Jesus. He has promised that if you trust Him, He will restore you and turn your consequences into good for your life. No longer relying on your own understanding – trust God to straighten out your life.

Proverbs 3:5-6 says,

"Trust in the Lord with all your heart and lean not on your own understanding; in all your ways acknowledge him and he will make your paths straight."

Wouldn't you rather walk on a straight path than try to navigate a crooked, rocky trail that threatens to trip you up or make you fall? This is what God promises to those of us who lift our eyes above our circumstances. We trust God, stop trying to figure everything out according to our own understanding, and acknowledge God in everything we do. He will straighten our path!

CHAPTER 9

If Only

"Ve grow too soon oldt undt too late schmardt."

DUTCH PROVERB

MY HUSBAND AND I RECENTLY attended a family reunion with his side of the family. A slide with the above quote was added to our family slideshow as it was his grandmother's favorite saying. One might need to be over 50 years of age to fully understand its meaning! The older we get, the less time we have to "fix" this area of missed opportunities.

Pain comes when we realize that there won't be more of those opportunities filling our life paths. Even if a few options do pop up periodically as we get into our 50's and 60's and 70's, there may not be resources or even energy to take advantage of them. Contemplation over what we wish we would have done can cause a very deep and painful form of regret. There is a hole in our lives. Nothing can fill it, nothing can change the past. We can't talk about it with others because our complaint would sound something like this:

"If only I would have gone to college! I would be so much more successful in my life. I don't know what made me decide not to study and choose a career. There is such a hole in my life because I didn't go to college."

How far would we get making those comments in a conversation with a friend? Soon into the discussion, the friend would blurt out, "There is nothing you can do about the past, make the best of it!" But nothing can remove the dull ache that reminds us that we missed an opportunity that we wish we would have taken.

How did it happen? How do we miss opportunities that later cause us to ask, "What was I thinking?" I believe the "missed opportunity" form of regret stems from one or more of the following:

a. We didn't understand the value of the option at the time it was presented
b. We believed the opportunity would present itself again and we would wait until it does
c. We made another choice that was more appealing and it replaced the missed opportunity
d. We resisted making a choice and time closed the door of opportunity

Sometimes we simply don't understand the impact of not choosing an option. When we're young, we subconsciously believe that there is plenty of time to add this choice to our lives. We choose a different option instead and over time, the new choice spills over into the area that was meant for the missed opportunity. Then there are times that we resist moving ahead with a decision, wrongly believing that we actually have control over when a door of opportunity opens and closes.

THE INVISIBLE MISSED OPPORTUNITY
It's easier to remember why we did something than why we didn't do something. We can remember our thought process in making a choice and taking an action. It is more abstract, however, to remember our reasoning for not making a choice. Dealing with something that never materialized into reality is much more difficult than dealing with something that we have actually experienced.

We can learn from pain that comes from a wrong choice. There are tools available to help people heal from past mistakes. Among them are books, support groups, talk shows, counselors, and programs. If we are wise, we choose to learn from our mistakes, become better, and move beyond regret. Or we can rationalize when there is a tangible experience to consider. We may come to recognize that some good resulted from the bad choice and we learn to be grateful in spite of the pain.

But it's hard to learn from something that was never experienced. Instead, we idealize what we believe *could have been* had we made that choice. Since we didn't actually choose the option, we dream about what it would have been like if we had made that choice. "If only I would have married my high school sweetheart!" Of course, we aren't aware of potholes and pain that could have riddled that path. No, we just contemplate how our lives would have been different and wish that we had not said "no" to something that we could have had.

We may view a missed opportunity as wrong action against our destiny, the fulfillment of what we were born to accomplish. The missed opportunity wasn't a "sin" against another person, it was a sin against myself! I am the one who missed out.

When we evaluate wasted opportunities, we may begin to realize that we have also wasted words, time, and money. We can become overwhelmed when we can't necessarily pinpoint one specific wasted opportunity. Instead, we could begin to experience regret over a *wasted life*. Pain sinks deeper into our souls as we realize that we had so much but didn't do much with what we had.

For some people, the "missed opportunity" form of regret actually turns into more than disappointment for missing a chance to do something. It slowly grows into a deep unhappiness with life. The unhappiness may be comprised of regret for missed opportunities, a bad attitude, and lack of hope for the future. These three ingredients combined make for a lethal recipe that poisons one's chance for a better future. The pain of a missed opportunity can cause remorse that may last for years and cause very real pain that needs resolution. The opportunity blew into our path and then disappeared like the wind, unable to be grasped, yet creating more pain as time goes on. Why does an invisible puff of a chance create such long-lasting regret?

The deepest form of regret
When we make choices that harm ourselves or others, it is sin. Sin can be dealt with and forgiven. God helps us and we move on. God works our circumstances out for good in our lives. We have hope as we move on from our past. We press ahead through bad circumstances created by our choices. But when we miss the chance to live a better life or become who God created us to be, we realize that we have missed the purpose of our lives. Time goes on, life continues, we grow older. The invisible missed opportunity begins to take form and shape and substance. It starts looking like our destiny is in the rear view mirror and there is no way to turn around and grab hold of it!

When we come to the realization that we didn't do much with what we had or we have missed God's purpose for our lives, the deepest form of regret begins to develop. A wasted life creates a form of regret that makes us feel bad about ourselves. We inherently know that life is a gift from God and we only have one life to live. We look back at the timeline of our lives and see wasted time and lost opportunities lining the path of our past. We realize we are less than what we could have been, we have displeased God, and there is no way to relive the past and do it again. What is the resolution for something that never materialized and will never present itself as an opportunity again?

Carrying the weight of "if only"
Because we are living the consequences today of yesterday's missed opportunities, it may seem that there is no way to eliminate regret

completely. It is a weight causing heaviness in our hearts; a burden that, at times, is impossible to bear. We may stubbornly carry the load of our regret on our backs or cry out in despair for God to take our burdens away. In Matthew 11:28, Jesus said, "Come to me, all you who are weary and burdened, and I will give you rest."

Not only does Jesus want us to bring Him our burdens, He wants us to *take up His yoke* and walk with Him through our difficulties. In the next verse, Matthew 11:29, Jesus says, "Take my yoke upon you and learn from me, for I am gentle and humble in heart, and you will find rest for your souls. For my yoke is easy and my burden is light." When we think of a yoke, we think of oxen yoked together so that they can walk at the same pace. When Jesus says, "take my yoke," He is referring to submission. We take His yoke, we submit to what He says, we walk with Him. Then He says, "learn from me." When we submit to Jesus and learn from Him, we will find that His yoke is easy and His burden is light. He is helping us carry our burdens.

We can bring our weighty burdens of regret and "if only" to Jesus, submitting to Him, learning from Him, and walking with Him every day. He will carry the weight of it and our regret will not crush us. On the contrary, our burdens will feel light, a much better feeling than trying to carry them for years on our own strength.

What's my part?

The yoke that Jesus speaks of refers to walking together. He doesn't say we'll ride on top of the yoke… no, we *take* His yoke and *walk* with Him. God partners with us in our healing of past regrets. Of course, He is able to touch us and miraculously make bad memories and painful feelings disappear. But typically, He doesn't choose to heal us in that manner. When Jesus walked among men on earth, many times He asked individuals to participate in the healing process. He wanted them, in some way, to express their faith and willingness to obey Him.

One of my favorite examples is told in John 5:1-9. Jesus met a man who had been paralyzed for 38 years. The man was lying near a pool that was believed to have healing powers for invalids. In verse 6 Jesus asked the man, "Do you want to get well?" I chuckle every time I read that verse. *Of course the man wanted to get well! Don't we all want to be healed of our problems?* But Jesus was asking something much deeper. I believe He was asking the man if he was willing to get up, trust Jesus, and participate in making his life better. When we realize what Jesus is really asking, do we find ourselves struggling to give the easy and predictable answer of "yes"?

The man answered by providing Jesus with a list of excuses and reasons why he could not move from his current situation. He blamed other people for not helping him. He even went as far as to explain that he had tried to get into the pool but everyone got in his way. Jesus paid no attention to the man's excuses. Verse 8 says that He said to the man, "Get up! Pick up your mat and walk." The next verse tells us that the man was cured immediately and he picked up his mat and walked.

When it comes to wasted time and missed opportunities, Jesus is asking us to "Get up!" We must quit wallowing in what was missed. He commands us to pick up the pieces of what is around us and… walk! We need to move on with what is in our life today.

If the man did not believe and did not want to be healed, he would have laid at the same place for the rest of his life. It was only as he responded and obeyed Jesus that he was able to experience healing and a changed life.

In John chapter 5 there were many invalids at the pool and only one man was healed and moved forward in his life. Jesus' invitation is specific and directed at each of us individually. Yet many people don't respond. They stay in the same place, day after day, week after week, year after year. It's time. Will you accept Jesus' invitation to get up, pick up your mat and walk?

PART 2

Moving Beyond Regret

CHAPTER 10

Repentance

*"Would you place a band-aid on a part
of your body that has cancer?"*

LAURIE DRIESEN

SELF-EXAMINATION — THE DOSE OF MEDICINE THAT BEGINS THE HEALING PROCESS

HOW CAN I BEST DESCRIBE this chapter? Is it the medicine that must be swallowed before the pain goes away? Is it the surgery that must be endured before experiencing the healing that is so desperately needed? Or the fire that stings and burns as the heat is turned up even hotter, boiling away the dross of sin and purifying the gleaming, precious gold?

There are many ways to deal with regret and move ahead in life, but we won't get very far without these: self-examination, repentance, responsibility.

In my late twenties I went through counseling during a long separation from my husband. Every week my very patient counselor asked me what I could do to change my situation. Every week I had a few good ideas about how my husband could improve. Or, I would come up with excellent suggestions on how I could help him change. I could try more, pray more, or talk more. I could make phone calls, pray, buy books, pray, or write letters and pray. One by one, my list of ideas became shorter and shorter, as I tried one thing after another. Finally, there was only one thing on my list. I answered her question, "Well, I can always pray." Soon after that, I entered her office and she asked me again, "Is there *anything* you can do to change your situation?" Finally, through my tears of frustration, I admitted, "No, nothing, I don't even have the strength to pray anymore." To my surprise, she responded, "Great! Now let's stop talking about him and get started working on you!"

My counselor gently led me through the process of learning to take responsibility for my choices and dealing with painful circumstances in a healthy way. She knew that unless I was ready and willing to examine myself and change, I was unlikely to make progress toward healing.

The dotted line through regret

It takes courage to examine ourselves. If we remove the rose-colored glasses, take a pencil and trace the dotted line from where we are today to our past, who is really to blame for our regrets? What actions or responses am I personally responsible for?

Self-examination is essential in our quest to move beyond regret. If we can't see or won't admit our mistakes or flaws, it's like going to the doctor without admitting our pain. We won't take the necessary medicine the doctor prescribes unless we first recognize we need it. In allowing the light to shine on our part in the intricacies of regretful situations, we can come to a place of repentance, the first step toward hope and healing.

Some might say, "But it is someone else's fault! What about calling another person to accountability?" Of course, that is a valid question. Your situation might be, in fact, due to choices that someone else made. Or, your situation may have been caused by circumstances that were out of your control. Taking responsibility means looking only at *your* role in the mess. It does not mean taking responsibility that belongs to others and loading it onto your back. The process of self-examination and taking responsibility focuses on your part in whatever regret you are working through. This is a thorough, personal examination that digs deep into your soul to identify and deal with everything that belongs to you.

A large corporation held a leadership training session and one of the speakers conducted an exercise. The attendees were instructed to write a paragraph about a time when he or she was a victim of a bad situation. After everyone was finished, the speaker then requested that the attendees write again about the same situation, but this time they were to include all of the choices they made that contributed to the circumstances. In other words, they were to examine their choices and consider how the situation could have been prevented. Many learned that they were actually not victims but played an active role in producing the painful circumstances by choices they had made or by ignoring warning signs of an impending bad situation.

Taking responsibility for what we allow

Years ago I dated a man who had some good qualities but the more time we spent together, the more I experienced situations that made it clear that he was not a respectful, caring person. When I look back, I realize that there is no point blaming him for his personal flaws. It was much more helpful to me to focus on why I allowed myself to become involved with a person who was not kind and caring.   If I want to be emotionally healthy, I cannot allow myself to become an angry, bitter person who blames others. Instead, I must face my responsibility. Why did I allow a person like that into my life? What can I learn from this situation? What needs to be dealt with deep inside of me so that I make better choices?

Many times we can trace regret back to decisions we made that helped create the unhealthy situation. We can evaluate our participation and where the breakdown occurred. Self-examination means that we scrutinize our mistakes and behavior. We may have had unrealistic expectations. We may have stopped taking care of ourselves spiritually, emotionally, or physically. The inability to set healthy boundaries is *my* responsibility.

Even if someone else is clearly in the wrong, I must examine my part in the complexity of regret. This is ultimately what I am responsible for, making sure I am emotionally healthy and right with myself, others, and God. I am also responsible for not setting expectations that are unrealistic for a person or a situation and realizing that I cannot change others.

TRUE VICTIMS

Unfortunately, there are times when a situation or a person inflicts pain on an innocent victim or creates circumstances in which the innocent suffer. There is much pain and suffering in this world from circumstances that are out of our control. If you are the victim of a crime, abuse, sickness, tragedy, or circumstance in which you had no control, you may need to seek professional help in order to work through the complexities of your situation. This section is not meant to provide answers for your situation, rather *principles* to consider as you work your way toward complete healing.

Some victims feel as though there is no hope for their future. They may feel that God failed to protect them; therefore, how can they turn to God for help? Some may blame God for circumstances that were authored and inflicted by Satan himself. If you are a victim who has lost hope, consider turning to the God who loves you. He promises to lead you from victim to victory!

While a true victim had no control over the pain inflicted on him or her, there is one thing that the victim is responsible for and does have some measure of control over. The victim is ultimately responsible for his or her *response* to the situation. Any circumstance that a person is drawn into, whether by choice or force, will cause either a healthy response or a response that can lead to deeper problems. In situations in which you are a victim, there is truly a fork in the road of responses. One direction will take you toward bitterness and blame and the other will lead you to healing.

ON THE BITTERNESS ROAD YOU WILL FIND:

Self-pity – the most natural and common response to unfair suffering
Complaining – much of which seems justified
Stagnation – staying stuck in the past
Jealousy – wanting what others have
Blaming – even though it doesn't produce an answer to the "why" question
"If only" mentality – fruitless and wasted time of wishing it never happened

ON THE HEALTHY ROAD YOU WILL FIND:

Thankfulness – gratitude in spite of circumstances
Positive attitude – for today and for the future – there is still good in life
Humility – trusting God even in our lack of understanding
Peace – God is in control even in confusing circumstances
Mercy – compassion toward others who are hurting just as you are hurting
Forgiveness – reaching the point of forgiving the perpetrator
Hope – walking closely with the Lord gives us hope for our future

There is a huge chasm between these two roads. They lead in two totally different directions. They are not one degree apart, rather miles apart with no gray area in between. There is no path that allows a little of Bitterness and a little of Healthy. No, they don't mix together at all. The Bitterness swallows up anything good, as a bad apple will sour the whole bushel. The chasm that lies between is filled with regret. Choosing the Healthy Road is the only way to avoid regret for the one thing you are responsible for as a true victim, Your Response.

When life settles down again and time passes and things begin to turn around for you again, Your Response to the injustice you suffered will be the crown you can wear. You won't wear it in pride, but it will be one of the things that will qualify you to actually reach out and help others. It will earn you the right to be an encouraging example to others and let them know that it's worth the effort to stay on the Healthy Road. And most of all, you won't be stuck in the mire of regret that lies waiting for true victims on the Bitterness Road.

It's tempting to blame, but it won't lead to emotional health. If you find yourself blaming others, consider taking the only medicine that is a sure cure: **Taking responsibility.** Whether it's facing our part in messy circumstances or choosing the right response to unfair suffering, we can't move on from regret unless we are willing to do this.

LOSING THE BLAME GAME

In Genesis 3:8-12, when Adam hid from God because of his sin, God asked him questions. The first question was "Where are you?" If we skim over the chapter lightly, we might believe that God, for some odd reason, couldn't find Adam because he was hiding behind a tree. But that is not the meaning of the question. The essence of the question was, "Where are you spiritually?" We can also take that to mean, "Where are you in relation to Me?"

Isn't that the first question God always prompts our heart to answer? Where are we spiritually? Are we hiding from God due to some sin in our life? Hiding is a natural response to guilt and shame. It is interesting that a person usually knows when his or her spouse has been unfaithful. Even without evidence, he or she senses the distance in the spouse, the hiding that comes from a separation caused by unfaithfulness. Sin separates us from the person we sin against. Pain, problems, and mistakes can cause us to feel unworthy of facing the Lord. Many people question where God is in the pain and why He allowed it to happen. If we don't know what

Scripture says, we can hide from the truth of God's Word and wallow in a set of lies that sound right. At some point, all of us must ask ourselves, "Where am I in relation to God?"

God also asked Adam if he had eaten from the forbidden tree. We know God is omniscient and, therefore, already knew the answer. God prompted Adam to recognize, talk about, and face the reality of what he had done. He wanted Adam to admit his sin and what he had done in disobedience. This is a concise snapshot of what we must do as we examine our choices. This process is imperative for us to take responsibility and fully comprehend the consequences of our sin.

I wish I could tell you that Adam immediately took responsibility and admitted his wrongdoing. That's not exactly what happened. When God asked Adam if he had eaten from the forbidden tree, Adam blamed Eve. In his blame game, he actually added God to the list by saying in verse 12, "The woman *you* put here with me – she gave me some fruit from the tree, and I ate it." (Emphasis added.) Then God asked Eve, "What is this you have done?" She was also quick to be a player in the blame game by answering that the serpent had deceived her and that is why she ate the fruit. How many times do we say some variation of the same thing? We blame others and ultimately fault God for causing or allowing whatever it was that caused our mess.

If we are brave enough to go through the process of self-examination, we will realistically identify areas that need to be changed in us. Change can't happen unless we recognize what needs to be changed. We should not be afraid of self-examination. It should not be the last resort or the last ditch effort to regain hope for our future. It should be done at the beginning of our quest for healing of regret. On the path to emotional and spiritual health there is a huge sign posted at the beginning of the road, "What's wrong with you? In order to have a better future, what do you need to change about yourself? Stop here, examine yourself, and find out!"

WRESTLING THROUGH SELF-EXAMINATION

Let me tell you the story of an individual who had much to regret and how he ultimately took responsibility for his choices. In Genesis chapters 25-32, the story of Jacob comes to life. As Jacob and his twin brother, Esau, were being born, Jacob's little hand was clutching Esau's ankle. Esau was born first, earning the title of "firstborn son." It appeared as if Jacob was struggling to be born first. If he were able to talk then, he might have said something like, "Let me out, I want to be the firstborn son!" Because of this, his parents named him Jacob, meaning "heel-catcher" or "he who supplants" or "deceiver." Jacob went on to live out the meaning of his name. When the boys were older, Jacob pressured Esau into selling him his birthright. At a later time, when their father, Isaac, was ready to pronounce his blessing on the firstborn son, Jacob again succeeded in "supplanting" Esau by tricking Isaac into giving him the blessing.

Needless to say, Esau grew very angry toward Jacob. This high level of anger threatened Jacob and forced him to flee for his life in order to separate himself from his brother. Jacob seemed to be living out the meaning of his name. He had cheated and tricked his brother and now was on the run for his life.

Jacob met up with a relative and fell in love with the young daughter. He planned to marry her but his relative tricked him into marrying the wrong daughter! Now he's getting a taste of his own medicine. In other words, life is dishing out exactly what he seemed to deserve in light of the way he had tricked others in the past.

Think about how Jacob's life has gone thus far. He has sown lies and reaped a whirlwind of deceit in return. The significance of this example is that Jacob could easily blame this on the circumstances of his birth. It wasn't his fault that he was grabbing onto Esau's ankle at birth, attempting to switch places. He was a baby! Nevertheless, his parents named him accordingly, "Jacob" or "Deceiver."   We can see during his life that he made very distinct choices to be just that, a trickster and deceiver. He began to suffer very painful consequences of those choices. We can evaluate his situation and comment about how terrible it was that he was "born" a deceiver. We feel sorry for him that having been given the name Jacob may have influenced his behavior to some extent. But ultimately it's very clear that Jacob began to make independent and willful choices that greatly affected his life.

This is significant because most of us consider our lives from a similar viewpoint. Part of the reason we are the way we are is related to the circumstances of our birth. We had no control over who our parents would be or in which city we would be born. So, we can blame those circumstances up to a certain point. Then, as we continue living our lives, we begin to make conscious choices, regardless of the circumstances of our birth. The blame game doesn't work for very long!

Genesis chapter 32 records Jacob's personal time of repentance and how God redirected his life. Jacob learned that his brother Esau was coming out to meet him accompanied by four hundred men. Jacob thought, as anyone in his situation would, that Esau was coming with an army to have final retribution. He thought he was going to be attacked and killed by his brother. Genesis 32:24-30 tells us that Jacob "wrestled" with God all night. I believe that the wrestling match may have gone something like this:

Jacob – "Why was I named Deceiver, Trickster, Liar?"
You are a deceiver and a liar.
Jacob – "God, it's your fault, I'm not in control over my birth! It's not my fault that my hand was on Esau's ankle when we were born."
You chose to lie and trick your brother.
Jacob – "Won't you help me? I know I made my brother mad and now he wants to kill me!"
You haven't called on me or honored me for years, why are you calling on me now? Are you just trying to save your life?
Jacob – "I don't want to die like this! Must this be my destiny? You are the only one who can change my life!"

> *Do you really want to change completely? Are you willing to honor me and follow me the rest of your life?*
> Jacob – "I want a different future. Please forgive me! I want to change completely. I want to serve you the rest of my life. Help me God, you're the only one who can change me!"

Back and forth, struggling, wrestling, questions, answers, more questions, begging, pleading. Why? Please! God forgive me! Help me! Change me!

Have you ever "wrestled" with God in prayer? Have you ever met God, face to face, and struggled through your questions, seeking God for answers? If so, you can identify very well with this picture of Jacob's long night of facing the Lord with tears and questions. I remember one long night of prayer and wrestling with God over an issue in my life. After lying in bed praying, questioning, and tossing and turning, I finally decided to get up in the middle of the night and "wrestle" with the Lord. I wrote in my journal that evening, "Lord, I don't understand what you are doing. Tonight I don't want to read the Bible or listen to my Christian music or listen to a sermon. I just want to talk to you, face to face. I need an answer to my problem. I want to know what you have to say." I sat in the living room at 2:00 a.m. in the dark praying for several hours. Finally, exhausted, I began to read the Bible and through my tears and through the words on the pages in front of me, God answered me. He turned my situation in a new direction that night. Through His Word, He gave me a promise regarding my problem. He also led me to a Scripture verse about trusting Him and not questioning Him. Oh yes, God gets very personal! And so, I felt He answered me that night and gave me hope. Sometimes we need to wrestle through our questions and ask God to meet us where we are in our problem.

Jacob told God he would not "let go" of Him until He blessed him. He would not give up until he was right with God. Jacob knew he had done many deceitful things and deserved the wrath of his brother, Esau. But he wanted to change and most of all, to be right with God.

God asked Jacob, "What is your name?" Remember how important names were to the Jewish people? Asking someone his name is the same as asking, "Who are you?" Jacob had no choice but to answer, "Jacob" (deceiver, supplanter, cheater). Jacob finally had to look at himself, admit his sin, face to face with God, nothing to hide, completely honest and truthful. He was basically saying, "I am a liar and a deceiver." I believe he was honest with God about all he had done, taking responsibility for all of his tricks and lies. Surprisingly, God answered him by saying that he would no longer be called Jacob and He gave him a new name, Israel.

God sets us free from our past

When we make big mistakes, some of us fear that we will be "known" by our mistakes. We fear that our identity has been molded by our failures. Jacob didn't want to be known as a deceiver. He wanted to become different! It is painful to be viewed and identified for a mistake in our past. For example, a person who is freed from prison may be referred to as "the guy that was in prison." How painful it would be for a woman who claimed bankruptcy to be known by others as "the woman who got herself into financial trouble." Our identity can easily be wrapped up in the regret we experience.

I recently attended a family wedding. I hadn't danced in years, but my daughter pulled me out on the dance floor and it didn't take long to remember how to dance. I stayed on the dance floor for two hours dancing and having fun. My nieces commented, "We heard all about you Aunt Laurie, and how you loved to drink and party!" Apparently their mom had entertained them with stories of my college years. I immediately told them, "That was before I was a Christian!" But it struck me that after 30 years of my Christian life, I could still be known and referred to as a party girl. I believe we should use others' misconceptions of us as a testimony to God's grace and mercy. We can use their comments as a chance to tell them about what God has done for us and how He has changed us.

When God gave Jacob a new name, He was saying to him, "You are no longer a deceiver, you are now a new person in my eyes." God gave Jacob a new identity! His new name was Israel, which means, "Triumphant with God" or "He who contended with God and prevailed." Then God declared a blessing over Israel. Wow! If you have regret in your past for sins and bad choices, wouldn't you love to have God Himself declare a blessing over you and grant you a totally new identity? If you are a Christian, God has already granted you a new identity. When we receive Christ, our identity is with Him, the old has passed and we are to walk in newness of life. But, in order to receive newness of life, we must go through the step of repentance.

New life – new sins – the continuous process of repentance

I wish I could say that after I repented, I never sinned again. I wish my personal testimony described how I gave my life to the Lord at age 25 and from then on, I lived a perfect, sin-free life. Unfortunately, the truth is that I made bigger and more serious mistakes as an adult Christian than I ever did as a high school and college student sampling what the world had to offer.

The fact is, when we repent and receive God's forgiveness, we are freed from the *penalty* of sin. Jesus has taken our punishment, what is due to us, upon Himself at the cross. When we repent and believe, we are forgiven and receive His gift of salvation. Jesus sends the promised Holy Spirit who indwells us and begins the work of sanctification in our lives. This process of sanctification, or making us more like Christ, takes place until the day we leave this earth and go to be with the Lord in Heaven. In a nutshell, this can be explained as follows:

- Salvation frees us from the **penalty** of sin as we are forgiven by God
- Sanctification frees us from the **power** of sin as the Holy Spirit works in our lives

- Glorification will free us from the **presence** of sin forever when we live eternally in Heaven

    This is the process that takes place in the life of every Believer. It is the second phase of this process that can be the most difficult. The process of sanctification is where we experience the most pain. As the Holy Spirit begins the work of pruning off old ways of thinking and patterns of behavior, we find that sanctification can be an ugly, painful process. It can be likened to the caterpillar, hidden in the cocoon where the grueling work of transformation takes place. We can't see or explain what is taking place or how it works, but we know it can be ugly before the beautiful butterfly is ready to be what it was created to be.

    At age 25, I was not an instant butterfly! Over the years, I have experienced the Holy Spirit working in the hidden places of my heart, revealing new areas that needed to be pruned. Although I had been freed from my past lifestyle, I went on to make fresh new mistakes, sometimes purposely and at times, unknowingly. The difference is that before I was a committed Christian, I *lived* in sin. After I became a Christian, I sinned but didn't live a *lifestyle* of sin. There is a big difference. Making a mistake is not the same as choosing to live against God's Word and under the power of a sinful lifestyle. As Christians, we are called to abide in Christ, respond to the conviction of the Holy Spirit and move on from our mistakes. We may sin for a season, or temporarily find ourselves in a lifestyle that isn't pleasing to the Lord, but as we immerse ourselves in the study of God's Word and submit to the pruning shears of the Holy Spirit, we overcome and experience victory over our sin.

    In John 13:5-10, Jesus gives a physical example of the ongoing cleansing that we need in order to walk with Him while living in a sinful world. Jesus began to wash the disciple's feet and Peter proclaimed that Jesus should never wash his feet. Verse 8 tells us that Jesus answered Peter by saying, "Unless I wash you, you have no part with me." Peter, who tended toward extremes, exclaimed in verse 9, "Then Lord, not just my feet but my hands and my head as well!" But Jesus explained that when a person has had a bath, he needs only to wash his feet because his whole body is already clean. He was showing the disciples that although they have been washed, forgiven, and given the "bath" of salvation, their feet would still get dirty with sin by walking daily in the mire of the world. Therefore, only the feet would need to be washed in order to be fully clean.

Sanctification reminds us that although salvation is a one-time experience, coming to the Lord in repentance is continually necessary as we get our feet dirty in a world of sin.

Confession vs. Repentance

I would like to shine a spotlight on a serious problem that affects most people at some point in their walk with the Lord – incomplete repentance. Many Christians wonder why they never seem to have victory over a specific sin in their life. Why do they fall back into the same problem, making the same stupid choice, knowing each time that consequences are never going to change? Consequences are stubborn, showing up without fail every time that choice is made. Some might say, "I confessed my sin, why do I still find no power to overcome this habit?" The problem is the lack of understanding that confession is not the same as repentance.

When we confess our sins, we come into agreement with God. Confess means to "say the same as." We say the same thing as God says about our sin. We agree with the truth. In other words, we finally agree with God!

Repentance is an action that takes us in a different direction. "Repent" actually means to "turn" or "turn away from." It is changing how we think about what we have done. We not only agree with God (confess), but we admit that our understanding and way of thinking is wrong and we surrender to God's truth. If we don't regret our *way of thinking*, we won't change our actions. If we do regret our thinking, confess our actions, and embrace the authority of God, He forgives us and redirects our destiny. Having turned from our ways, we begin to live a new lifestyle and make better choices.

Confess	**Repent**
Agree with God	Change my way of thinking
Say the same thing as God	Turn away from doing the same thing
"Say"	"Do"

We think if we feel shame, remorse, and regret that we have repented. We feel sorry and guilty and believe that those feelings mean that we have repented. Then we wonder why we do not experience the victory that God promises. No, being sorry is not true and complete repentance. True repentance brings me to the point of breaking my will and surrendering my choice to do that thing. *I turn and move in another direction because my mind has changed.* Repentance is a deep work in our spirit causing us to lose the desire to do the same action again. How do we know if we haven't fully repented of a specific sin? Simply, we'll flirt with that sin again. We will rationalize until we are back into it. We'll say the same thing we said the first time, "I have needs, I want them to be met, the way I want, and it has to be now." As long as we refuse to allow our will to be broken, we will not truly repent.

LEARNING TO REPENT WELL

King David, the second king of Israel, committed serious sins including adultery and murder. Yet God called David, "A man after my own heart." David is mentioned more in the Bible than any other person, aside from Jesus Christ. He was brave and loyal and had a deep love for God throughout his entire life. He wrote dozens of Psalms that serve as praise and encouragement for us today. David had a heart for the Lord and a strong faith that developed in him from the time he was a shepherd boy. How could a person like David, a man after God's own heart, be capable of falling into such great sin? He committed some of the worst sins recorded in the Bible, including indulging in an adulterous affair with Bathsheba, which resulted in a pregnancy. When he couldn't hide the adultery, he had Bathsheba's husband killed in battle, then hid the entire situation for a year.

How can someone who did such things be considered a man after God's own heart? The answer is because David *repented well*. We learn from this that the key to intimacy with God isn't perfection and a sin-free life, rather a contrite heart that seeks the Lord above all else. After David had been confronted by the prophet Nathan regarding his adultery with Bathsheba, he wrote Psalm 51. In this beautiful Psalm of repentance, David pleads for the Lord to forgive and cleanse him. His heart is cut open and laid bare on the pages of Scripture as an inspiration to us in our prayers of repentance.

"Repenting well" means to be quick to respond to the conviction of the Holy Spirit of sin. Quickly means right away! As soon as the prophet Nathan charged David with, "You are the man" in 2 Samuel 12:7, David confessed that he had sinned against the Lord. Repenting well also means to repent completely. Psalm 51 reveals the thorough repentance of David with the words in verse 2, "Wash away all my iniquity and cleanse me from my sin." And verse 4, "Against you and you only have I sinned and done what is evil in your sight." Finally, in verse 10 David says, "Create in me a pure heart O God and renew a steadfast spirit within me." David wanted God to give him a whole new heart, not just fix up the old one!

Someone might say, "I don't have anything to repent of, my regret is another person's fault!" Your regret might be the fault of someone else, but we all are called to repentance. Romans 3:23 states that, "...all have sinned and fall short of the glory of God." Acts 17:30 says that God commands "...all people everywhere to repent." God promises the following to those who repent:

- Restoration, right relationship with God (Jeremiah 15:19)
- Forgiveness, God will "wipe out our sins" (Acts 3:19)

- Eternal life, God takes no pleasure in death (Ezekiel 18:32)
- Relationship, we can now approach the throne of God with our prayers and we receive grace (Psalm 65:2, Hebrews 4:16)
- Freedom, God sets us free from the law of sin (Romans 8:2)

If we don't repent, we remain in the following state in relation to God:

- Separation, there is a veil between you and God (2 Corinthians 3:16)
- Eternal death (Romans 6:23)
- Slavery to sin (Romans 6:19)
- God does not hear our prayers (Psalm 66:18)
- Loneliness, we cannot enter the presence of God (Psalm 51:11, 101:7)

Just as surgery opens an area that needs healing, self-examination cuts us open and takes us deep into the places where regret began. We dig into the pain and examine each part, pulling out and dealing with all of the decisions, actions, and responses that belong to us. Taking responsibility is the necessary surgery, facing the truth, admitting our faults, and accepting our role. With a thorough examination, honesty, and a little bit of courage, we can take responsibility for our part. Repentance brings true healing as we turn from our old ways, change our behavior, and live free of regret.

CHAPTER 11

Forgiveness

When we consider the ingredients of choices and mistakes that brought us to where we are today, forgiveness is an absolute necessity in cleaning up the mess! We experience regret when we live out the painful consequences of our choices. How can we change things? How can we start over? The "punishment" seems so much greater than what is deserved. A small choice produced a harvest that grew out of control. So we learn from the past and begin to make better decisions. We attempt to add new healthy choices like fresh ingredients to the mix of destructive choices made years before. But the old is still there, poisoning the taste of the life we hoped to live. Can things ever be right when our past is riddled with choices that still affect where we are today?

God offers an ingredient that will change the entire flavor of our lives. Forgiveness. It is a gift from God that breaks all the rules of nature, consequences, punishment, and regret. Forgiveness is the one thing that can interrupt the path of the storm. It can make situations right that are wrong. It can turn circumstances that are upside down right side up again. It can heal relationships. It softens hearts. It can bring people back together again. It is the key that unlocks closed doors. It gives us a new start. It redirects our destiny. Forgiveness.

Forgiveness – a cleansing relief

Forgiveness was not "Plan B" when Adam and Eve sinned in the Garden of Eden. God did not create forgiveness to accommodate sinful man. He knew that giving man the gift of free will would result in sinful choices. His answer for sin is forgiveness and salvation. God's plan for redemption was revealed immediately after Adam and Eve sinned, hid from God, and broke fellowship with Him. The story in Genesis did not end with condemnation. On the contrary, God immediately killed an animal in order to provide skin for a covering for Adam's and Eve's nakedness and shame that resulted from their sin. The two deserved the punishment of death for their sin but God chose a substitute to die instead. We shouldn't pass over this principle lightly. God required that the life of an innocent animal be sacrificed in order to atone for the sin committed by Adam and Eve. This is a picture or a shadow of the plan of redemption that God established at the beginning of the world. After sin entered the world, separating us spiritually from God, He paved the way back to Him through the sacrificial death of the innocent. If we understand that principle, it will deepen our understanding of Jesus' ultimate sacrifice, shedding His blood to atone for your sin and mine.

Why can't God simply wipe away our sin? Why did blood have to be shed as payment for our sins? Why is death the punishment for sin? If God is all powerful, why couldn't He just wipe it all away and forget about it?

Before I answer those tough questions, let me ask you to consider a few questions. When you hear of a school shooting in which innocent students are killed, how does that make you feel? What about when a child is kidnapped and murdered? Do you want God to wipe away the perpetrators' actions with no consequences? Do you want terrorists to receive forgiveness and then we'll all just forget the horror?

Our sense of justice that rises up, demanding to be satisfied, burns in our hearts because we were created in the image of God. We experience feelings, emotions, anger, and a sense of justice because that is how God created us. We feel a strong sense of anger toward others when they do evil things. We want justice! When someone takes something from us or harms us, they "owe" us. They have created a debt that needs to be repaid. Our society has formed a judicial structure that attempts to accommodate this system of payment or restitution for breaking laws and causing harm.

What we don't want is justice for our own sin and our own mistakes. We don't want to experience consequences or punishment for the things we have done. But God's justice is complete and thorough. We owe God a huge debt for our sin against Him. Reconciliation with God only comes when that debt has been satisfied. If we believe that God can and should wipe away sin with no payment, we lack understanding of our sinfulness and God's Holiness. Because God is Holy, He cannot reside where there is sin. It must be atoned, paid for, and punished in order to satisfy His wrath against all of the evil that has permeated our world.

If we want to know how angry God is about all the sin in the world, all we have to do is study the crucifixion of Jesus. The Bible tells us that God's wrath for our sins was poured out on Jesus at the cross. Jesus bore the wrath of God that was meant for us. Christians call this the "Divine Exchange." Paul explains this in his letter to the Corinthians, "God made him who had no sin to be sin for us, so that in him we might become the righteousness of God." (2 Corinthians 5:21) Jesus took the punishment for our sin (though He didn't deserve it) and we become righteous in God's eyes (though we don't deserve it).

Because God's anger was satisfied at the cross, we can be reconciled to God. John 3:16 tells us that in order to receive this wonderful gift of free righteousness, we must believe in Him. "For God so loved the world that he gave his only son, that whosoever believes in him will not perish but have eternal life." The passage goes on to say in verse 18, "Whoever believes in him is not condemned but whoever does not believe stands condemned already because he has not believed in the name of God's one and only Son."

Forgiveness from God must be accepted and received by each of us. God offers us the free gift of forgiveness but many people don't accept the gift. Those who don't receive or experience God's forgiveness fall into one or more of three categories:

1. They reject God's offer of forgiveness because they do not want to be cleansed of their sin. They want to continue on the path they are on. Forgiveness means change, and they do not want to change.
2. They believe in the forgiveness of God but have not accepted His forgiveness personally in their lives. They feel they don't deserve God's forgiveness. They reason that they must pay something to earn God's forgiveness.
3. They still experience the consequences of their choices; therefore, they don't "feel" forgiven by God. They are basing their assessment of God's forgiveness on their ability to *feel* cleansed and forgiven.

Forgiveness is an essential part of healing from regret. Forgiveness goes to the heart of the matter of regret, beyond just feeling better about our choices. Forgiveness takes care of the sin that caused our poor choices and reconciles us to God. Without reconciliation, we have no hope of living out our true purpose in life. God is the one who helps us reach our potential and live a life free of regret.

FORGIVING OTHERS

When we believe and experience the forgiveness of God, we are commanded in Scripture to go and forgive others for what they have done to us. Remembering how much God has forgiven us should make it easier for us to extend that same forgiveness to others. The parable of the unmerciful servant in Matthew 18:23-35 shows us that God desires that we forgive as we have been forgiven. The servant owed his master a huge sum of money. The master was going to throw the servant in prison but the servant begged the master to be patient. The master took pity on him and canceled the debt. Then the same servant went out and found another servant who owed him a small amount and demanded repayment. The fellow servant fell to his knees and begged for mercy but the servant refused and had him thrown in prison. He was unwilling to extend the same mercy he had received to the person that owed him. Jesus told this parable to illustrate how we should continue to forgive others and not hold unforgiveness in our hearts.

But where does justice fit in God's command for us to forgive? If we forgive those who hurt us, is that the same as wiping away their sin? Certainly not! We are keeping our hearts free from grudges, resentment, anger, and bitterness. Many people misunderstand what God commands regarding forgiveness of others. They believe that when God says that He "forgets" our sin, that we should also "forget" the sins of others. Jeremiah 31:34 tells us that when God forgives, He chooses to "remember our sins no more." We know that God is omniscient; therefore, He knows everything. The passage doesn't mean God actually forgets our sin, but He deals with the sin in our lives and then *chooses* not to hold it against us any longer.

Jesus is our example of how we should forgive others. He also explained exactly what we should do when someone sins against us. In Luke 17:3, Jesus says, "If your brother sins, rebuke him, and if he repents, forgive him. If he sins against you seven times in a day, and seven times comes back to you and says, 'I repent,' forgive him." Rebuking or confronting a person who has hurt us should be done humbly, speaking the truth in love. (Ephesians 4:15) Jesus encourages us to hold people accountable. If the person repents, we forgive him. We will not forget what he did but it does mean that we choose not to treat him or her on the basis of the wrong done to us.

Forgiveness does not erase consequences

When we are forgiven by God, it doesn't mean that we won't suffer consequences. God can heal and restore us but for some, the ultimate healing and restoration will not take place until they get to Heaven. When we forgive others, we won't necessarily hire the person back in our business or reunite in an intimate relationship. Reconciliation and rebuilding what once was may not be possible even though the debt is canceled and the forgiven person's slate is clean. What became broken along the way may not be able to be repaired. The trust has been damaged. Forgiveness is a gift, but trust must be earned. Forgiveness doesn't mean that there are no consequences.

Forgiving the unrepentant

What do we do if our sibling, friend, parent, child, spouse, boss, coworker, or other person sins against us and does not repent? How do we handle a situation where the other person continues to hurt us and does not admit any wrongdoing?

Jesus modeled what our attitude should be toward those who hurt us, even if they don't repent. He taught that we should love our enemies, pray for them, and do good to those who have hurt us. This should be our attitude toward those who hurt us who aren't aware that what they are doing is wrong, or refuse to repent and change. An attitude of forgiveness will keep our hearts free of bitterness and regret. We can extend grace to those around us, not expecting perfection and remembering that there have probably been times when we have hurt others without realizing it.

The ultimate example of forgiveness for the unrepentant is when Jesus was hanging on the cross. There is no record of anyone standing around repenting while Jesus was dying. Yet He prayed, "Father, forgive them for they do not know what they are doing." (Luke 23:34)

When we extend grace to others, we can turn the situation over to God, who will avenge where necessary. We are placing in God's hands the consequences and outcome of the other person's hurtful actions. Romans 12:19 says, "Do not take revenge but leave room for God's wrath, for it is written, 'It is mine to avenge, I will repay,' says the Lord."

Forgiving ourselves

One of the hardest things to do when we are angry over our past choices is to extend to ourselves the same forgiveness that God has given to us. Some people grow to hate themselves for their choices, holding themselves to a higher standard than they hold others. Many who are living in regret simply can't let go of past mistakes and feel they must "pay" for them somehow. They feel that self-forgiveness, a cleansed conscience, and a new start are not options. It is possible that they believe one or more of the following statements:

- I feel that I deserve to continue being punished for what I did.
- My choices affected many people. How can I forgive myself and move on when other people are still angry about what I did?
- I'm not just angry because of what I've done, I'm mad at myself for who I have become.
- I would forgive myself but I can't get rid of the guilt and shame over what I've done.
- My standards for myself have become higher than my standards for those around me.
- I believe God has given up on me. I don't believe He has forgiven me. If God can't forgive me, then I won't forgive myself.
- If I forgive myself, I will have to learn to accept and love myself again. I don't deserve this after what I've done.
- I'm still suffering the consequences of my choices; how can I forgive and forget when I'm reminded every day of what I did?

If we have repented, we are forgiven by God. We should not dwell on our regret, sin, and mistakes when God has chosen not to remember them. Learning from our mistakes is an absolute necessity. We remember what we've done and use our new wisdom that we've gained from the pain to avoid making similar choices. But other than that, the only benefit to remembering our sins is when it reminds us of the forgiveness we received from God, prompting us to extend the same forgiveness to others.

When we are filled with regret for our choices, why wouldn't we take God up on His offer of forgiveness? What a relief to be able to stand before my Creator free of guilt! He loves each of us and wants an intimate relationship with every person that He created. Forgiveness is God's answer for us to be in relationship with Him.

You may believe that you are too bad to be forgiven or reconciled to God. Have you considered that not accepting God's forgiveness reveals a prideful spirit? You are basically expressing to God that His forgiveness is not good enough. Jesus' payment for your sin was not complete. His humble and excruciating sacrifice on the cross wasn't good enough to cover all sin. It was only powerful enough for a few small sins, but not great big sins. You know better and you'll hang on to the mistake and pay for it until you feel cleansed on your own. Proverbs 16:18 warns us that a haughty spirit will bring destruction to us.

You see, whether we have sinned a little or a lot, we are still separated from God and in need of a Savior. No matter what the size of the sin, the separation from God is the same. And guess what? The answer is still the same! The answer is the same for your sin and my sin and all sin… **Forgiveness.**

CHAPTER 12

The Power of the Past

*"Yesterday we deposited experiences
into today's bank of memories."*

Anonymous

Memories...

God wants us to be persistent in facing forward and pressing on toward the goal of our Christian life. He wants us to know that we have been forgiven, cleansed, and are walking in newness of life with Christ. But even as we press forward, we still may be experiencing the aftermath, the consequences, the fallout of bad choices. And those painful little things called "memories" float to the surface periodically and don't ever seem to be erased completely. The fact is, sometimes it is hard to move on because our memories hold us back. Even though our slate is wiped clean and God chooses to "remember our sins no more," our memory is still very much intact.

At times, memories can be so strong that they elicit the same feelings and emotions in us that we felt years ago when the choice happened. This phenomenon is actually a beautiful gift from God. It is the gift of "nostalgia." As we get older and life becomes more limiting, pleasant memories of the past give us wonderful things to talk about and treasure. But when our past is filled with bad choices, the gift of memory doesn't feel like a gift. It feels more like a curse! We relive the situation as if it happened only yesterday. The bad memories bring bad feelings and the bad feelings bring negative emotions and before we know it, we are living in regret.

This is also true of memories of sins that a person committed that become fresh in his mind and cause temptation again to make the same choice. For example, if a person made a bad choice sexually, he can revive the feelings of the experience by reliving the details of the memory. The feelings are real and the temptation to relive the memory is powerful.

Jesus had strong words for a person who nurtures sinful thoughts. He said in Matthew 5:28, "But I tell you that anyone who looks at a woman lustfully has already committed adultery with her in his heart." Jesus considers our thought life just as important as our actions. In other words, what we think about is just as important as what we actually do.

Why are our memories so strong in certain areas of our lives? Why do certain situations seem so real for us today even though they happened years ago?

Science has revealed through studies of brain activity relating to memory that the more adrenaline present in the brain at the time of the action, the stronger the memory relating to that incident will be. This is why people can remember exactly where they were and what they were doing when, for example, the twin towers fell on that fateful day of September 11, 2001. Or a person says, "I remember vividly what I was doing when the phone call came with the tragic news." In other words, an extreme situation that elicits powerful emotions causes adrenaline to be released which produces a stronger memory of the event. In turn, when we relive the memory, we essentially release the adrenaline into our system once again.

This is a helpful physical explanation of why our memory banks are so strong. But what about the spiritual and practical solution to memories of what we regret?

THE ONLY ANSWER FOR A HIGH BANK ACCOUNT OF PAINFUL MEMORIES

There is an answer that frees us from the pain of the past and the powerful memories that keep us trapped in regret. When we come into close relationship with the Lord and begin to fill our minds with His truth, a new thing happens to those poisonous memories. They begin to fade as the reality of our relationship with Christ grows stronger.

GOD OF THE PAST, PRESENT, AND FUTURE

Many people say, "Yes, I believe in God." They may pray and depend on Him in their everyday lives. But did you know that God is not only God in your life today? He is also God of your past and your future.

"Is God able to go back into my past and change it?"

Maybe that is the wrong question. The right question might be, "Was God in my past?" Or better yet, "Is He God of my past, present, and future?" And the answer to those questions is, "Yes!"

One aspect of the natural world that we take for granted is time. Time was created by God. The past, present, and future are simply points in a timeline created by God. With our limited understanding of Almighty God, we may fail to realize that, although we are bound by time, God is not. It is a law of nature, like gravity, that was created by God as part of the natural system in which we exist. We understand events in terms of beginning and end. It is difficult to comprehend that God has no beginning. Jesus said in John 8:58, "I tell you the truth… before Abraham was born, I am!" He was essentially saying that He has no beginning and He is God.

How does this truth apply to our regret for an unchangeable past? I believe that as we receive God into our lives, we can invite Him into our past, present, and future. God is able to help us deal with the pain of the past, even though the timeline of life has cut off my ability to go back and change things.

During my first week as a new Christian, I invited God into my past. I spoke with a pastor who said that even though I lived life for years without the Lord, I could go back into my past and invite Jesus into that part of my life. If I sinned, I could ask Him to forgive me. I needed to come to the realization that He was always with me, even when I wasn't walking with Him.

When I was alone at home, I closed my eyes and pictured everything I could remember from my past, especially my college years. I brought every memory I could think of up to the surface of my mind, only this time, my memory included Jesus in the "picture." As I pictured myself walking through all of my experiences, I envisioned my hand in His, walking together. Of course, it was painful exposing to Him all of the things that I had done, but didn't He already know all of it? It was a very healing experience to bring God into my past, experience His forgiveness, and know that my past was not "cut off" from Him because I did not walk with Him at that time in my life.

I encourage you to do the same; invite Jesus into your past. Close your eyes and with your hand in His, walk through all of your memories. Talk to Him as you walk through your memories and ask for forgiveness as you go along. Talk to Him about the chances you missed along the way. Talk to Him about your struggles today. Open your heart to Him as you face the memories of the past.

An outcast meets Jesus

Do you remember the woman that Jesus spoke with at the well when He traveled through Samaria? In John chapter 4 we learn that this woman went to the well at about noon, when she knew not many others would be there. After we learn of her past, we realize why she felt like an outcast and wanted to go to the well when the least amount of people would be there. But Jesus arrived, thirsty, and asked her to draw some water and give Him a drink. They began a conversation and eventually Jesus confronted her about her past. He revealed to her that He knew about her past, that she had been married five times and the man she was now living with was not her husband. He surfaced the very thing she was trying to run away from. He was not condemning her and she replied that she recognized that He must be a prophet, since He knew all about her life. They continued their conversation about spiritual worship and verse 25 tells us that she said, "I know that Messiah (called Christ) is coming. When He comes, he will explain everything to us." Then Jesus said to her in verse 26, "I who speak to you am he."

Wow! Jesus revealed to a sinful woman that He was the long awaited Messiah! In just a brief conversation, He helped her face her past and lead her right to the heart of who He was. I believe she was repentant because she didn't deny Jesus' statement about her past. She didn't run away or argue. Instead, with an open heart, she talked with Jesus, believed Him and listened to what He had to say. This had a profound effect on her as she went back to the town, proclaiming to the people that she had encountered the Christ. Her meeting with Jesus changed her from being a shamed outcast to proclaiming to the town that she had met the Messiah! The chapter tells us that many of the Samaritan people believed in Him because of the woman's testimony.

The Samaritan woman's life changed radically as she faced her past with Jesus and believed who He said He was. Then she moved forward, never to be the same again. She had a testimony and shared it with others. The chapter tells us that Jesus stayed two days in that town, teaching the people. Many became believers and said, "...we know that this man really is the Savior of the world." (John 4:42)

PRESSING FORWARD PAST THE PAST

You and I and anyone else who wants to be free of the ball and chain around our ankle that threatens to hold us to our past need to take on the challenge of "pressing on." The Apostle Paul tells us in Philippians chapter 3 that there is one thing he had to do... "Forgetting what is behind and straining toward what is ahead, I press on toward the goal to win the prize for which God has called me heavenward in Christ Jesus." (Philippians 3:13-14)

There is only one direction to face as we attempt to break the power of the past. FORWARD! What this means is that after we have been forgiven and cleansed of our past, we press forward, not allowing memories, guilt, and shame to drag us backward. And the further we travel forward, away from our past, the less power it will have over us.

CHAPTER 13

The Battlefield of Choices

I QUIT SMOKING WHEN I was 25 years old. To be more accurate, I should say I "decided" to quit smoking when I was 25. I didn't actually conquer quitting until several years later. I had smoked throughout high school and college and was as hooked as anyone could be. I loved smoking. Cigarettes had become my friend. But when I committed my life to the Lord, smoking was one of the first things God began to deal with in my life. I began to feel pangs of guilt when I smoked and felt the Holy Spirit convicting me that this habit of mine needed to go. I knew if I didn't quit, I would grow into an old woman with a smoker's cough and a raspy voice, wishing I would have quit years before. I envisioned myself at age 50 sitting in a doctor's office with a serious man in a white coat, shaking his finger at me saying, "Now you know you should quit smoking!" Because, in my mind, quitting was inevitable at some point, I came to the grand realization that I should go through the pain and trouble at my young age and get it over with.

It took about three years of all-out war between my flesh and my spirit. My flesh craved smoking yet my spirit longed to be free of any addiction. Every day was a battle. I would begin the day, cigarette-free, until about 4:00 in the afternoon and then the battle would begin. I'd fight the urge for a few minutes, reminding myself that this would be difficult. I needed to resist and be strong. But as the urge got stronger, I would give in, unable to overcome the craving. It was a tough, daily battle. But soon each day got better and better. I would fight a little harder, resist a little longer, until I finally reached the point where I lasted all day without smoking. Then the same battle would take place every few days, soon only every few months, then at last, I quit! Now, in my 50's, I look back in relief at what a smart decision that was for me.

My story about quitting smoking portrays, in a small way, how our lives become battlefields between our flesh and our spirit, wise choices and poor choices, and ultimately, between good and evil.

The struggle between wanting and doing

When we become Christians, we receive the promised Holy Spirit who indwells us and guides us. Our spirit is strengthened and we want to follow the Lord. We begin to study God's Word and we soon learn that how we think and live is not in line with what Scripture teaches. James 1:23 tells us that God's Word is like a mirror. We have sin (imperfections) but until we look in a mirror, we don't even see them. Then we look into the mirror of God's Word and our sin becomes clear and we know we have to deal with it. If we never look into a mirror, we will never know if we have areas we need to address. If we don't study the Word of God, we will not have a clear understanding of what we need to change. If we do look in the mirror but take only a fleeting glance, we will miss things.

It is very frustrating to me when I put my makeup on in the morning, only to look in the mirror later in the day and see a blotch of black mascara on my eyelid. Wouldn't it be silly for me to see that mistake and simply respond, "That's too bad that I missed my eyelashes. Oh well, I'll just pretend that the blotch is not there." Of course I'm not going to leave it there; I'm going to fix it to the best of my ability.

James 1:22-25 says that if we look intently into the mirror of God's Word and do what it says, we will be blessed. He tells us that we deceive ourselves if we listen to the Word and don't do what we know it is saying to us. So, we make up our minds and decide to change. We soon learn that there is a gap between what we desire and what we are able to actually do. A struggle begins to take place in our minds as we come to realize that what we want to do isn't the same as what our body/flesh wants to do.

We continue learning more by studying God's Word. The battle gets even stronger. It has extended to our flesh, which is accustomed to getting what it wants. We desire to do the right thing but our flesh cries out in pain when we begin to withhold some of its satisfaction and indulgences. Soon we find we are in an all-out war against the sin that trips us up and threatens to steer us back to our old ways.

The main reason our struggles increase as Christians is because we now know more about God's view of right and wrong, wise and unwise choices. Before coming into a relationship with Christ, we essentially did as we pleased and followed our own desires. As followers of Christ, we now live to please Him and try to live as He directed, "denying ourselves, taking up our cross and following Him." When we truly deny ourselves, guess who becomes the most irritated? Our flesh! Our motives are pure and we desire to do good, but our flesh screams out to be pleased by the things of the world.

In Romans 7:15-25, the Apostle Paul talks about his struggle with wanting to do what is right yet not having the ability to carry it out. His heart is right but his actions are wrong. He says in verse 15, "I do not understand what I do. For what I want to do I do not do, but what I hate I do." In verse 18 he continues, "I know that nothing good lives in me, that is, in my sinful nature. For I have the desire to do what is good, but I cannot carry it out." He wants to do good but his sinful nature keeps him from doing it. He loves God but the sin within himself keeps surfacing. Finally, after his discourse about this struggle, he exclaims in verse 24, "What a wretched man I am! Who will rescue me from this body of death?"

How many times have we experienced that same frustration? We try our best and struggle to make good choices but there is something powerfully at work within us that holds us back from victory. What is the answer?

After honestly laying out his conflict and pain on the pages of Scripture, Paul gives us the one and only resolution to his struggle. In verse 25 he answers his own question. "Who will rescue me from this body of death? Thanks be to God – through Jesus Christ our Lord!"

THE TRUE BATTLEFIELD

When Paul describes the battle between his flesh and his spirit, the battlefield where the fight takes place is clearly in his mind. Our thoughts are crucial to winning the battle over the temptations that flood our daily lives. Before I decided to quit smoking, I enjoyed my cigarettes. I felt happy when I smoked. I liked having a cigarette whenever I felt I wanted one. Before my battle to quit smoking, I began to *think* differently about my friend, the cigarette. I *thought* about what my future would look like if I didn't quit. I *thought* about the benefits of eliminating smoking from my life. I *reasoned* that if I quit, I would be happier in the long run. Those thoughts strengthened my resolve to begin the fight to quit.

The battle in my mind would take place when I began to argue with myself. The argument went something like this:

I'm going to quit smoking, starting today.
Oh no, I feel the urge to have a cigarette!
Well, maybe I'll have one cigarette and then start quitting again tomorrow.
Why am I quitting anyway, I like smoking!
I've already thought about it, I have to quit smoking. It's a bad habit and I want to be healthy.
God is not going to stop prompting me to quit this habit. If I don't deal with it today, I'll have to deal with it in the future.
I can't stand it – I need a cigarette. How am I going to go through the day without one?
I want to quit.

I can't do it.
Resisting is too hard.
I don't want to smoke anymore.
What I want to do I don't do, but what I hate I do. I want to do what is good but I can't carry it out. Who will help me? Thanks be to God, through Jesus Christ!

Paul's struggle is our struggle. We have all felt this same struggle when our flesh wars with our spirit, with the battles taking place in our thoughts.

THE PRACTICAL RESCUE

Let's get practical. How does God, who lives miles away in Heaven, actually rescue us and help us in our struggle to overcome making bad choices? Is this just a hopeful platitude with no substance? No! I have experienced the very practical and real way that God helps me make the right choice when my flesh is screaming to be satisfied with something I don't want to do.

First of all, when we don't walk with the Lord, there is only one road. The road we follow is the one in front of us, the one that makes the most sense and the one we want to follow. We can make very bad choices on that road. Jesus, however, offers another path – should we choose to take it. He offers an alternative. We add that alternative to the mix and then our menu of choices widens. There is another option! What is the option that Jesus offers? The option of following His Word. For example, when I was in the battle to quit smoking, the option of following God's leading was now on the table.

My strength came from the Holy Spirit living inside of me. God is not miles away, He lives within me! I felt the Holy Spirit prompting me, encouraging me, and letting me know that it was His will to eliminate smoking from my life. I *chose* the option of following His leading on the matter.

God strengthens us to do what He is prompting our hearts to do through the power of the Holy Spirit. The Spirit works in our hearts, unseen, but definitely there, strengthening our resolve to continue the battle all the way to victory.

CHAPTER 14

The Process of Healing

In our "now" society, we do not like to wait for anything. Not only do we want it now but we can have it now! Why wait? Systems are in place in our society for immediate gratification and pleasure. Credit cards keep our material stash overflowing. Cell phones allow us to be immediately in touch with people. Computers keep us informed of what is happening all over the world in real time. We stomp our feet when our internet connection is slow. We groan in frustration when we drive through a dead zone and our cell phone drops a call. It's no wonder that people don't have patience anymore. If you are chuckling and nodding your head as you read this, I'm laughing with you because I fall prey to all of these things.

Even some preaching and teaching today offer the hope that not only do you deserve a great life of blessings, but if you believe strongly enough, you'll get it! Those who cling to this philosophy end up frustrated and find themselves asking, "Why doesn't that work for me?"

We need to study God's Word so intensely that we recognize false doctrine, even when it's woven in tightly with threads of truth. I've heard that when investigators are trained to identify counterfeit money, they do not study all of the various counterfeit bills, they instead study the real thing. They know the genuine money so well that they can easily recognize a counterfeit. Studying God's Word and asking the Holy Spirit for discernment are the only ways to sift through all of the ideas and teaching that come at us on a daily basis in today's world.

It is not Biblical to say that we won't suffer as Christians. It is not Scriptural to say we can have anything we want. On the contrary, Jesus looked at His followers in the eye and told them they would suffer. When He taught them to pray, He said they were to pray according to *His* will, not according to *their* will.

THE GOD OF MIRACLES

I believe in miracles. I don't think a person can believe in the God of the Bible without accepting the fact that He is a God of miracles. God is able to do immediate miracles in our lives, breaking all the rules of nature that exacerbate our problems. I've seen miracles in people's lives and I've experienced miracles in my own life. But God doesn't always choose to answer our problems with immediate miracles. The truth is, I have been forced to work through most of my problems little by little, step by step, day by day, changing my mindset, changing my actions and maturing through the process, until I reach a better place in my life.

When I attended support groups during one of the most difficult times of my life, the group members would constantly say, "One day at a time!" We were always encouraged not to try to solve everything at once, just take things a day at a time. In the worst of those days, I remember saying, "Are you kidding, one day at a time? For me it's more like one hour at a time!" I could handle what was heading my way in the next hour, but not what I needed to face in the next 24-hour timeframe. Then, of course, as each hour came to pass, I found the strength to keep going.

We need to understand that God's way of taking us through pain and on to the other side is typically through a process. Although at times we'll be blessed with a wonderful miracle, most of life is a process, step by step, hour by hour, and day by day.

I love the story of Naaman the leper in 2 Kings, chapter 5. He was a highly regarded Commander in the army of the King of Aram. But he had leprosy, the deadly disease for which there was no cure. The young

Israelite girl that served as slave to Naaman's wife claimed that if only he would see the prophet Elisha in Samaria, he would be cured. That comment began a series of events that enabled Naaman to take a trip to Israel to seek out the prophet Elisha. When he arrived at the prophet's home, Elisha instructed Naaman to wash seven times in the Jordan River, and then he would be cured.

The Bible tells us that upon hearing this instruction, Naaman went away angry. He expected a grandiose miracle! Naaman's expectation was that this famous and powerful prophet would raise his hands toward Heaven and call down the power of God and miraculously heal him. It would be a profound and spectacular sight that he would never forget. Instead, Elisha told him to walk to the river and wash himself seven times in the dirty water. Verse 12 tells us that Naaman stormed off in a rage. He responded by saying the rivers back home were much better and if he was going to wash, he would have just stayed home! In verse 13 one of his servants talked some sense into him. He said, "…if the prophet had told you to do some great thing, would you not have done it? How much more, then, when he tells you, 'wash and be cleansed!'" He convinced Naaman to at least try doing what Elisha instructed.

Naaman went to the river and dipped himself once, nothing happened. Then again and nothing happened. Again, nothing. He dipped himself six times in the water and nothing changed. Then, the seventh time he dipped, he rose out of the water and his flesh was restored – like the skin of a child. Naaman returned to Elisha's house and proclaimed in verse 15, "Now I know that there is no God in all the world except in Israel!" He went on to say that he would never worship any other God but the Lord.

Why did God heal Naaman through the process of dipping himself in the river rather than simply having Elisha lay hands on him for immediate healing? In order for Naaman to receive his healing, he had to throw away all of his expectations. It was not going to happen in the way he wanted or thought he deserved. The only chance he had at receiving his healing was to do it God's way.

When we have a problem and beg God to help us, don't we face a similar crisis? We can either choose to follow God and go through the process of healing that he has laid out for us, or we can walk away in anger and disappointment. It's almost as if suffering is like a sword, cutting right through to the heart of the issue. Will I give up on my expectations and trust the Lord or will I cling stubbornly to what I want? What a quick, clean, and immediate way for God to eliminate pride and bring us to a place of humility. Naaman was brought to that crisis of belief, and it was God's purpose to humble him.

There is another reason that God desires us to walk through the process of healing. It teaches and develops us in a more in-depth, permanent manner than if we receive something immediately, without experiencing the stages of learning. If God miraculously heals us in one day, we will say, "Wow, God is great!" But if we walk through our problem, day by day, little by little, hand in hand with God, experiencing the victories, seeking His guidance, and being sustained with His strength, we will say, "I *really* know God is great! He sustained me every day through this tough time. He worked things out for the best and gave me His strength and grace." Our foundation of faith becomes stronger for the next problem or trial that comes our way and we have come to know God better in the process.

Which will you seek? The miracle or the process? What if the process is really one long, stretched out miracle?

GOD WANTS TO ELIMINATE OUR PERSONAL ENEMIES

God wants us to overcome our weaknesses and the character flaws that cause us to make bad choices. It was a process that caused us to make mistakes, as the branches of our choices jutted out in new directions that we never meant for them to go. It takes a process to "undo" a process!

Our dysfunctions can drive us to make decisions that lead us straight toward a situation that we will later regret. Many people can give firsthand testimonies about how their personal weaknesses and dysfunctions led them down a path of pain. Rather than say, "I made bad decisions," I can more accurately state, "I was dysfunctional; therefore, bad decisions came naturally to me!"

The process of healing exposes the things that God wants to deal with in our lives. We may be hard on ourselves and take the full brunt of the blame for our actions that led to our regret. But I would like to offer a suggestion that might soften the harshness with which we treat ourselves as we deal with regret. It is a concept that can be difficult to believe or accept. Take a deep breath… our God is so loving and merciful that He may have allowed me to make a bad choice in order to reveal the things in me that need changing. I'll go a step further with that line of thinking. God may even have *led* me down a path that would surface my weaknesses and dysfunctions in order to prune them off once and for all.

If you have a problem spending money that you don't have, God may have chosen not to spare you from bankruptcy court, rather to allow you to face your enemy of spending head on. God may have led you straight into the path of a struggle in order to provoke the level of pain that would drive you to change how you will make future choices.

When God led the Israelites to the Red Sea in Exodus chapter 14, their enemies showed up in chariots, trapping them at the edge of the sea. The Israelites could not understand why God would lead them to the edge of the sea, only to be trapped by their enemies. When God parted the waters of the Red Sea and Moses told them to move on to the other side, the people would not have crossed the seabed without the threat of death looming at their heels. If their enemies were not approaching, forcing them to keep moving forward, they would have camped where they were and complained that they would never get to see the Promised Land because the sea was in the way. But God *purposely* led them to what we would describe as "between a rock and a hard place." They couldn't go back to Egypt or they would be killed. Their only option was to move ahead through the parted waters of the Red Sea. So they moved ahead on the only path open to them.

When the Israelites reached the other side, their enemies followed, eager to capture them. When the enemies tried to cross the sea, the walls of water fell and drowned every one of them. After going through the process, the journey through the crisis with the Lord leading them, the Israelites witnessed the destruction of their enemies. They would never see those enemies again; they were permanently destroyed.

One day I was reading Isaiah 43 and ran across verse 17. The verse states that God *drew* out the chariots and horses, luring them to follow the Israelites. I pondered this idea and questioned why God would "lure" the Egyptians to follow the Israelites. Then it hit me! God placed the Israelites in such a situation that would tempt and lure their enemies to come after them, bringing them to a place where God could destroy them completely. If God would have simply helped the Israelites reach the Promised Land using the easy route, their enemies would surface again and again, causing many future wars and problems. So God routed everyone to the edge of the Red Sea, where He would help His people through, and destroy their enemies forever!

If you are suffering from regret, God may be after the things inside of you that caused you to make the choices you made. He longs to deal with those age-old enemies of yours once and for all. It is possible that God led you straight into a place between a rock and a hard place. It is His way, at times, to lead you right into that difficult situation and make things so uncomfortable that you have no choice but to move ahead through the parted waters. If you press forward through the process and allow God to do a great work in your life, you will find those enemies destroyed once and for all. They won't be retreating and discouraged by your success, only to raise their ugly heads again later in life. No, they will be dead, never to be seen again. And you will be on the other side of the problem, with no desire or ability to cross backward to the same place you came from. The Israelites could not even consider going back to slavery in Egypt, the sea was closed off!

God longs to close off the path backward in our lives. The process is a miracle, in slow motion, that heals the deepest part of us. Forward, to the Promised Land, is the direction He calls us to travel!

CHAPTER 15

Dealing with Ourselves

IMAGINE THE FOLLOWING DESCRIPTION OF a woman:

She's been married three times, alone more years than married, single mom for many years, dated the wrong men, and experienced financial ups and downs in her life.

If you told me about this woman, I would respond, "She really made some bad choices. What is wrong with her?"

Arrrggghhh! That woman is me! But I don't see myself as that person. I believe I'm a good person, competent, bright, organized, responsible, and successful. But my past testifies against me. My past tells a whole different story.

We may view ourselves in a positive way but our history reflects something totally different. We believe we are good and we try to make right choices. But the reality of our past is a witness against us. We look back and we see a messy road that is filled with bad choices.

Our choices disappoint us. Our past history shoots down the idealized version of who we think we are and who we were trying to be. When reality shouts over the soft voice of self-idealism, regret begins to wash over us like a wave threatening to knock us off our feet.

Then there are times we think too lowly of ourselves. We swing to the other extreme and consider ourselves to be failures because of the shameful chapters of our life story. We fail to remember the good choices, the successes and accomplishments that also line our paths. We forget that we also have talents and abilities that we have put to good use many times in our lives. As I periodically wallow in the lowly thoughts of myself, I fail to think of the good choices I made over the years:

I was a responsible single mother and I raised a smart, hardworking, and wonderful daughter.

I worked hard to afford to buy a home in a nice neighborhood to raise my daughter.

I sacrificed to pay tuition for my daughter to attend a Christian grade school.

I have been a dependable hard worker who sought to always do my best with integrity.

I nurtured my relationship with God through prayer, participating in Bible Studies and actively serving at church.

I built a successful business and had a good income for many years.

Those were good choices! The reality is that I made good choices and bad choices. The good brings fruit and the bad produces consequences. The effect of bad choices is what fosters regret. Sometimes the aftermath of our bad choices overshadows the good choices that we have made.

Specific self-talk

When we are overcome with regret, we may tend to deal with ourselves harshly. We reason that we deserve the harshness because deep inside we feel we deserve to be punished.

When we begin our self-talk during moments of regret, it is important to be careful not to talk in generalities. Instead we should focus on specifics. For example, if I say "I should not have done that, I'm a bad person," I am talking in generalities. It is simply self-condemnation that brings about no constructive change or improvement. It would be much more constructive to say, "I should not have gossiped about my friend, it was wrong to do that." Or, "I should not have spent that money, it was wrong of me to overextend myself." Speaking to ourselves in specifics and identifying our particular mistake provides clear guidance as to what we must do in order to avoid making the same mistake again. If we rely on general accusations and negative self-talk to process our regret, we will add to our hopelessness because we simply can't "fix" ourselves. If I believe I am a bad person, how am I going to make myself a good person? If I condemn my entire being for a mistake, how am I going to work on the specific issues that led me to the point of making that choice? We can't deal with a problem that we are not able to identify. Identifying choices that brought about regret is the best way to get us onto the road of healing.

Conviction vs. Condemnation

This principle of "specifics" is God's way of dealing with us throughout our lives. When we suffer from our choices, Satan condemns us by accusing us in generalities. He wants us to have the general overall feeling of condemnation and guilt. The Bible describes Satan as the "accuser of the brethren."

The Holy Spirit *convicts* and Satan *condemns* us. Romans 8:1 states that there is "no condemnation for those who are in Christ Jesus." We are not to feel condemned if we belong to the Lord.

Satan condemns	Holy Spirit convicts
"You're a bad person for talking like that"	"You should not have spoken to him like that"
"You are no good, you are worthless"	"You need to repent"
"God could never love you"	"You need to change the way you communicate"
"You'll never change"	"You can rely on Me to change you"

THE ATTITUDE THAT CREATES REGRET

When asked if she had any regrets, a woman answered, "Sometimes I feel that I have many regrets, but God has been so good to me that I really don't think I have regrets anymore. Actually, what I regret the most is how I acted when I had regret!"

How we act during times of regret can pile on more regret to the already painful situation we may be facing. Our attitude during hard times can determine the depth of pain we experience. God places a high importance on our attitude and level of faith while we walk through hard times.

OUR OWN WORST ENEMY

Is it possible to limit God's activity and blessings in our lives? The Bible makes it clear that the answer to that question is a resounding "YES"!

Am I my own worst enemy? By my attitudes am I keeping myself from moving beyond regret?

LIMITING GOD BY OUR UNBELIEF

When the Israelites wandered the desert for 40 years, there is one word that describes their roadblock to the Promised Land. Unbelief. In Exodus 3:17, God promised them a land flowing with milk and honey. But because of their murmuring, complaining, and disobedience, their destiny turned into 40 years in the desert. Why did they murmur and complain? Because of unbelief. If they would have believed God's words to them, they would have been thankful and trusted God through the journey. What blessings are we missing out on by not trusting the Lord?

In Scripture, unbelief is blamed as the main reason for not receiving blessings from the Lord. Hebrews 3:19 explains that the Israelites missed out on the Promised Land because of their lack of belief. "So we see that they were not able to enter, because of their **unbelief**." (Emphasis added.)

Revelation 21:8 lists those who don't believe with those who are headed toward eternal hell: "But the cowardly, the **unbelieving**, the vile, the murderers, the sexually immoral, those who practice magic arts, the idolaters and all liars — their place will be the fiery lake of burning sulfur." (Emphasis added.)

Unbelief, which is essentially lack of faith in God, turns me into my own worst enemy.

"Without faith it is impossible to please God...." Hebrews 11:6

When we choose to have faith, we open wide the path to be healed from regret. Why must we have faith? Because we can't forge ahead on the road of healing while holding ourselves back with negative self-talk.

"I want to be emotionally healed but I'm too bad of a person for God to help me."

"I want to have faith but I don't believe God will help me."

How can that person move ahead through the healing process when his attitude is going in two opposite directions? He wants to move ahead but his attitude holds him back. God wants us to have single-minded faith, keeping our eyes on Him to guide us through the healing process.

"I want to be emotionally healed and I'm trusting God every step of the way."

"I have faith that God will do what He says in His Word, that He will guide me, strengthen me, and help me to live out His will for my life."

It may not feel natural to us to exercise faith but the more we practice speaking statements of faith and truth rather than negative lies, we will find that our faith will grow. The Bible tells us in Romans 10:17, "...faith comes from hearing the message and the message is heard through the word of Christ." If we know that God requires faith, why not inundate ourselves in His Word, which He promises will grow our faith?

CHAPTER 16

Following God

LET'S FACE IT, THERE ARE some things that the Bible is clear about when it comes to right and wrong. We know it's wrong to murder, lust, covet, worship other gods, etc. Most of us don't need convincing that those things are wrong. We agree that they are sin. The Bible also makes clear what is right. It is good to repent, worship, love others, help our neighbor, forgive our enemies, and follow the Lord Jesus. Where we struggle is the array of choices in the vast gray area that falls in between Right and Wrong. How we spend our free time, which movies to watch, what hobbies to choose, which books to read, where to go to college, when to take a vacation, are examples of areas that are not defined in Scripture. They are left to wisdom, discernment, and conscience.

CONSCIENCE – A GIFT FROM GOD

The definition of conscience is the "inner sense of what is right and wrong." Our conscience "impels" us to right action. Our conscience is a gift from God. We didn't ask for it and we had nothing to do with implanting it within ourselves. God placed it there as a tool for the Holy Spirit to use in guiding us and leading us. Our conscience was given to us by God for our protection! Parents know that the conscience is a valuable tool for protection as they teach their children the difference between right and wrong. They want their children to feel the prick of a guilty conscience when disobeying. The development of a child's conscience is heavily influenced by his or her parents. As a child grows older and begins to be influenced by peers and eventually by society, the sensitivity of his conscience will be changed depending on the nature of those factors.

CAN YOU ALWAYS TRUST YOUR CONSCIENCE?

We've all heard it said, "Just let your conscience be your guide." In many ways, we do let our conscience guide us through decisions. But because of the pliable nature of our conscience (the ability to influence it and harden it), our conscience cannot always serve as a trustworthy guide for our choices. This explains why the consciences of two different people can react totally differently to the same choice. In the gray area of life, rather than be led by our feelings, we should do what we know is right and avoid what we know is wrong. The problem is, at times, we <u>do</u> what we know is wrong and we <u>don't do</u> what we believe is right. It is then that we enter the area where we begin to influence and eventually corrupt our conscience.

Our corruptible conscience can steer us toward wrong choices resulting in much regret. For example, a man believes that viewing pornography is wrong but pushes past that initial inner conviction because of the temporary pleasure. The next time he surfs the internet and views pornography, it becomes easier to brush off that inner warning, quieting the voice of conscience within him. The next time and the time after that become easier for him. He is, in effect, "training" himself to ignore his conscience. The Bible refers to the extreme disregard of conscience as "searing" our conscience as with a hot iron (1 Timothy 4:2). We are warned that the conscience is not to be ignored. It is our helper as we navigate life's gray areas using God's marvelous gift of free will.

How does our free will and desensitized conscience lead us into regret? At times it leads us straight down a road heading directly into regret. At other times, it takes us down a winding path of justification, convincing arguments, and momentary pleasures that finally cause us to end up in that place where almost everyone arrives at one time or another – REGRET.

Correcting the conscience

There is only one way to correct a conscience that has been desensitized and changed by the influence of peers, society, and other factors. As a builder uses a plumb line to measure whether the building he is constructing is perfectly vertical, we can go to Scripture to measure whether our beliefs are right or wrong. The Bible is our plumb line that we can trust to see if our conscience and our choices measure up correctly to God's standards.

When a builder's plumb line is not perfectly vertical, he does not change the plumb line to fit the building because he knows that the structure will be in danger of toppling over. He must adjust the building to the plumb line if he wants the construction to be successful. A person who attempts to adjust Scripture to fit his life choices is in danger of pain and failure because his life is not set securely according to the plumb line of God's Word.

I might be so bold as to say that many people intentionally do not study the Bible for the simple reason that they do not want to be faced with the reality that they need to make changes in their lives. They do not want to measure their lives against the True Plumb Line. Some people believe that the less they know, the more free they'll be. Yet Jesus tells us in John 8:32 that the truth will set us free. We may not see bondage, pain, and regret ahead of us on the road of our choices, but God knows that things that appear good can lead us down a wrong path. Even in the gray areas of permissible choices in life, the things we can enjoy are also the same things that can trap us into bondage.

God says in Hosea 4:6, "…my people are destroyed by lack of knowledge." Throughout Scripture we are exhorted to seek knowledge and be determined to be wise. We are to embrace wisdom and be filled with knowledge. When we study the Word of God, we come to know His mind on the matters that concern us. As we begin to understand what God says is right and wrong, we will begin to feel convicted of the areas where we have fallen short. As we recognize our shortfalls and ask for forgiveness, our conscience becomes increasingly sensitized to God's standards. We become better equipped to be led by the Holy Spirit through our choices.

GOD'S PRINCIPLES FOR THE GRAY AREAS

I believe there are two important reasons that the gray areas of life are not clearly and specifically defined in Scripture. The first reason is that our God is a God of principles. Throughout 30 years of in-depth Bible study, I have learned that the principles laid out in Scripture reveal God's mind on many matters that fall in the gray area of life. God never says, "Thou shalt not smoke." But He does reveal His mind on the stewardship of our physical bodies. Therefore, I can safely say it's not good to smoke. God wants us to live by principles rather than a set of black and white rules in the gray areas of life. When we learn God's principles and begin to live by them, we gain wisdom to make better choices using our free will. The principles that God gives us in the gray areas allow us freedom to choose, freedom to follow, and freedom to take part in God's plan for our lives.

The second reason that God does not lay out specifics in the gray areas of life is because He desires to guide us and sanctify us *individually*. When I gave my life to the Lord at age 25, the Holy Spirit convicted me to completely change my lifestyle. I met other Christians who watched movies that I felt I could no longer watch. They didn't seem to have the same convictions in their hearts. Yet I knew what God wanted me to do. God does not deal with Believers in the exact same way in the exact same moment any more than a master gardener would prune two rose bushes in the exact same way. He will prune each according to what is necessary to cause the best roses to flourish. God knows each of us so deeply that there are things He may prune off of my life that He may not prune off of someone else's life. The Holy Spirit may lead a person who has a tendency toward alcoholism to never take a drink. On the other hand, He may not lead someone else to total abstinence. The gray area of life is the area where the Holy Spirit guides, prunes, and sanctifies us each *individually*.

Because there is so much freedom in the gray area of life, the Bible teaches us to be careful that we don't use our freedom as a cloak for sin. In other words, we need to make sure we don't justify what we do by saying that we are free to do it. If I believe the Lord is leading me to quit doing something and I do it anyway, then it is sin in the Lord's eyes even though the Bible doesn't explicitly say I shouldn't do that thing. We need to be sensitive to the Lord's personal leading in our lives.

We also should be careful not to judge others when we are convicted in an area of our life. This is where we see strife even among Believers. No one knows our motives and weaknesses and potential areas of downfall better than the Holy Spirit. We need to let the Holy Spirit lead us and lead others. He may lead one person to stop going to movies. He may lead another person to stop playing video games. The Holy Spirit knows what He needs to do in each of us to sanctify us.

I'm very thankful that God didn't just come at me with his pruning shears and prune off everything in the first year of my walk with Him. No, He takes His time and prunes as He sees fit and when it is the right time.

Another important consideration in the gray area of freedom is what Paul addressed in 1 Corinthians 10:23. He tells the Corinthians, "Everything is permissible, but not everything is beneficial." He doesn't mean everything is permissible, he means that everything that is *lawful* is permissible. We know this because Paul would not disregard all of God's moral law and claim that he could do anything he wanted. No – he meant that within the realm of the gray area, everything may be permissible but it certainly isn't all beneficial. That is where wisdom comes in.

There are certain activities that inherently have the possibility to become stronger in our lives and rise up to control us. What has the potential to control me may not be the same thing that could possibly control you. The activities that tend to become stronger in our lives usually relate to satisfying the flesh or pleasing our desires in some way (for example, sex, alcohol, materialism, or the use of credit). We must ask ourselves this necessary question when deciding whether to do something, "Is this beneficial to me?" We also may add another dimension to that question, "Will this lead me into addiction?" "Will this eventually become a problem in my life?" "Will this slow me down in reaching my goals?" If we are willing to be honest, we know the answers to those questions. And if we really don't know the answer, we will continue to make bad choices until the consequences begin to teach us the right answers.

Relationship vs. Rules

Mankind. We say we don't like rules, but then we create rules. We say we don't want anyone telling us what to do and then we tell everyone what to do. In many ways we love rules because then when we follow them, we think we chalk up points for ourselves. We like roadmaps pointing the way toward success. We want maps to make things clear to us. Unfortunately, that is not how life works. The Bible teaches that life with our Lord is about a Relationship, not Rules. Jesus spent much of His time on earth rebuking the Pharisees for their inability to see past the system, rules, and traditions they had created. He clearly showed people that He was all about *relationship*.

When we realize that God wants a relationship with each of us, we may begin to understand why God doesn't "zap" us when we make wrong choices. We want a lightning bolt to come down from Heaven and knock us off our feet when we are about to make a wrong life-changing decision. We want God to write it across the sky in big bold letters, "Don't go there!" When God seems passive about our choices, we think He doesn't have an opinion. We think if He cared, He'd speak up – and loudly!

When Elijah fled from Queen Jezebel in 1 Kings 19, he was exhausted from his great victory on Mount Carmel. Now, Jezebel threatened to kill Elijah and he was afraid. The Lord told Elijah to stand on the mountain because He was going to pass by. There was a powerful wind that "tore the mountains apart and shattered the rocks." Verses 11-12 tell us that the Lord was "not in the wind." Then there was an earthquake, but "the Lord was not in the earthquake." Next there was a fire, but the Lord "was not in the fire." Finally, there came a gentle whisper; it was the Lord speaking to Elijah, giving him instructions on what he was to do next.

Why does God speak to us in a whisper? Maybe because He wants us to be still and quiet in order to hear Him. We have to quiet our anger, passion, will, and desire in order to hear the voice of the Lord. We need to be very humble to listen and obey a whisper. We don't have to be humble to obey the mighty force of a powerful earthquake. Anyone will obey that loud voice simply out of fear! No, it takes humility and patience to seek the still, small voice of the Lord. And humility and patience are exactly the character traits that God desires to grow within us.

Because God doesn't choose to lead us with flags, banners, earthquakes, and fire, we find it hard to follow Him. We walk down the wrong path and there is no road sign that says, "Bad choice, turn around or else!" Instead, there is the aftermath and the repercussion, those hidden consequences that don't raise their ugly heads until we are well underway on the wrong road. The picture is one of a harvest when the wrong seeds have been planted and then watered with more choices. What else can grow but what was sown into the ground? God has built in consequences for our actions, whether good or bad. We are free, that is certain. We are free to choose – but we are not free to choose the consequences of our actions.

The good news is that God still wants a relationship with us, even when we are sitting in the messy field of weeds, bristles, and gravel. He wants to heal our wounds, lead us, and work with us to accomplish His purpose in our lives.

THE GUIDANCE OF THE HOLY SPIRIT

A relationship with God is not like any other relationship. When I want to talk with my husband, I talk, he listens, he talks, and I listen. If I want physical attention, I hug him and he hugs me back. We laugh, we go places, we eat together, and work together. My relationship with God is so different! I can't see Him and I can't touch Him, yet He is closer to me than any human relationship. Why is that? Because He lives within me, in my spirit. God has given me His Holy Spirit, just as Jesus promised after His resurrection.

My communication to God is through prayer. His communication to me is through His Word, preaching, circumstances, and the Holy Spirit. The Holy Spirit guides us, prompts us, convicts us, counsels us, and strengthens us.

The Bible also teaches us that our motives, thoughts, and actions can hinder the work of the Holy Spirit in our lives. 1 Thessalonians 5:19 admonishes us not to put out or quench the Spirit. The word "quench" means to suppress, as one would extinguish a fire. If we ignore and push back the voice of the Holy Spirit, we are quenching Him. When we are rebellious and going our own way, ignoring the promptings of the Holy Spirit, we grieve Him (Ephesians 4:30) and He limits His work in our hearts.

THE FEAR OF THE LORD

The fear of the Lord is a necessary factor in following Him. Many people, very simply, do not fear God. I am amazed by the lack of reverence and respect for God in our world. People make jokes about God and use Jesus' name as a swear word.

Quite possibly, they have the wrong idea about who God is. He is not a Santa Claus or a "softie" sitting in Heaven. We need to have a reverential fear and respect for Almighty God, the Creator of the universe. The Bible tells us in Proverbs 1:7 that, "The fear of the Lord is the beginning of knowledge."

Fear of God doesn't mean that we need to tremble in terror and avoid His presence. The definition of fear of the Lord is, "awe, reverence, respect." The beginning of wisdom and the place that we need to start in our relationship with God is an understanding of His greatness and power. Those who fear the Lord are called "friends of God."

> "And do not be afraid of those who kill the body but cannot kill the soul. Rather be afraid of the One who can destroy both soul and body in hell." Matthew 10:28
>
> "Fear God and keep his commandments, for this is the whole duty of man." Ecclesiastes 12:13

"The Lord confides in those who fear him; he makes his covenant known to them." Psalm 25:14

"How great is your goodness which you have stored up for those who fear you...." Psalm 31:19

"Blessed is the man who fears the Lord, who finds great delight in his commands." Psalm 112:1

And my favorite verse on the fear of the Lord:

"He will be the sure foundation for your times, a rich store of salvation and wisdom and knowledge; the fear of the Lord is the key to this treasure." Isaiah 33:5

The proper reverence, respect, and awe of God is the key to the treasure of true wisdom. The fear of the Lord is the beginning of understanding that He is God and we are nothing without Him. The fear of God destroys the pride within us, the sense of self-sufficiency that keeps us walking in our own ways. We keep God first and foremost in our hearts and minds because He is awesome and we revere Him, knowing that our very existence, past, present, and future are in His hands. We are driven to obedience by our commitment to this Holy, Just, and Powerful God. We worship Him for who He is, not because of what He does for us. The fear of the Lord keeps things in perspective. For those who have traveled far away from this first step of wisdom, reading and reflecting on the Psalms will bring you back to this very important foundation of following God.

The problem of lack of reverential fear of the Lord may also reside in the hearts of mature Christians who have walked with the Lord for many years. For some Christians, God becomes familiar as they have made Him such a big part of their lives. What happens in many relationships can happen in their relationship with God – they begin to take His friendship for granted or they simply lose the vibrant love or passion they once had for God. They don't notice the distance between themselves and God. They take God's love for granted and feel that if they sin, the grace of God will cover them. This is true but it's not an excuse to sin. We need to remember that although God extends His grace to us, the price of forgiveness and right relationship with God was the blood of Jesus Christ. God's marvelous plan of bringing people into relationship with Him reflects His love, justice, mercy, and power. He is worthy of our worship, awe, reverence, and respect every day of our lives.

Fear not

If we are to fear God, then what does God mean when He says, "Do not fear"? There are two types of fear: reverential awe for a Holy God (as discussed in the previous section) and the fear that keeps us from obeying God. When God told Joshua to enter the Promised Land, He told him to be strong and courageous and to "fear not" because God would be with him. The fear in this sense is anxiety, apprehension, dread, and lack of courage. When God leads us to do something, we are not to fear. We are to obey with courage knowing that God is with us and strengthens us. We are not to live as fearful people who don't trust God. We are to live courageously, following God's commands and living by the power of the Holy Spirit in all that God leads us to do.

Living a life of obedience

Following God means living a life of obedience to His Word. If we are obedient in little things, God will entrust bigger things to us. This is a principle that is woven throughout Scripture. Someone may ask, "Why don't I hear from God? Where is He? Why doesn't He help me?" I would answer by asking, "What was the last thing God directed you to do? Did you obey? If not, go back to the last thing God said and begin there." If God leads us to pray more and we don't do it, we will stay stuck until we obey what God has already said. If God leads us to spend more time studying His Word and we resist doing it, we will feel stuck until we obey His leading. God leads us through the power of the Holy Spirit. He will not change His mind on what He wants us to do. This is why studying Scripture is so important. If we don't know what God is telling us, how can we be obedient? We will stay stuck until we learn what God has to say and obey what we understand. When we are obedient to what we *do* know, God will grant us greater understanding and insight into His Word.

The Holy Spirit will speak to our hearts and lead us with His gentle whisper as we seek God through prayer and study of His Word. He will lead us individually to do what God has for us to do. I am amazed that when I read Scripture, God leads me to passages that speak right into my circumstances or convict me of something that I need to change.

Our obedience to God is the proof that we love Him and want to be in relationship with Him.   Jesus said in John 14:15, "If you love me, you will obey what I command." In other words, if we love Jesus, we will prove it by following what He teaches.

OBEDIENCE IS FOR OUR GOOD

God's rules, laws, and principles are not in place because God enjoys pounding the gavel as a strict judge and setting limits to the enjoyment of his people.   On the contrary, obedience is for our good! Obedience is required because our lives will be blessed and fruitful following the One who knows all things and can see the consequences down the road of our choices.   Isaiah 48:18 says, "If only you had paid attention to my commands, your peace would have been like a river…."   God doesn't place limits to make us unhappy or to keep us from enjoying life; His laws keep us from pain and destruction of our happiness.

The Israelites in the Old Testament followed a cycle of disobedience that went like this:

1. Disobedience
2. Suffering
3. Repentance
4. Forgiveness
5. Peace

Then the cycle would begin again:

Disobedience – suffering – repentance – forgiveness – peace

Isn't that typical of many of our life patterns? We know what's right, we go our own way, we suffer, we repent, and God forgives. Then we do the same thing, over and over again. God is faithful and forgiving but in the meantime, we fill our lives with complex and painful issues that overwhelm us and threaten to destroy any hope of accomplishing our true life purpose.

If we walk closely with the Lord, follow the voice of the Holy Spirit daily, and obey the Word of God, we will experience the peace that God promises. It may not be easy but there are only two choices available. Following God or doing things my way. Which will you choose?

CHAPTER 17

Blessings in the Midst of Pain

As there are many layers to life, circumstances, situations, and relationships, so there are more layers to the skeleton version of my personal story in Chapter 1. So, let me put a little meat on the bones by adding a few details. Where I've left some blanks in the consequences of several of my choices, you can imagine how deep the pain must have been. Consequences can be temporary or they can last a lifetime. If we lay bricks on the path we wish to follow and each brick builds upon the previous brick, what happens when we start laying a few crooked bricks? Or we lay one or two heading off in another direction? Sometimes, we actually don't even know we are on the wrong path until we've arrived at a totally different destination than we expected.

At times, something good comes along that wouldn't have happened unless we had deviated. Some blessing comes directly from that crooked road and we wonder if maybe we were meant to take that "detour" after all. In fact, I would argue that not all deviations from our main path are mistakes. Many times the new road is exactly where God is leading in order to accomplish His purpose in our lives. Maybe our plan isn't the same as God's plan. Our plan may be a pain-free, successful life filled with blessings and happiness. God's plan is to develop each of us into an instrument worthy of being used by Him. There are many tools in God's toolbox to accomplish what He desires, and believe me, detours are among them!

Remember my earlier story? At age 25, I took a trip to Mexico and fell in love. I eventually moved to Mexico, against my family's wishes, to pursue my new relationship. As I made my way through my new life, 2,500 miles away from my familiar support system, I spread my wings and found myself growing by leaps and bounds. It was almost as if all of the restraints of my sheltered, suburban, comfortable upbringing melted away as my eyes opened to a whole new world.

Free of familial expectations, I began to feel a level of confidence I had never felt before. I was in a foreign country, soaking up the language, and relishing in new friendships. I had never felt such freedom as each day opened up new experiences.

BLESSINGS IN MY DETOUR

One of the first blessings I experienced was the deep connection with the members of my boyfriend's family. I developed many unique and vibrant relationships within the family. My future mother-in-law was a wonderful, spirit-filled Christian and we marveled at how the souls of two such different people from two different parts of the world could meld and understand each other so beautifully. We became more than close friends; we were "gemelas del alma" (soul sisters). We prayed together and talked about our spiritual experiences. I loved that she was so free and joyful, enjoying her relationship with Jesus. My veil of misunderstanding about how much God loves us melted from my heart the more I was around her. The simplicity and genuine nature of her relationship with the Lord taught me a great deal.

I spent many months in Mexico learning and growing. I bought Spanish Bibles for people I met and witnessed to them. It was the closest I came to becoming a self-employed missionary!

My boyfriend and I married in the United States and settled on the U.S. side of the border. I experienced God's hand in many areas of my life. God provided a strong support system as I made many close friends. I obtained a wonderful job in management and grew in my career. My daughter was born and I loved being a new mother. Spiritually I was growing through many in-depth Bible Studies that involved homework and deep study of the Old and New Testaments.

Later, as my marriage began to fall apart, I became devastated by the unraveling of the threads of the life that I so desperately wanted. The tapestry of my dream was being torn apart, thread by thread, never to be repaired. I tried to follow God and trust Him in spite of all of the confusing new circumstances in my life. I was fearful at the prospect of my future alone… what was God's plan for me?

During that time, I was consumed by my suffering. I was meeting with a counselor and attending support groups. All I felt was pain. I could not see the future and felt void of hope. I wasn't able to recognize God's blessings because of the heavy cloud of pain. It wasn't until later when I looked back that I realized that the blessings God had poured out on my life were simply too many to ignore. In fact, I have never felt that I would want to trade those memories, relationships, and blessings for a pain-free life. God showed me that He was with me and helping me even through the valley of pain and suffering. I look back with thankfulness!

BLESSINGS, EVEN WITHOUT ASKING!

Is it possible to be blessed without feeling like you're being blessed? I believe the answer to that question is "YES"! When we are in the hospital receiving treatment or undergoing surgery, is that a curse or a blessing? When the rosebush is being pruned, is it experiencing pain or becoming beautiful?

When I moved back up north to Wisconsin with my daughter to be near my family, I began my new life as a single mother. I found a position with a nice company and loved my job. I had friends where I worked and began to be a very successful recruiter placing people in jobs. Then, after several years, the owners announced that all employees were required to sign a non-compete agreement. As a single mother, I felt that I could not limit myself in the way the contract was written. In one day, the security and benefits of my position were taken away from me. I was given an ultimatum, sign or lose my job. I knew I couldn't sign it and yet the only other option I could see was a cliff and me standing on the edge with nowhere to go but the unknown.

Well, I chose not to sign the contract. I jumped off that cliff into the unknown and decided to start my own recruiting business. I set up a card table in my extra bedroom, bought a desk and a newspaper. I poured through the help wanted ads to see which companies were hiring. I began to make phone calls to sell my placement services and within a month, my business was born.

I ask myself, was that time of darkness heading into the unknown a curse or a blessing? It was difficult and scary and I felt very alone. But it was part of God's bigger plan for me to own a business and have the flexibility I needed as a single mother. At the time I didn't feel as if I was being blessed but ultimately, wasn't it a wonderful blessing from God?

The faithfulness of God

Sometimes God's blessings are invisible to us because of the pain in our lives. When we enter a new season in life, we look back and see that God was with us all along. God is faithful as He leads us through tough times and helps us to become stronger, wiser people. While we are struggling with the ups and downs and twists and turns of circumstances, God helps us, strengthens us, and changes us. He is faithful because of His "hesed" love for His people.

The word "hesed" is used almost 250 times in the Bible. It is a Hebrew word for love that means "steadfast, loyal." It has the sense of stubbornness, refusal to let go. That describes the love that God has for us. God is faithful to us because of His "hesed" love for us. In spite of our mistakes, poor choices, and imperfections, God is faithful to His people and He will never leave us.

I am amazed that God's hesed love is continuously poured out on unfaithful people. At times we make mistakes and end up at dead ends. We do what God hates or we are obstinate and don't obey God's Word. Yet God continues to be faithful and bless us in spite of ourselves! If God removed all of His blessings from our lives, we would sink in the quicksand of pain and regret.

Even unbelievers, many times, experience the blessings of our God who loves them. When I see an unbelieving mother give birth to a new baby, I think to myself, *Does this young mother realize that she has just experienced one of the most miraculous blessings of all? The gift of a child, new life, the miracle of participating in the procreation of God's masterpiece!* A child is a gift from God, even to those who don't care about Him or believe in Him.

GOD'S PROMISE OF BLESSINGS FOR THOSE WHO TRUST IN HIM

If we belong to the Lord, through faith in Jesus Christ, God promises that He will bless us. But in order to experience the fullness of the blessings that God has for us, there are two very important things that we must do:

1. **Trust**
   "Whoever gives heed to instruction prospers,
   and blessed is he who trusts in the Lord." Proverbs 16:20
   "Taste and see that the Lord is good;
   blessed is the man who takes refuge in him." Psalm 34:8
   "But blessed is the man who trusts in the Lord,
   whose confidence is in him." Jeremiah 17:7

2. **Obey**
   "Blessed are they who keep his statutes
   and seek him with all their heart." Psalm 119:2
   "For I command you today to love the Lord your God, to walk in obedience to him, and to walk in his ways, and to keep his commands, decrees and laws; then you will live and increase, and the Lord your God will bless you in the land you are entering to possess." Deuteronomy 30:16

> "Blessed is the man who does not walk in the counsel of the wicked or stand in the way of sinners or sit in the seat of mockers." Psalm 1:1

Scripture teaches us that we play an important role in receiving the fullness of the blessings that God has for us. If our role can be boiled down to one word, it would be, "Choices." Deuteronomy 30:19-20 says, "This day I call the heavens and the earth as witnesses against you that I have set before you life and death, blessings and curses. Now choose life, so that you and your children may live and that you may love the Lord your God, listen to his voice, and hold fast to him."

Even if we are in difficult circumstances or living in the midst of the consequences of our choices, we are still given opportunities every day to trust and obey the Lord. These are things that we can do every day, no matter where we are on the road of life. Seeking the Lord above all else, striving to be closer to Him, and studying His Word are the ways we can learn to Trust and Obey.

GOD IS WITH US IN THE PAIN

If we trust and obey God even in the midst of trials, His blessings will be evident to us. God has done miraculous things for His people who have placed their trust in Him. Take a look at this brief list of the amazing blessings that God has given some of His followers who were on lonely, painful roads during their lives:

> **Moses:** When he fled Egypt and tended sheep for 40 years, God appeared to him in a burning bush, giving him his assignment to lead the Israelites out of slavery.
> **David:** During the time he was a shepherd, David took food to his brothers on the war front and ended up personally fighting the giant Goliath. With God's help he killed Goliath and gained victory over the Philistines. God eventually raised up David to be the second king of Israel.

Daniel: When he and his three Hebrew friends were taken into captivity in Babylon, God granted them His favor. He miraculously saved Daniel's three friends from the furnace of fire, saved Daniel in the lion's den, and raised Daniel to the second highest position under the king.

Joseph: He was sold into slavery in a pagan nation, but God showed him favor and blessed all that he did. Joseph was promoted to be in charge of Potiphar's household. Then when Joseph was falsely accused and thrown into prison, he was promoted to be in charge of the prison. Eventually God miraculously raised him to the second highest position in the land under Pharaoh.

Thankfulness every day

During the times when I have tripped over the rocks in my life path and fallen in the mud, I learned to stay in God's Word. When I couldn't see the blessings around me because of the dark clouds of pain, God was always faithful in providing hope and encouragement through Scripture. I am amazed that, in spite of my choices and detours, God has still blessed my life in so many ways. I learned over the years that even in pain and regret, I should still be thankful every day. If we begin each day with thankfulness, we will begin to become sensitive to all of the blessings that God provides.

Thank you that we have the Bible, God's written Word, so that we can learn the Truth.

Thank you for sending Jesus to be the sacrifice for my sin, canceling my debt to God, providing atonement for me, and making a way for me to have eternal life.

Thank you God, for good health.

Thank you for hot water!

Thank you for my job.

Thank you for my husband and my family.

Thank you for your beautiful creation.

Thank you for food, plenty of food that is available to us!
Thank you for my home.
Thank you for your forgiveness and patience.
Thank you for your faithfulness.
Thank you for the ability to help others around us.
Thank you for giving me the ability to financially support ministries extending all over the world, helping those in need.
Thank you that we always have hope!

If you can't see the blessings because of the pain and you can't think of what to be thankful for, you may borrow from the above list. Many of the things listed are blessings that you have right now in your own life. Without these blessings, circumstances would be even more painful. God is gracious and provides more blessings than we can count. Our part is to keep our eyes on Him and be thankful.

The greatest blessing of all

I am sure that at the end of my life, I will look back and affirm that the greatest blessing I experienced throughout my life was the faithfulness of God. He never gives up on me and He always helps me. He has even blessed me with unexpected gifts just to make my life better. God's faithfulness, His stubborn "hesed" love for me, is the greatest blessing of all.

CHAPTER 18

Prayer – Answered and Unanswered

"The more you submit, the less you'll regret."

LAURIE DRIESEN

INTIMACY WITH GOD

PRAYER IS A GIFT FROM God. It is our lifeline of communication with our Creator. Through prayer, we are invited to close communication and continuous intimacy with God. The gift of prayer is God's way of showing how much He loves us and wants an intimate relationship with us.

Why doesn't God simply do what He wants and give us what we need without requiring that we become involved through prayer?

Relationship is more important to God than just supplying all of our needs. Imagine parents who send their daughter off to college and they say, "Don't bother calling or texting, in fact we don't have to communicate at all. We'll just deposit money in your bank account and make sure that you have all that you need. Have fun at college!" Well, that wouldn't be very realistic. The parents would most likely want to stay in close touch, learn about what is happening for their daughter and encourage her. In fact, their relationship with her would always be more important than simply giving her whatever she needs as she goes off to college. They would want to continue to be involved in her life.

If God intervened with all of His people with no communication through prayer, He would end up with a world full of happier people who still have no intimacy with Him. That is not what God desires. He wants an intimate relationship with each of us, but He will not force Himself upon us. It is clear in Scripture that He wants to be *received* into our lives. God may intercept our path and intervene in our circumstances in order to get our attention, but we need to open our hearts to Him. He will "court" us and invite us into a relationship, but we must respond and participate. The most important way we participate is through choosing to spend time in prayer.

I believe that lack of prayer (which is the result of a lack of faith) is one of the causes why many people make choices that they eventually regret. When we lack faith, we may not take time to pray. We don't believe that God cares. What is the point of praying to a God that doesn't care?

Much of the regret that I have experienced is the result of choices that I made that were not fully covered in prayer. Looking back, I believe I may not have prayed diligently over certain choices because praying means changing. Praying means I want God's answer. Maybe some people don't pray because they really *don't* want to hear God's answer! Praying means submission to God.

Now, I can truly say from experience:

The more I submit – the less I regret!

Without submission to God through prayer, we continue our attempts at a successful life without God's power. We can have the right attitude to move beyond regret, but we will not experience the power of God in our lives without prayer. The following options are helpful but they don't tap into the power of God:

> ***Positive Thinking***
> ***Psychology***
> ***Human Effort***
> ***Great Knowledge***

These things may be necessary and good, but without prayer, we miss out on an intimate relationship with God who has the power to transform us and our circumstances. He has chosen this avenue of communication to exhibit His power in our lives and in His world. When we experience His power in our lives, our faith becomes stronger and we develop into more effective servants and witnesses for the Lord.

GOD'S TERMS FOR PRAYER

I've heard it said that people tend to pray, "Listen Lord, thy servant speaketh," rather than, "Speak Lord, thy servant heareth." We do more talking than listening, more begging than thanking, more complaining than praising.

Our definition of prayer might be: We close our eyes, thank God for His blessings, pray for others, and then pray for what we need and want for ourselves. Then, we are done praying and go on with life, hoping God will answer our petitions. Sometimes this works, sometimes it doesn't. When God doesn't answer our prayers, we may give up, feeling distant from God. After all, if prayer doesn't work, where else can we turn?

But the Bible reveals so much more about this lifeline of communication called prayer. There are many examples in Scripture of God's life-changing and history-influencing answers to prayer. Prayer is powerful and… prayer is a choice. It is an act of our will. It's our response to the God who reaches out to us and invites us into a relationship with Him.

Maybe that's why God works so powerfully through prayer. It's a choice on our part and many times, it's a sacrifice. When I set my busy life aside and sit in a quiet place to pray, isn't that one way of showing the Lord that He has priority in my life? Prayer involves me personally with God and involves God personally with me. Prayer keeps my faith alive! Through an intimate prayer life with God, my faith increases as I dig into Scripture and ask God to reveal His thoughts on the matters that concern me.

When we don't cover our choices with prayer, we rely on our own wisdom and ability to choose. Inevitably, we may make poor choices that lead us into regret and then we come to God in prayer to "fix the mess."

It takes commitment and humility to pray over our choices. Prayer keeps us humble. It shows God that we are submissive to Him. When we realize that we may be on a wrong road, we need to pray for God's direction and strength to make the needed change. Through prayer, we seek to know God's will and avoid the detours that cause future regret.

Praying according to God's will

When we pray according to God's will, we can have confidence that God will answer. John tells us in 1 John 5:14, "This is the confidence we have in approaching God: that if we ask anything *according to his will*, he hears us. And if we know he hears us – whatever we ask – we know that we have what we asked of him." (Emphasis added.)

How do we know God's will? In John 15:7, Jesus says, "If you remain in me and my words remain in you, ask whatever you wish, and it will be given you." To remain means "to abide." If we abide, or walk closely with Jesus and live by His words, we will have a much greater chance of recognizing His will on the issues that we are praying about. The closer we are to the Lord and the deeper knowledge we have of Scripture, the more our prayers will be aligned with the will of God. When we pray and add, "if this be your will" or "let your will be done," we are submitting to God's ultimate decision according to His good and perfect will.

Praying in Jesus' name

Jesus said something very powerful in John 14:13. He told His listeners that if they pray for anything **in His name**, He would do it for them. Wow – anything? If we really understand what it means to pray "In Jesus' Name," we might not be so quick to pray for anything we want. Jesus said, "And I will do whatever you ask in my name, so that the Son may bring glory to the Father. You may ask me for anything in my name, and I will do it."

Imagine that someone arrived at your front door and said, "I'm here in the name of the President of the United States and he requests your presence at an event this evening." Would you say, "I'm sorry, if the President wants to see me, he'll have to call me himself!" No – we understand that the person is acting on the President's behalf. A person who comes in the President's name has the authority to speak for him. Acting on behalf of someone else and in the person's name means that everything he says represents exactly what the other person would want.

Praying in Jesus' name means praying with His authority. It means praying for things that honor and glorify God. If we pray in Jesus' name, we are praying what Jesus would pray if He were standing right here. We pray only for things that would honor His name.

Reasons for unanswered prayer

Isaiah 30:18 tells us that God longs to be gracious to us. He wants to answer our prayers! If this is true, then why do so many of our prayers seem to go unanswered?

At one time or another, most of us have experienced unanswered prayer. We feel as if our prayers are bouncing off the ceiling and not reaching Heaven. It can be very frustrating to reach out in prayer to the One who can help, only to realize that He is not listening! We might prefer that God answer "no" or "wait" if He will not say "Yes" to what we are asking. At least we know He is there, listening, responding, interacting. But silence? No response at all? Why would the God of the universe, who loves us so much, not listen to or answer our prayers?

Some throw their hands up and abandon God. Others, however, are driven deeper into His Word, desperate for an answer. Is this what God is after in His silence? Is God actually drawing us into deeper spiritual water? Is He testing our faith? I believe the answer to all three questions may be "Yes." God does test our faith. Unfortunately, we don't always recognize when we are being tested. Is God leading us into a deeper relationship with Him? When we go deeper into Scripture with a seeking heart, we will learn what God is after in us. He shines the light on passages that speak clearly to our issues. I'm not referring to opening your Bible and letting the pages fall open and reading whatever you see. God wants us to be diligent and *search* the Scriptures for understanding.

UNBELIEF

Believing is a choice. When we study the facts about something, we form a belief about it. Paul tells us in 1 Thessalonians 5:21 to "…test everything. Hold on to the good." My faith grows stronger as I learn more about God through His Word. I choose to believe what the Bible says. The more I experience God's faithfulness and learn that what He says is true, the stronger my faith becomes.

Jesus told His listeners in Mark 11:24, "Therefore I tell you, whatever you ask for in prayer, believe that you have received it, and it will be yours." Jesus is commanding His listeners to believe and not doubt. However, this is not a free ticket to have anything we ask for in prayer. With any subject that we examine in Scripture, we need to take the whole of God's Word and "correctly handle the word of truth" (2 Timothy 2:15). If what we are praying for is God's will, we can be confident that we will receive it.

God wants us to believe Him regardless of what is going on around us. Unbelief is the same as saying to God, "I don't believe what you say." Unbelief is the same as doubting the integrity of God. James 1:6 says that

"…he who doubts is like a wave of the sea, blown and tossed by the wind. That man should not think he will receive anything from the Lord.…"

Sin

Another reason for unanswered prayer is SIN. God wants to get our attention and convict us of sin in an area of our lives. He will not ignore our sin, even in the midst of our crisis. He will not set our sin aside, deal with our problem, and then allow us to retreat, unchanged. Isaiah 59:2 says, "But your iniquities have separated you from your God, your sins have hidden his face from you so that he will not hear."

When God's silence comes in response to our pleas, we ask ourselves, why? And if there is sin that we have not recognized or chosen to deal with, we begin to wonder if that is the roadblock. The sin gets our attention and we feel convicted. Yes, sin is a block to answered prayer. God's silence gets our attention and demands that we deal with sin in our lives.

Do we have to be "perfect" before God will hear our prayers? If that were the case, no one could pray because no one is perfect! No, we do not have to be sinless to pray. But if we are living a blatantly sinful lifestyle, such as committing adultery, and refusing to submit to God's will, our sin will certainly cause a roadblock in our prayer life. I'm not referring to individuals who are repentant yet continue to struggle to overcome a lifestyle or addiction. It's a matter of the heart. If we submit to God, seeking His strength and help to change, we are faced in the right direction.

David states in Psalm 66:18, "If I had cherished sin in my heart, the Lord would not have listened." Notice that David used the word "cherished." The real question is whether we are holding on to the sin in our hearts or whether we are willing to give it up. We will never be perfect while we are here on this earth, but the condition of our hearts is what is important to God. Will we be repentant and submissive to His will or continue to guard the hidden sin in our hearts and hope the Lord won't notice? The Apostle Peter tells us that obedience is necessary for an answer to prayer. In 1 Peter

3:12, he tells us, "For the eyes of the Lord are on the righteous and his ears are attentive to their prayer, but the face of the Lord is against those who do evil." Our disobedience is a certain block to answered prayer.

WRONG MOTIVE

Another block to answered prayer is a wrong motive. James tells us, "You do not have, because you do not ask God. When you ask, you do not receive, because you ask with wrong motives, that you may spend what you get on your pleasures." (James 4:2-3) God's silence prompts us to examine our motives. Some questions we can ask to test our motives include:

"How will the answer to my prayer glorify God?"

"If God says no, what will my attitude be?"

"Will I watch and pray for His will to be done?"

I admit that many times I pray without examining my motives. Then, when time goes by with no answer, I begin to ask myself these questions. It causes me to consider what I am praying for and, at times, change my prayers.

GOD'S GLORY IN THE SILENCE

When God is silent and we can't identify any blatant sin or wrong motive in our heart, there may be another reason for His silence. Believe it or not, at times God is silent in order to display His glory to us. You may ask, "How can I see His glory if I can't even find Him?" Nevertheless, God chooses to take us to an empty place where there are no distractions, only God Himself.

Have you ever felt so hopeless that there was nothing to hold on to except God? Have you been in a place where no thread of hope was evident and there was nothing to cling to except the words on the page of your Bible?

Sometimes I hear people who are suffering say, "There's nothing left to do but pray." Or they say, "I have nowhere else to turn but God." I imagine God in Heaven responding, "Nothing but prayer? Prayer is powerful! Nowhere to turn but to Me? I'm all you need!" I sometimes even imagine that God exclaims, "Yippee, she has nowhere else to turn but to Me!"

Yes, when we have no place to turn and there is nothing else holding us up, we learn that God Himself is enough. In reality, we prefer to rely on crutches such as encouragement from friends, evidence of change, threads of hope. But when all of the crutches we cling to disappear and there is nothing in our circumstances to lean on, that's when faith exists in its purest form. Faith in something when there is nothing. Faith in God when we don't hear Him or feel His presence. Faith in His Word when what we see and experience is the opposite of what we read on the pages of Scripture. Just pure, simple faith. When we learn to say to God, "I trust you," with no proof, no crutches, no evidence, no hope, then we have pure, true faith.

Hebrews 11:1 says, "Now faith is being sure of what we hope for and certain of what we do not see." Faith gives substance to our hope. Faith tells God that we don't need proof, His Word is good enough. And that pleases God! Our faith tells God that we trust Him to work out our problem in His way and in His time.

In the silence of unanswered prayer and through the passing of time, we come to learn that what God is taking us through actually *is* an answer to prayer. For example, recently I was praying earnestly about a situation and in the next few days, things happened that appeared to take the situation even further from what I was praying about. I wanted to begin complaining to the Lord but suddenly I realized that the new turn of events actually could be an answer to my prayer. It wasn't that God hadn't heard me, He could very well have been answering my prayer but I just didn't see the answer yet!

God's glory shines brightest when there is nothing else but Him in the resolution of our circumstance. When we know our situation is hopeless and impossible and God comes through with a mighty work, He gets all the glory. We can't say it was coincidence, it would have happened anyway, or something else made things work out. It was impossible, remember? God brings us to the place of darkness, silence, or impossibility in order to manifest His glory in an even greater way in our lives.

GOD'S GRACE AND BLESSING IN A LIFE OF REGRET

When the Apostle Paul prayed to God to remove his "thorn" in 2 Corinthians 12:7, God gave Paul an entirely different perspective on his suffering. Paul says in verses 7-9, "To keep me from becoming conceited because of these surpassingly great revelations, there was given me a thorn in my flesh, a messenger of Satan, to torment me. Three times I pleaded with the Lord to take it away from me. But he said to me, 'My grace is sufficient for you, for my power is made perfect in weakness.'"

Paul had been mightily used by the Lord and was given visions and revelations. In order to keep him humble, God allowed Satan to inflict upon Paul some type of physical ailment. Paul earnestly prayed for God to heal him. The term Paul used in this passage was "pleaded" or "implored." Paul didn't just ask the Lord once to remove the pain, he went through three *seasons* of prayer concerning the thorn. God, knowing how Paul was suffering, chose not to relieve him of the pain.

Paul's specific sickness is not identified by name in this passage. He may have purposely left it unnamed because it doesn't really matter what it was. It was pain! And the principle that God taught Paul applies to any type of affliction in our lives.

God's answer to Paul was that His grace was going to be sufficient in Paul's suffering. He further explained that in Paul's weakness, God's power would be made perfect. God's grace and strength would be manifested in a *greater* way because of Paul's weakness. Then Paul continues in verses 9-10 by saying, "Therefore I will boast all the more gladly about my weaknesses, so that Christ's power may rest on me. That is why, for Christ's sake, I delight in weaknesses, in insults, in hardships, in persecutions, in difficulties. For when I am weak, then I am strong."

When God revealed to Paul the answer to his prayer, Paul understood and responded with joy and thankfulness because he recognized the purpose in it. Paul learned that Christ's power would be more evident to others through his own sufferings.

I believe that there are times when we must personally come to a deep realization that God has heard our prayer and He knows about our regret and suffering. But we surrender to God, knowing that He wants to accomplish something greater in us than pain-free living. He wants us to learn that, ultimately, His grace is sufficient for all of our needs. When we are at our weakest, with nothing of our own to get in His way, His power is perfected. There is nothing to dim the light of His grace. Sometimes this is God's answer to our prayer. And when we are empty, the only thing left for people to see is Christ.

CHAPTER 19

The Sovereignty of God

MOST PEOPLE BELIEVE IN GOD. Most people believe that God is all powerful and knows all things. Some, however, believe that the free will of man has caused this world to become out of control. Because of confusion and unanswered questions, some believe that God is passive, not always actively involved in His creation and the events of His world.

Because we have made poor choices, we may feel that our lives have become out of control. Somehow we kicked God off of His throne and we messed up what was previously under His control. We interrupted the flow of His ruling authority. We look around at the troubles throughout the world and we see this on a bigger scale. Man is obstructing God's plan! Why doesn't God put everything back as it should be?

Nothing could be further from the truth. The Bible teaches that **all** things are under God's control and **nothing** happens without His permission. For those who believe that God is passively sitting on the sidelines watching the world self-destruct, here are some Scripture verses to align your thinking to the truth:

> "I am God, and there is no other; I am God, and there is none like me. I make known the end from the beginning, from ancient times, what is still to come. I say: My purpose will stand and I will do all that I please." Isaiah 46:9-10

> "He does as he pleases with the powers of heaven and the peoples of the earth. No one can hold back his hand or say to him: What have you done?" Daniel 4:35
> "Are not two sparrows sold for a penny? Yet not one of them will fall to the ground apart from the will of your Father. And even the very hairs of your head are all numbered. So don't be afraid; you are worth more than many sparrows." Matthew 10:29-30
> "…who works out everything in conformity with the purpose of his will.…" Ephesians 1:11
> "Our God is in heaven, he does whatever pleases him." Psalm 115:3
> "There is no wisdom, no insight, no plan that can succeed against the Lord." Proverbs 21:30

The Bible assures us that God is not only in control of His creation but that He is actively involved in every aspect. God not only knows about everything in our lives and in the world, but He is the ruler of all things. The Biblical teaching is that God rules by personal and proactive involvement with His people and the events of His world.

What is the purpose of God's providence? If we believe that God has created each of us with the sole purpose of making us fulfilled and happy, then our view of God's providence will be limited to a small sphere of understanding. Yes, God longs to bless us, be gracious to us, and give us an abundant life. But that is not the primary purpose of His providence over our affairs. The purpose of God's providence is that His name would be glorified and that His will would be accomplished. He works in our lives for His glory and for the good of those who love Him.

The doctrine of God's providence is clear in Scripture. God is sovereign. He is above all things and works in all things. Nothing can thwart His plan or purpose. He directs everything to accomplish what He desires. The forces of evil that are set in opposition to God are subject to and are restrained by God's sovereignty.

Thy Kingdom come

Jesus taught us to pray that God's Kingdom would come and His will would be done. When we say, "Thy will be done...," we are inviting God into our lives and situations to do His will. This should be our greatest desire. Jesus taught us to ask God to accomplish His will. As I have considered this further, I realize that Jesus is also telling us to ask God to help people to do His will. We are, in essence, saying, "Please God, let your will be done through me and others on this earth." We are asking God to help us and help others to do His will. What an important thing to pray! God is always accomplishing His purposes but man is not always doing God's will. Man can't thwart God's ultimate purposes but he can cause a lot of suffering along the path of history. God's plan will prevail, albeit through many tears and pain in the lives of people who live on earth.

God's Kingdom is different from any other kingdom we can possibly imagine. That is why Jesus used many parables to help His listeners gain a greater understanding of the uniqueness of His Kingdom. God is always working to bring about His purposes in the affairs of men and in the events of the world. He is bringing about His Kingdom on this earth!

God's Kingdom within me

While we don't see clearly or understand completely how God moves in the affairs of His creation, we can experience God actively moving in our personal lives. God's Kingdom is so unique that when questioned, Jesus answered the Pharisees, "The kingdom of God does not come with your careful observation, nor will people say, 'Here it is,' or 'There it is,' because the kingdom of God is within you." (Luke 17:21)

When God's Kingdom is established, God drives away the forces of evil and takes His place as King. Isn't that what God does in our hearts and lives? As Jesus walked on earth healing people and driving out demons, so He drives out the sin from our lives and establishes a new Kingdom. He does this right within our own hearts!

As we study what Jesus says about God's Kingdom, we can pray the Lord's prayer in Matthew 6:9-13 with a better understanding of what we are actually praying for:

> "Our Father in heaven,
> hallowed be your name,
> your kingdom come,
> your will be done
> on earth as it is in heaven.
> Give us today our daily bread.
> Forgive us our debts,
> as we also have forgiven our debtors.
> And lead us not into temptation,
> but deliver us from the evil one."

HOPE FOR REGRET

As Christ establishes His rule in our lives, the power of regret diminishes. The light of Christ in our hearts dispels the darkness of regret. There is no place for pride or defeat. We are secure knowing that our failures and mistakes are under God's control. We are ultimately victorious because God is on the throne. If I could focus on one reason alone that we should not have regret, it is because of this truth – God is sovereign. He is above everything that we have done.

Because of God's sovereignty, we can be secure knowing that no matter what happens, what we do, what we choose, what others choose, what circumstances befall us, God is above it all. He knows what is happening in our lives and in every corner of the world. None of it is out of His control. We may not understand why He doesn't stop certain actions or circumstances because we can't see the bigger picture.

The doctrine of God's providence is mysterious yet cannot be ignored if we trust and believe God's Word as revealed in the Bible. In our limited human ability to comprehend God, we simply can't imagine how

He can possibly have control over all things. Yet this remains as a solid Biblical truth: God is in control.

THE FREEDOM TO CHOOSE

Equally as mysterious as the providence of God is man's freedom to choose. It is clear that man has freedom to make choices every day that affect his own life and the lives of other people. In fact, one could even accurately state that many of the things we enjoy and/or suffer from in our world today are a direct result of man's choices from years or even centuries ago.

How can free will exist if God is in control?

This is a mystery.

Because this mystery is "God-sized," our scope of human understanding limits our ability to comprehend how man can choose yet not override God's sovereignty.

The Bible teaches that God is sovereign *and* that man has free will. How can both of these statements be true? Doesn't one end of the spectrum nullify the other end? My answer to that question is… only God knows. We are not able to comprehend the omniscience of God Almighty. There is a realm that is higher than us and more complex than our intelligence can comprehend.

On a personal level, the deeper I get into Scripture and the longer I walk with the Lord, the more the concepts become clearer to me. I look back on my life and know for certain that God has changed me and guided me through the power of the Holy Spirit. On the other hand, I know without question that I made many choices that were not in alignment with God's will. I traveled on roads that God never intended for me to take. I also know that God has worked things out for my good to such a degree that I wonder if He actually led me down a path that I thought was a detour. I also know that many of my choices were wrong and cost me many blessings that God may have planned for my life. Do you see how both principles are true in our lives?

I believe God would rather have us focus on doing what He tells us to do (trust and obey) than strive with all of our intellectual might to figure out how He manages to be in control while allowing us the freedom to choose.

The proof is yet to come

We can't always make sense out of circumstances until much later when we can look back at the situation from a different perspective and all of the confusing pieces are in place. Then we see things much more clearly. When we look backward, we can see how God worked things out, resolved things, or helped us reach a new place in life.

In a similar way, the proof that God is in control of our world is yet to come. Right now, we see a world that is filled with injustice, chaos, and pain.

God has revealed to us how He will put an end to pain, suffering, and sin on earth. The book of Revelation tells us the end of the story. The story that began in Genesis will end with a triumphant conclusion when the events described in Revelation take place. God's Kingdom will prevail and Jesus is coming back in full power and glory to put an end to sin. Satan will be cast into Hell, never more to tempt, kill, and destroy. The questions that we all want answered will be answered with one event and one Person, Jesus Christ. Justice will prevail over the people of this earth. The Bible says that all judgment is in the hands of Jesus. He will separate the "sheep from the goats" (Matthew 25:32), placing those who belong to Him on one side and those who don't belong to Him on the other side. Justice will ultimately be done and we will understand that God had a plan all along. He was always in control, leading the forces of history, nations, kings, and people toward His ultimate conclusion.

When the future is here and God is triumphant and Jesus judges and rules as promised, we will all witness and understand that it is true, God is sovereign!

CHAPTER 20

God's Gift of Grace

Mercy – Not getting what I deserve
Grace – Receiving what I don't deserve

GRACE – GOD'S GIFT FOR REGRET

DO YOU KNOW THAT GOD loves you? Often we hear it said that God is Love. We know He loves people. But do you know how much God loves you *personally*? Psalm 139 is a beautiful psalm about how intimately God knows each of us and that we cannot flee from His presence (v. 7). We were "knit together" in our mother's womb (v. 13).

When people live out the consequences of their choices, they can feel unloved, unwanted, and unworthy. It becomes easy to ask, "How can God love me when I don't even love myself?" But the Bible assures us that God does love us. In fact, He loves people so much that He was willing to suffer and take upon Himself the punishment for sin that each of us should have paid personally.

Ecclesiastes 3:11 tells us that God has "…set eternity in the hearts of men." We know that there is something beyond this temporary life on earth. People long to have an answer for the question of where they will live for eternity. The answer is in John 3:16. "For God so loved the world that He gave His one and only Son, that whoever believes in Him shall not perish, but have eternal life." Our part is to believe in Jesus. The promise for those who believe is eternal life. Our salvation, the free gift of God, is only ours by faith – believing in Him who did this wonderful thing for us.

Do you believe? Do you know how much God loves you?

Two holidays showing God's love

There are two important holidays that show God's love in action. I'm not sure which holiday I love more, Christmas or Easter.

Christmas: Jesus set aside His glory and was born in a manger in the little town of Bethlehem. He chose to be born into this world and walk among men. He is called "Emmanuel" which means "God with us." He is the promised Messiah, foretold by the prophets in the Old Testament, the One who would come to save His people. God desired to be among us, live with people, and teach us the truth about Himself. He chose to be confined to the limitations and frailties of human flesh. He experienced hunger, temptation, ridicule, beatings, torture, and death. Why did He subject Himself to these things?

Easter: After a three-year ministry of teaching, performing miracles, and preparing His disciples for service, Jesus was betrayed and turned over to the authorities for multiple unfair trials. He was questioned, mocked, spat on, and beaten. He was put on display before the crowd for one final vote that sealed His fate of death. The people rejected Him as Messiah and shouted, "Crucify Him!" He was then sentenced to crucifixion on a cross, that old Roman form of tortuous execution that our word "excruciating" comes from. He died on the cross and was placed in a tomb, the entrance blocked by a heavy stone, sealed, and guarded by Roman soldiers. Three days later, Jesus was no longer inside the grave. He rose from the dead! Why did He submit Himself to a death that was assigned to criminals?

What would cause God to set aside His glory and walk among sinful men? What would motivate Him to endure suffering for us? The answer is simple: **Love.**

THE $20 LESSON ON LOVE

Many years ago, I was in my pastor's office discussing with him the subject of God's love. I was going through a difficult time and my view of God's "tough" love was affecting my personal relationship with the Lord. I felt that I always had to learn things the hard way and didn't experience God's gentle love. Pastor Mike asked me, "Does God love you?" I replied, "He loves all mankind, He died for us. He wants me to serve Him." Pastor Mike asked more specifically, "Does God love you personally?" I wouldn't answer. I was serving God and trying to do all the right things but I felt empty inside. Pastor Mike explained that I was trying to earn God's approval. He said that God's love is unconditional and there is nothing I can do to earn it. I listened silently.

Finally, Pastor Mike reached into his wallet, pulled out a $5 bill and placed it in front of me. "It's yours," he said, "I want you to have it." I told him I couldn't take it but I understood what he was attempting to prove. He was trying to show me that God's love is free. He insisted, "Take it, it's my gift to you." I laughed and pushed the bill back to his side of the table. "I understand. I get the picture, but I can't take your money!"

He slid the money back in front of me and left it there as we talked for a while longer. He told me that I would have to learn how to receive something without working for it. He explained how I needed to accept God's gift of love for free and rest in it.

Then Pastor Mike reached over and took the $5 bill and put it back into his wallet. *What a relief! I'm so glad he took it back. I knew he couldn't have been serious. He can't just give me money. Besides, I wouldn't take it anyway!* But instead, he pulled out a $20 bill and said, "This is my gift to you, I want you to have it." He must have thought I needed a bigger lesson. If I couldn't keep the $5 bill, it certainly would be harder for me to keep the $20 bill! Again I replied, "I understand the lesson but I'm not taking your money!" But it was too late, he left in a hurry saying that he was late for another appointment and didn't have time to talk about it. *That's OK, I got the message, it's a great example. I'll just catch up with him later and give it back to him.*

When I left Pastor Mike's office, I anticipated a feeling of guilt and began to plan how to return the money. I thought it would feel "unspecial" because I didn't do anything to earn it. But that's not what happened. On my way home, I suddenly found myself smiling… finally I understood! The lesson would only be complete if I kept the money. If I would simply accept it as a gift, I could enjoy it. If I did not *receive* the money, then it was only a nice theory about love. It would only become a reality when I actually accepted it as a gift. I had to receive it and keep it!

I put the $20 in a separate place in my wallet so it wouldn't get mixed up with other bills. This money was special because it was a gift. *Maybe that's what I need to do with God's love, just receive it in my heart!* After all, the transaction of a gift is not complete unless and until the receiver accepts the gift from the giver.

Is there something in your heart that is preventing you from receiving God's love? Do you feel that you don't deserve His love because of your past choices? Are you allowing past experiences to close your heart to God's gift?

I still have that $20 bill. It brings a smile to my face and reminds me of God's personal, unconditional, and free gift of love to me.

LOVE AND GRACE

God extends grace because He loves us so much. As long as you have breath and life, you have an opportunity to experience the grace of God. If you feel that your choices cannot be covered by God's grace, then you are relying on your own limited understanding of God. Jesus told several parables in Luke chapter 15 to address this very question of how important every person is to God. He told the parable of the lost sheep and how the shepherd leaves his flock to seek after the one lost sheep until he finds it. Then he rejoices and celebrates with friends. Jesus compares this scene with the rejoicing that happens in

Heaven when one sinner repents. He then proceeded to tell the story of a woman with ten silver coins who lost one coin. She searched and searched until she found it and called her neighbors over to celebrate.

When one of our children is lost, do we as parents ever feel complete? Will we not pray and seek out that child until he is safely home? Won't the shepherd risk his own life to bring his helpless lost sheep that he has loved and cared for back into the fold?

The love of a father for his prodigal son
The story of the prodigal son is the third example of God's love for us in Luke chapter 15 and is one of the most powerful pictures of God's grace. Jesus told this parable, using characters that represent 1) us – sinners, 2) God, and 3) Pharisees. A man had two sons and the younger said to his father, "Give me my inheritance." That seems a little bold, don't you agree? It is almost as if he was telling his father that he couldn't wait until he died or that he wished he were dead. He just wanted the blessing that was "due" him. Before we judge that young man too harshly, however, we should examine ourselves. How many times do we ask for or even demand blessings from God without acknowledging Him as our Father?

So the father divided the property and gave the younger son his portion. The son packed up all he had and set out for a distant country. The fact that he took everything reveals that he was not planning to return. It was a permanent move, not a vacation. How painful for his father! The father could have withheld the inheritance, the result of many years of hard work. But the father granted the freedom rather than forcing the son to stay. What joy would it be to have a son in the house who constantly longed to be out in the world? The father recognized that his son was already gone because his heart had left the home.

The younger son traveled to a foreign country and began to spend his money frivolously. He created a lot of regret with some very bad decisions. He spent all of his inheritance and began to experience the consequences of his choices. A famine swept over the land and soon there was no food available. So the son hired himself out to feed pigs. By now, as Jesus is telling this story, anger is rising in members of His audience at how this young Jewish boy betrayed his father. The boy wasted everything that was given to him. On top of that, Jews were not permitted to eat pigs and now this starving boy was not only feeding unclean animals but craving the pods of their food. It was an insult to the Jewish tradition.

Circumstances became so bad for this young man that he finally "came to his senses." He realized that even his father's servants had food to eat. So he planned to return to his father and ask for forgiveness, saying "Father, I have sinned against heaven and against you. I am no longer worthy to be called your son; make me like one of your hired men." Wow, what a transformation of attitude! When he left home his demand was, "Give me," and now his desire was to humbly say to his father, "Make me." He would ask his father to make him a servant. Isn't that exactly what God wants from us? Rather than demanding selfishly for blessings with no regard for God as our Father, how wonderful if we would approach God with a heart that says, "Make me your servant!"

The young man headed toward home. The Pharisees listened and burned with anger. Those who believe in salvation by works will feel the same anger toward this young man who wasted all of his father's hard-earned money on foolish, wasteful living. The boy hadn't done anything deserving of forgiveness. He only earned himself retribution and punishment. In fact, the ancient Jewish law held that if a son was stubborn and rebellious against his parents, he would be stoned at the city gate. It was a serious offense. Justice! That is what the Pharisees were hoping for and expecting.

Now we learn that the father saw the young man while he was a long way off. Was the father waiting at the city gate daily, watching, expecting, and hoping? Only a father with a great love for his son would do such a thing. When he saw his son, he was filled with compassion and ran to him. That is the picture of the Father's love that Jesus wanted to portray in this story. The father ran to the boy, intervening in the expected and deserved punishment that would happen at the city gate, and he showered grace and love on his repentant son. He hugged and kissed his son. In verse 21 the son cried, "Father, I have sinned against heaven and against you. I am no longer worthy to be called your son." We are filled with joy and relief as Jesus continues the story. The father called his servants to quickly bring the best robe and put it on the young man. He placed a ring on his finger and sandals on his feet. The robe indicated that the young man would not have the status of a servant, but that of a son. The ring symbolized authority in the household. The father commanded that they kill the fattened calf, the one saved for only a very special occasion, such as a wedding. They would have a feast of celebration!

The Pharisees didn't understand – how can this be? Grace? Undeserved? The story continues... the older brother heard the music and dancing and asked what was going on. A servant explained that his younger brother had returned safe and sound and that was the reason for the great celebration. The older brother was so angry that he refused to go in. His anger and lack of compassion would not allow him to participate in the celebration of grace. Verse 28 tells us that he said to his father, "All these years I've slaved for you, and this son of yours wasted all of your property!" In his desperation he was essentially saying, "It's not fair, I deserve the celebration because I'm so good, and he deserves nothing but punishment!" The father again showed his heart of grace in verses 31-32 by reminding the older brother that all that the father had belonged to him. His younger brother was "dead and is now alive again" and that was the reason for the celebration.

God rewards humility, not self-righteousness. This story shows the heart of compassion that God has for a repentant sinner who humbly returns to the Lord. God showers grace on him as a son and forgives him, restoring him to a right relationship with Himself. But what about the inheritance? It is gone. The younger son could never pay it back. Nothing can change the consequences of the wrong choices. But in the Father's care, the consequences are softened by grace and a right relationship with God.

TOO GOOD TO RECEIVE GRACE?

Ephesians 2:8-9 says, "For it is by grace you have been saved, through faith – and this is not from yourselves – it is the gift of God, not by works so that no one can boast." The doctrine of grace is hard to understand because there is something deep in us that wants to earn and deserve what God gives us. That something deep inside is the opposite of humility. It is PRIDE. We do good works and then we want to present them to the Lord to prove we deserve salvation. But God will not allow pride to be part of his Kingdom. Pride lacks compassion and is like a cancer that grows until it causes us to want to be "god" of our own lives. As sinful human beings, we resist submitting to God and giving up our selfish desires. We prefer to do a few things wrong and make up for them by doing more things right. We like the scales of justice and try to pile up good works on one side in order to outweigh our mistakes and selfishness on the other side. So we resort to a works-based theology. But the passage in Ephesians shoots that theology down. We are offered salvation by grace alone – it's the only offer on the table.

When Jesus was in the Garden of Gethsemane, He prayed, "Father, if you are willing, take this cup from me; yet not my will, but yours be done." (Luke 22:42) The Bible tells us that Jesus sweat drops of blood and was in agony as He prayed this prayer. He was essentially saying… "If there is any other way Father, take what is about to happen from me." Isn't it clear that if there were *any* good works that you or I could do to save ourselves, God would have responded, "OK, let's have them do some good works for their salvation and You won't have to die on the cross as payment for their sin."

TOO BAD TO RECEIVE GRACE?

If you believe that your list of sins and regrets is too bad to qualify for this offer of grace, then I recommend that you read Acts 8:1-3 and Acts 9:1-31. Before his conversion, the Apostle Paul had worked hard to destroy the newly born Christian church. He had Christians arrested, jailed, and put to death. He was on a rampage to eradicate Christians and all remnants of testimonies about Jesus.

Acts chapter 9 describes Paul's conversion to Christianity, which took place only by the intervention of Jesus in his life.   God not only forgave Paul but shed His grace on Paul's life, calling him to be an apostle for Christ.

You may ask, "Where is the justice? What about all those people Paul had jailed and killed?" As you read the story of Paul's conversion in Acts chapter 9, note that after he was struck blind on the road to Damascus, he did not eat or drink for three days. I believe these days were a time of deep conviction and personal grief over what he had done. It was a time of repentance and one-on-one transaction with the Lord regarding how wrong Paul was in his former life path. God calls each of us to a time of repentance. But He knows that there is nothing we can do to make up for the sin. Big sins and small sins all place us in the same category: Sinners. If you have one little germ or a lot of germs, you are still sick. You still need to be healed in order to be well. You can't ignore the germ just because there is only a small amount. It will grow and contaminate your entire body.

A few good works will not erase our sin record. It is clear in Scripture that God does not accept works as payment to make the scales of justice even again. There is only one payment that He accepts: death. The sentence for our sin is death! That is why Jesus set aside His glory, walked among men on earth, and willingly paid the price that was required. The spotless lamb, as described in the Jewish law, would serve as the substitute and its shed blood would count as remission for sin.   Here is what the Bible says about our sin:

> "...all have sinned and fall short of the glory of God and are justified freely by his grace through the redemption that came by Christ Jesus." Romans 3:23
>
> "For the wages of sin is death, but the gift of God is eternal life in Christ Jesus our Lord." Romans 6:23

> "Therefore, since we have been justified through faith, we have peace with God through our Lord Jesus Christ through whom we have gained access by faith into this grace in which we now stand." Romans 5:1

Was justice served? Yes! God is a God of justice. He does not wipe away sin as if it never happened. No, He dealt with it thoroughly in order to satisfy His wrath for all of the pain and suffering sin produces. If a person wallows in regret, feeling that his sin is too great to be covered by Jesus' death on the cross, he diminishes the great sacrifice that Jesus made.

Maybe we would have written the story differently or come up with a different sort of plan for redemption, but there is no other plan offered by God. This is simple and humble enough for anyone in the world to understand yet deep enough to cover even the most heinous of sins.

CREATED FOR GOOD WORKS

Where do works fit into this plan of salvation by grace? Does grace mean that we don't have to worry about what we are doing? As recipients of the grace of God, we lose our desire to continue sinning. Our repentance causes us to turn away from our former sinful lifestyles. The Holy Spirit gives us a desire to please God. Good works are the *fruit* of the grace that we have been extended. **Good works do not earn our salvation, they are the result of salvation!**

Ephesians 2:10 says, "For we are God's workmanship, created in Christ Jesus to do good works, which God prepared in advance for us to do." We were created to do good works for the Lord, not as payment for our sin, not as a wage for our salvation, but as *service* to a God who has saved us and given us hope. Our hands and feet are the extension of Jesus' work of service and compassion to a dying and helpless world. The evidence of our salvation is displayed in our actions. James tells us in chapter 2 verse 18, "Show me your faith without deeds and I'll show you my faith by what I do." Faith without deeds is dead faith. Good works = faith in action!

Accept the gift of grace for your regret. Submit to it and don't trample on it as worthless compared to your good works. It is a mighty gift of God that overflows because of His great love for you. When you experience God's undeserved blessings in spite of past choices, Grace will become the most precious and meaningful gift to you.

Putting it off causes more regret

Believe it or not, there are some people who say, "Yes, I believe in the grace of God. I believe in it so much that I know I can wait until I'm ready and then I'll get right with God. I'll believe later and do what I want now." Grace is not a free pass to sin. We are not to presume God's grace or take it for granted. Deuteronomy 6:16 says, "Do not test the Lord your God...." In other words, do not test the extent of His grace by knowingly sinning, believing that it doesn't matter because God will always forgive.

The gospel of grace in the teaching of many churches sounds too easy. Some teach that all you have to do is say the right thing and it's that easy, you will be saved. But Romans 10:9 gives two conditions for salvation, "If you confess with your mouth Jesus as Lord, and believe in your heart that God raised Him from the dead, you will be saved." In addition, we must understand the whole teaching of Scripture on the matter. Without repentance and turning from our sin, we will not receive the salvation for which we think we are "eligible."

We are told in Hebrews 10:31, "It is a dreadful thing to fall into the hands of the living God." God is all powerful, awesome, and just. If you don't believe in God today, what makes you think you'll believe later in life? Our hearts get hardened with sin and rebellion. Consciences become seared. And we can't avoid the obvious question, will you even have tomorrow? There is no guarantee the option of choosing the Lord will be available to you. If you do believe in God today, you are responsible for what you know to be true.

Here are some verses that encourage us to receive salvation today:

"…now is the day of salvation." 2 Corinthians 6:2

"Today, if you hear his voice, do not harden your hearts as you did in the rebellion." Hebrews 3:15

"Do not boast about tomorrow, for you do not know what a day may bring forth." Proverbs 27:1

"Seek the Lord while he may be found; call on him while he is near." Isaiah 55:6

And the most important verse of all, an invitation from Jesus:

"Here I am! I stand at the door and knock. If anyone hears my voice and opens the door, I will come in and eat with him, and he with me." Revelation 3:20

THE INVITATION OF GRACE

The free gift of grace is just that: it is free and it is a gift. Jesus' invitation in Revelation 3:20 is for anyone who *will* receive Him into their hearts. He sends His Holy Spirit to live within us, just as He promised in John chapters 14 and 16.

Not only are we saved by grace, we live by grace. Since God does not accept our works as payment to earn salvation, why would we think that He would accept works as payment to keep our salvation? We live by grace, through the power of the Holy Spirit.

"Thanks be to God for his indescribable gift!" 2 Corinthians 9:15

PART 3

Preventing Future Regret

CHAPTER 21

God Turns Regret Upside Down

GOD TURNS PAIN INTO GAIN

DURING MY MANY YEARS AS a single mother, there was much to enjoy in my life. I started a business, which allowed me time to be flexible for the needs of my daughter. I owned a home in a nice neighborhood and had family living close by. I was faithful in attending church and Bible Studies on a weekly basis. I felt that leading small groups would force me to be diligent in completing the study homework and would encourage me to minister to others, so I led small study groups for many years. Being in a leadership role helped me to commit myself to be disciplined and proactive in staying as close to God as possible.

There were also some very difficult times during those years. I developed several dating relationships that I thought would be positive in my life, yet they were difficult and depleted me emotionally when they ended. At one point during one of those disappointing and painful seasons, the calling committee of my church contacted me and asked if I would serve on a leadership board. Before giving an answer, I spoke with the pastor about it. I told him that I didn't believe it was a good time for me to serve because I was going through a difficult season. I didn't think I would have a lot to offer the board and honestly, I felt that I didn't have a lot of emotional stamina to be a good leader. The pastor replied with an answer that I hardly expected. He said, "Oh that's perfect, that's the best place to be for God to use you!" I thought to myself, *What? Do you mean to tell me that God wants to use me because I'm weak and broken?*

I knew in my heart that the pastor was right. God prefers to use a broken vessel than a strong person who plows ahead forcing his or her own agenda. A broken person is much more pliable, humble, and moldable. Yes, God can and will use a broken person. I realized that God called me to a higher level of service to Him not necessarily because I'd be such a great servant for the church, but to change me and use me. During those years of service on the Diaconate and Elder Boards, I grew spiritually and learned firsthand about the faithfulness of God as He strengthened me to serve Him.

Allowing regret to work for us — not against us

God took those years that could have been wasted on self-pity and sadness and turned them instead to fruitful years of service. There were two sides to my situation, one side was heartache and pain and the other side was healing, change, and growth. On one hand, I was broken and suffering, yet on the other hand, God saw me as a useful servant.

Let's turn regret upside down for a moment, examining it from the viewpoint that it is a good thing. Let's not look at it from the perspective of how to get rid of it, rather how to make it work for us. We consider our pain and regret to be BAD. At times, we are just plain broken by our suffering. We wish certain things would not have happened in our past. We look at the tapestry of our lives and see countless messy, frayed, and broken threads. But we are looking at the wrong side of the tapestry. If we turn it over and look at it from the other side, we would see something beautiful with every thread perfectly in place to form an exquisite masterpiece.

If I look at my pain from a different perspective, I come to the realization that the times I have felt the closest to the Lord and have grown the most spiritually have been during the darkest times of my life.

God turns things upside down for His purposes. He takes pain and turns it into blessing. He turns bad things that happen to us into good. In my life, God has done this in so many ways that at times I look back on mistakes and think, "God must have wanted that to happen because if it weren't for that mistake, I wouldn't have arrived where I am today!" Although God does not desire that we sin and make dreadful mistakes, He takes what we do and our painful circumstances and weaves them so masterfully into His plan that we stand back in awe, marveling at how things all worked out. God can take whatever circumstances come our way and choices that we make and turn them upside down.

REGRET TEACHES US

While writing this book, I asked many individuals about the regret they have experienced in their lives. I was surprised that a few people claimed to have experienced no regret at all. As I pondered how some people could feel that their "slate is clean" and have no regret for anything, I realized that there may be a few reasons for this:

1. The person has such a positive attitude and is so happy with life today that he or she experiences no regret.
2. Some people are ashamed of their choices and do not want to revisit the past by admitting their mistakes.
3. Young people may not have experienced the consequences of their choices yet, and therefore, regret hasn't settled into their hearts.
4. The person has reached the ultimate state of emotional and spiritual health, has worked through past mistakes, and therefore, experiences no regret.
5. Some people harden themselves to the past, living in denial and refusing to reflect on how they got to where they are today.

I believe that everyone should have some regret. Yes, you read correctly! No one is perfect; we all have made bad choices at some point in our lives. Therefore, everyone should have some regret for mistakes they made in the past. Here is a list of what regret can do for us:

- Regret teaches us lessons.
- Regret humbles us and helps us realize that we're not perfect.
- Regret helps us to be sorry for what we've done.
- Regret causes us to ask for forgiveness from God and others.
- Regret causes us to treat others with more empathy and compassion.
- Regret leads us to better choices.
- Regret shows us what doesn't work in life.
- Regret forces us to change.
- Regret motivates us to try a better way.
- Regret prunes off our dysfunctions.
- Regret refines good qualities in us.

I have a sense that some people are ashamed to admit regret because it is equivalent to admitting that they made mistakes. Many people can't handle looking back at their past to learn from mistakes; they instead harden themselves to the past. They live as if their choices were not wrong, forging ahead without letting regret do its work in their lives.

In other instances, some young people may not have experienced the full consequences of their choices yet. Regret doesn't always manifest itself right away when we make our choices. We enjoy the short-term benefits, like spending more money than we can afford. Then the seeds of credit and overspending sprout a harvest bigger than we are able to manage and it begins to stifle and restrict other areas of our lives. Soon we lose our freedom because we have planted a crop that becomes out of control or grows too big to maintain.

Regret reminds us of the wrong path and gives us wisdom in making new choices. Even though it's painful and brings back memories we would rather forget, the reminder should cause us to act differently, think differently, and arrive at a different conclusion concerning the same set of circumstances. A woman who made a bad choice about a dating relationship will want to evaluate her choice critically. How can she make a better choice the next time around? What was it that caused her attraction to the wrong person? Even if she never faces the exact same set of circumstances again, she can begin to develop new decision-making skills that will work for her in other situations.

Stopping regret in its tracks

The natural path of regret is to travel from our past into our present and into our future. It doesn't seem to stop on its own. If we don't stop regret in its path, it will grow bigger as time goes on. We can block the natural flow of its negative impact by allowing it to work for us and teach us its useful lessons. When we recognize that God turns our regret upside down into something positive, the pain of the past loses its power over our lives.

CHAPTER 22

Sacrificing Our Future

"We must all suffer from one of two pains: the pain of discipline or the pain of regret. The difference is discipline weighs ounces while regret weighs tons."

JIM ROHN

REDUCE REGRET – CONTROL YOUR HABITS

DOES ONE CIGARETTE CAUSE CANCER? Does one bite of cake cause the scale to go up? Does one credit card purchase cause bankruptcy? When we are filled with regret, many times we can trace the dotted line directly to our habits, those pesky little things we do that can cause so much damage.

We all were born with appetites. Humans have an appetite for food, sex, love, entertainment, and many other things. We feed our appetites and they continuously need to be satiated. The more we feed an appetite, the stronger it becomes. If we have an appetite for salt, the more we eat salty foods, the more we crave saltier foods. Sex is an appetite that, when satiated, causes people to crave more sex. Is it wrong to eat, have sex, and spend money? Only when the appetite draws us into sin. God's Word is the instruction book on the boundaries of our fleshly appetites.

There is only one way to change or control an appetite. That is to NOT feed it! Cause it to starve and the craving will soon die. This is what Jesus refers to when He speaks of "dying to self." When our appetites cause us to sin against God, we need to "die" in that area of our life. We no longer keep that appetite alive by nourishing it and feeding it. Instead we resist the temptation to satiate it and we cause it to weaken its hold on us. That particular appetite loses its strength and weakens until it dies. Is this easy to do? Oh no, there is pain involved when our body screams for more of something that we deny it. That is where our choice to "pick up our cross" causes us to have victory in a problem area.

Jesus said in Luke 9:23, "If anyone would come after me, he must deny himself and take his cross daily and follow me." When we are faced with a choice, even as small as a bite of something to satiate a demanding appetite, we can resist, pick up our cross and follow Jesus to ultimate victory.

The cross is painful but the reward is great. What is the reward? It is freedom from being a slave to something that will hinder our true happiness. It is freedom from something that rules over us and prevents us from experiencing God's best in our lives.

Which pain do you prefer?

When we choose the wrong path, it feels good initially but pain comes later. When we choose the right path, there is pain first and blessing comes later. Pain that comes from obedience and self-control is not the same type of pain that regret brings. The pain from regret brings a sick, shameful feeling. The pain that comes from obedience and self-discipline makes us grateful. It is the opposite of regret. Rather than saying, "I wish I would not have done that," we can say, "Thank God I did the right thing!" Which would you rather say:

"I wish I would have quit smoking."

or "Thank God I went through the pain of quitting!"

"I wish I would not have gained so much weight."

or "Thank God I went on a diet!"

"I wish I wouldn't have had sex with that guy last night."

or "Thank God I said no!"
"I wish I wouldn't have charged up my credit cards."
or "Thank God I controlled my spending!"

Nothing compares with the good feeling of having made right (albeit hard) choices. The pain of self-control brings greater reward for us later. Our reward for choosing the pain of self-discipline over the pain of regret is a better life. We have a much better chance for happiness when we follow the truth of God's Word.

Preventing bad habits

There is something that we must do if we are going to make good choices in areas that we are the weakest. I call it "pushing through." When I set my mind to do or not to do something, inevitably I face the temptation to do the opposite of what I decided. If I can "push through" the amount of discomfort it takes to resist, I end up a little bit stronger for the next time. Eventually, I develop a better habit and it becomes a lifestyle and I am happy to be free of the struggle.

The Biblical or formal term for the same principle is "self-discipline." I like the term "pushing through" because in my experience, that is exactly what it feels like to exercise self-discipline. For example, when I gain weight, it's usually because I follow whatever my stomach and my mouth dictate. I love to snack and if I'm not careful, I can put on a few pounds very easily. When that happens, I realize that I must exercise self-discipline and not eat everything that is available to snack on. So, when I'm really serious about controlling what goes into my mouth, I stop and think for a minute before beginning to eat. Inevitably, I have an argument with my flesh which is crying out to be satisfied. If I push through the pain and resist the temptation to eat what I am attempting to avoid, the result is a greater sense of happiness and stability in my choice. When I do this, I am effectively "training" myself to obey my will and my mind rather than the superficial and fleeting desires of my body. I believe this is what the Apostle Paul is talking about when he says that he brings his body under control. Paul explains in 1 Corinthians 9:27 that he disciplines and trains his body to do what it should.

Deciding not to eat something may not seem like a big deal, but I believe it is. It is the snacking, the small bites, the giving in to every hunger pang, grabbing every tasty thing in sight that eventually causes us to put on pound after pound. So, making a small choice about a small bite is a BIG deal! We can "snack" on one or two dates with the wrong person, one or two small purchases, one or two drinks. It's the snacks that create the appetite for bigger servings of the same. And bigger servings of the same bad choices take us down a road that we regret later.

The more I resist the small bites of snacking, the more I am practicing not only to eat well but to control myself. In most cases, becoming overweight is due to an overall lack of self-control over the food we choose to put in our mouths. Pushing through the desire to eat what I shouldn't eat strengthens me for the next round of temptations. If I keep it up, I begin to develop a habit of thinking before grabbing and resisting the desire to give my body a momentary bit of pleasure.

SMALL CHOICES MAKE A BIG DIFFERENCE

Because regret does not always come from one big bad choice, it's important to examine each thread that makes up the tapestry of our lives. We may begin to notice threads that formed a pattern of how we make our choices. The mindset, reasoning, and skills that we use when making a big decision are the same as what we employ when making small choices. If we don't learn to make better choices in the small things in life, we simply won't have the skills to make the right choices on a bigger scale. I believe that God wants us to practice in the small things and develop the self-control that we need when faced with big decisions that have the potential to destroy our lives. If we are faithful in small things, we can be trusted in bigger matters. If we fail in the big issues of life, it is probable that we have failed in many small things.

A few years ago I read the story of a woman who had embezzled a large sum of money from her employer. When she was caught, it was discovered that she began with small choices to do little dishonest things. Then the choices became bigger as she was drawn deeper into the deceitful activities. She was sentenced to serve time in jail for her crime and her life changed forever. Little choices become big choices!

Paying tomorrow for bad choices today

If you reconsider the story of Jacob and Esau in Genesis chapter 25, let's focus on Esau's actions. Esau came in from hunting and was famished and asked Jacob for some of the stew that he was preparing. Jacob's answer was essentially, "Sure, you can have some stew, but first sell me your rights as firstborn son." I don't think this was the first time that the issue of Esau's birthright came up. It's possible that Jacob had argued for years about how unfair it was that Esau had the birthright and that Jacob should have been born first. From the time of their birth Jacob had been trying to "supplant" Esau. This had been on Jacob's mind and he used the situation in this story to bring it up again, hoping to finally get what he wanted. He could see that Esau was in a weakened, hungry state and he demanded Esau's birthright in exchange for a bowl of stew. In verse 32 Esau gave in and agreed, saying he was about to die and "what good is the birthright to me?" Jacob told Esau to swear an oath, which Esau did, formally relinquishing his birthright to Jacob. Then Esau ate and drank, got up and left, and the Bible tells us in verse 34 that he "despised his birthright." Now, you might be asking, "What in the world does Esau's stupidity in selling his birthright have to do with my life in the 21st century?"

Esau was famished so he gave in and made a grave choice that would permanently and negatively affect his destiny. You may insist, "I would never do that. I would never sell my future for something as small as a pot of stew!" I beg to differ with that statement. Most people, including the author of this book, have done just that in many different ways. In fact, most of our bad choices are a direct result of responding to a strong, immediate appetite for love, sex, happiness, material blessings, power, revenge, justice, money, relationship, alcohol, drugs, or _____ (you fill in the blank). Our natural human inclination is to closely follow our appetites and do whatever is in front of us that will satiate us. We usually choose the path that we believe will bring us the most immediate happiness. What's worse is that many times we don't examine carefully whether the path aligns with where we desire to be later in life. The less we are willing to wait and consider how a decision may affect our future, the higher the risk of making a choice that may bring bad consequences. In other words, many regrets come from sacrificing the future for the pleasure of the moment.

These ancient Bible stories teach us principles and encourage us to make right choices and avoid bad choices (as God's people have experienced throughout history). The birthright was Esau's future. He was the eldest son and that gave him precedence over the other siblings, as well as assured him of a double portion of the inheritance. The birthright could be bartered which is what Esau chose to do. Swearing an oath in those days was similar to having a written contract in our day. It was a serious thing. My first question is, I wonder if Esau always made decisions based on what his appetite dictated? It certainly appears as if the decision to give up his birthright came rather easily. After the stew incident in Esau's life, how many times did he look back in regret and say, "Why did I give up my inheritance just because I was hungry? The stew took five minutes to eat and now I'm suffering for the rest of my life because of it. How could I have done something so impulsive and stupid?"

Many people have asked themselves the same questions when they gave in to momentary pleasures and then lost out on future blessings because of their choices. A man has a one-night stand with a woman he doesn't love and she ends up pregnant, changing both of their lives forever. A woman spends money she doesn't have and gets into credit card debt, robbing her future of financial security. A man takes drugs for the momentary high and then spends his future focusing on breaking the addiction. A woman eats to soothe her emotions and trades a healthy future for medical issues. The list of examples goes on and on.

We might question why one small choice has the ability to affect so much of our lives. But if we think about it realistically, it's more than one small choice. If Esau did not have the mindset of following his appetite, he would have resisted the temptation to give up something so important for five minutes of relief of his hunger. Esau probably had the habit of living pretty closely to whatever suited him for the moment. His mind was on the present, not on his future. He didn't seem to value how his inheritance would affect his future. In those days, a birthright was more than just extra money out of the inheritance. It had position and responsibility attached to it. When the father passed away, the eldest son would take over as head of the household, take charge of the family property, care for the mother and unmarried sisters, and have authority over the family. If Esau had valued his destiny and responsibility as the eldest son, there would never have been a question in his mind as to what the right choice would be when offered a bowl of stew in exchange for his future. So his bad choice wasn't so impulsive after all. It was the fruit of his mindset and values. Given the right circumstances, this was bound to happen.

God's principle of waiting

There are many principles that are woven throughout the books of Scripture. The more we study the Bible, the more we learn God's ways and the principles that He wants us to apply to our lives. One of the most prominent principles in the pages of Scripture is the principle of waiting on God. The more we are ruled by our appetites, the less we like the idea of waiting on God. When we let our appetites rule us, we tend to make bad decisions. We are convinced that if we want something, we have to have it now and we deserve it now. We have no assurance that if we wait, what we want will actually come our way.

So we try to make it happen while we can. Many of us yield to what is before us rather than trust the Lord to provide what will be good for us in His way and His timing. God doesn't always ask us to wait, but He does lead us to wait enough times throughout our lives that we must learn to become good at it.

One of the characteristics of temptation is the urgency for having it now. The power of temptation says, if you don't make this happen or take this, you'll never have the chance again. Then, if I reach for it and take it ahead of God's timing, disastrous results can happen. I've experienced this pattern many times in my life. I've spent money that I should have saved for my future because I "had to have it now." I've been in relationships that were wrong for me because I didn't have the patience to wait for the right person in God's timing. The pressure of the immediate was strong. I didn't stop to ask, "How will this decision affect God's plan for my life?" "What are the future consequences of this choice?" Many prisoners say this, "If I had only known where this would lead, I would not have done it." If we immerse ourselves in God's Word, we learn about the consequences that await decisions made by feeding our appetites. Then, if we're wise, we'll heed the warnings in Scripture and wait.

There are several valid questions regarding the issue of waiting. The first one is, "Why?" Why do I always seem to have to wait for the things I want out of life? "When?" When is God going to act on my behalf and provide what I need? "What if?" What if I wait and God never gives me what I want?

Waiting proves that we are submissive to God. Being impatient is the same as saying, "I don't trust you." Psalm 119:74 says, "...I have put my hope in your word." We are to ask God for direction with our decisions. The Psalmist is waiting for God to speak. God may ask us to wait in order to prompt us to seek His guidance.

Time builds our trust in God. It is one of the mechanisms that God uses to test our faith. Will we seek Him? Will we trust His Word?

Moreover, will we trust His Word when the circumstances display exactly the opposite? When life is confusing and painful and the situation gets worse, the problem can soon rise above God in our eyes. We begin to rely on what we see and we are tempted throughout the waiting time to succumb to the problem. This is the juncture where we must learn to lean on God. Our faith is strengthened when we choose to trust God in spite of what we see.

God exposes our motives while we wait on Him. Is it lust? Is it greed? Is it pride? Is it selfishness? Maybe what we want isn't what we should want at all. God knows our deepest desires and needs better than we do. I remember years ago complaining to the Lord in a prayer that went something like this, "Lord, why haven't you let this situation work out? Why haven't you given me what I wanted?" Immediately I felt in my spirit that God answered, "I did give you what you want!" I realized that although my desire was for this situation to succeed, my deeper desire was for God's will in my life and that God would keep me from something that wasn't good for me. Years later I looked back in gratitude that God answered my deeper desire rather than give me what I thought I wanted.

We are conformed to the likeness of Jesus while we wait. Conformation is not fun. If a beautiful rose could talk after being pruned, it might say something like this, "It really hurt to have those leaves and branches snipped off and to have the gardener work on me with those pruning shears, but look at me now – I'm the best rose I can be!" We need to understand that in the mix of our circumstances, desires, and needs, God's greatest goal is for us to become like Jesus.

THE PROMISE OF GOD TO THOSE WHO WAIT

Isaiah 64:4 says, "Since ancient times no one has heard, no ear has perceived, no eye has seen any God besides you who acts on behalf of those who wait for him." God promises that those who wait on Him will never be disappointed. Psalm 25:3 says, "No one whose hope is in you will ever be put to shame." Isaiah 30:18 tells us, "…Blessed are all who wait for him." Yes, we had better get very good at waiting if we want God to act on our behalf.

LEARNING TO WAIT WELL

Waiting is something that does not come naturally to us, it is something that we must learn. Unfortunately, the only way to really learn how to wait is to do just that… wait. It's similar to learning patience. I've heard it said that we should never pray for patience. God won't just give us patience, rather He will place us in circumstances that produce patience. I know from experience that the circumstances that produce patience are not comfortable. It is the same as learning how to wait on God. We learn to wait by waiting. We sense the Lord is leading us to wait in a certain area that is important to us. We want to obey so we begin to wait. Some time goes by and nothing happens. Then our flesh starts to cry out! Our faith begins to be tested. Questions rise to the surface. "Are you sure you should be waiting? Is God really leading you to wait on this? Why should you wait when you could do something to alleviate this pain right now? What if God forgets about your situation? What if He makes you wait for years? What if you don't like what He gives you after you've waited so long?"

Yes, God used circumstances to teach me how to wait. I had never waited well and it was about time that God created a special lesson plan for me. Unfortunately, I didn't earn extra credit as I would have liked. I passed the course, but not with flying colors. I was faithful in serving the church but complained and grumbled about being single for so many years. Through God's special lesson plan for me, I studied much about the Israelites at the edge of the Red Sea and their 40-year trek through the wilderness before reaching the Promised Land. All but two of the original group that came out of Egypt never made it into the Promised Land. They took 40 years to make an eleven-day trip. What was the reason they didn't go into the Promised Land? Unbelief! They grumbled and complained every time they struggled. The core of their complaint was that they didn't believe God's promise to take them to the land He destined for them. They didn't trust Him, even after He had already freed them from slavery, miraculously opened the Red Sea, and provided manna in the desert.

Learning to wait well is all about faith. We say we believe, we say we have faith. But in the desert, the waiting time, the years of seeing nothing but sand with no skyline of the Promised Land in the horizon… will we allow our faith to grow? Lack of faith can cost us our future as we wander in the desert complaining. Exercising our faith pleases God because it proves that we believe Him. Believing God is what we're called to do. That's why we are called "Believers"!

CHAPTER 23

Busyness – The Business of Being Busy

*"If Satan can't get us to sin against God,
he'll just make us too busy for God."*

ANONYMOUS

WE ARE BUSY, BUSY PEOPLE. I've heard it said that if Satan can't get us to sin, he'll just make us busy! I'm sure Satan is very pleased when people are so overloaded with activities, commitments, and work that they are unavailable or uninterested in accomplishing God's will on earth. What better way to render people useless for God's Kingdom than to distract them with busyness? Our attention can be easily diverted off of the things of God as we struggle to keep all of the pieces of our lives functioning successfully.

Our busyness has created so much stress in our lives that close to 80% of doctor visits are for stress-related illnesses. In spite of that statistic, people in general view busyness as something to be proud of in their lives. It's a badge of honor that we wear when people ask, "How are you?" The common answer is, "Really busy!" It's almost as if the word "busy" means that we are not lazy; we are important and successful. It tells people, in one word, that we are doing something worthwhile and productive. Who wouldn't want that in their lives? We reward people with compliments for overloading themselves, while raising children who are equally as busy with school, sports, and hobbies. We are a competitive, accomplishment-driven society made up of people whose time is bulging with work, activities, and more work and more activities.

I fall into this trap of busyness at times. When asked how I am, I answer, "Busy!" And I am answering honestly because often I am just about as busy as the next person. There can be many demands on us. We feel that we have no choice but to enslave ourselves to the demands of work, family, home, school, and outside activities.

We consider that busyness equals productivity. That is the message behind our "badge of honor." But why, at the end of the day, do we feel depleted and unproductive? We can become exhausted by our busyness. We wonder why our lives seem out of balance. Our busyness comes with a price. We find that the cost includes losing time with our children, failing to nurture relationships, missing opportunities to help others, and not spending quiet time with the Lord. When I ask people if/where they go to church, I often hear the answer, "I need my sleep on Sunday mornings because I'm so busy during the week." Many people do not spend time reading their Bibles or praying, except on the fly when there is a crisis in their lives.

BUSYNESS - THE BLOCK TO OUR SOURCE OF POWER

When we are bogged down with busyness and don't make time to seek the Lord, our intimacy with Him is weakened. When it becomes too weak, our intimacy with God can be broken. For Christians, this doesn't mean we lose our salvation but it does mean that we lose the faith, wisdom, and strength that we need to navigate our lives. When we spend time in prayer, we are exercising our faith by sacrificing our time to talk to God. We study His Word and are filled with wisdom for the challenges of the day. When we "eat" of the Word, it nourishes and strengthens us spiritually to do what we need to do. In our intimacy with God we witness His faithfulness and our walk with Him becomes stronger and more solid.

I was just outside today trimming bushes in the front yard with an electric trimmer. It's a long heavy trimmer with two sets of blades. Needless to say, I am very careful when I walk with it and use it. When I was finished cutting the bushes, I unplugged the electric trimmer. Finally, I could relax! I wasn't worried anymore about being too careful and keeping my hands far away from the dangerous blades. I knew I could handle the trimmer without fear because it was totally cut off from electricity – its power source.

Busyness has the potential to cut us off from our power source. We don't have time to nurture our relationship with God and we begin to cut ourselves off from the very thing we need to survive, flourish, and bear fruit. Just as the electric trimmer could not do what it was meant to do without electricity, I will not be able to do what I am called to do if I am cut off from my source of power.

THE PRICE OF BUSYNESS

The following list shows some of the blessings we miss out on when we are too busy to think about the things of God:

- **Worship/Praise**
- **Giving time to help others**
- **Financially supporting church and missions**
- **Spending quiet time with God**
- **Serving Him using our spiritual gifts**
- **Fellowship with God's people**
- **Learning what God has to teach us in Scripture**
- **Following His plan for my life**
- **Getting nourishment for our souls through His Word**

What is the price of busyness? **Regret!**

Regret is a high price to pay for our busyness.

"But I have to work, take care of the kids, and do a million other things! I don't have time to learn about God. There are too many demands on me. There is nothing I can cut out of my life." Have you said these things?

CLEAR THE LANDSCAPE OF YOUR LIFE

We all want the best life possible. We seek after it and strive for it. Unfortunately, in working and striving for it, we fill our lives with so many good things that it becomes unmanageable. We don't want to cut anything out because it's all good. We operate under the false assumption that because something is good, it needs to stay in our lives. This is not necessarily true. Even a master gardener tending to his rose bushes will prune off good roses in order for the best roses to flourish. We, on the other hand, are afraid to cut out good things, so we continue to pack our lives with busyness. We may miss the best because we are too busy tending to the good!

The book of Joshua describes the Israelites taking possession of the Promised Land. In Joshua 17:14 some of the people asked Joshua for more land. Joshua responded by telling them that what they wanted was already right in front of them. He instructed them in verse 15 to clear the trees from the land. Joshua was telling the people that land was out there, they just couldn't recognize it because of all the trees cluttering the landscape. He told them to cut the trees down and get rid of what was distracting them from seeing the goodness of the land.

I wonder how much clutter we each have in our own lives that needs to be cut out in order for us to experience the blessings that are already right in front of us? Unnecessary clutter can be defined as anything that has the potential to overtake us, become stronger in our lives, or distract us from our ultimate goal. These are the things that need to be cut out. We may be asking God for more blessings and more territory. If we clear the territory we now own, we might find that we already have our answer.

Joshua was also telling the people that it would be advantageous to cut the trees down because their enemies could be hiding in the forest.

They would not be able to properly defend their land with so many places for their enemies to hide. Bad habits and time wasters are enemies that can hide behind the activities that are jam-packed into the landscape of our lives. Maybe it would be beneficial to take an actual inventory of the hours in your day, and then try to identify the clutter that can be cut out of your life.

Write the number of minutes or hours that you spend doing the following:

Activity	How much time usually spent	Amount of time that is wasted – possible to cut out
Working		
Eating		
Shopping		
Exercising		
Socializing		
Watching TV		
Sleeping		
Hobbies		
Computer/Tablet		
Other		

We should continually evaluate what is cluttering up the landscape of our lives. I believe that electronic entertainment is the biggest culprit as a "time waster." Not only do we keep our days busy with activities, we keep our minds busy! We enjoy having our minds constantly stimulated. We may believe we are "resting" when we are entertained by the TV or computers, but we are actually energizing our minds and thoughts. We process and react to all of the scenes and action we are watching. Our feelings and emotions are stimulated. We push the cares of the day out and fill our minds with an alternate form of busyness. Unfortunately, we are replacing our cares with, for the most part, entertainment that is void of true meaning.

Our internal engine goes 100 miles an hour all day to keep up with our responsibilities. When are we going to settle our minds and hearts down to pray and listen to the Lord? He is not going to shout over the noise and activity in our lives. He is not going to speed up to walk with us at our pace. No, we will have to slow down, be quiet, turn off the noise, and open the Bible and our hearts to hear God.

In addition to quiet time with the Lord, there are many opportunities to learn God's Word through unlimited online resources. Rather than using our smart electronics for idle pastimes, why not access Bible teaching podcasts or watch a video of an online sermon?

DON'T SERVE GOD THE LEFTOVERS

I believe we are to give God the first and the best of what we have to offer, not the leftovers. Therefore, it is my practice to begin my day with the Lord. Of course, we can spend time with God at any moment during the day and I have spent many quality hours in the evening working on Bible Study homework over the years. But the principle in Scripture is this: God desires the firstfruits of what we give to Him, including our worship, money, and time. What is firstfruit? It is the *first* of our fruit. It's not the leftovers after we have used up, eaten, or spent our fruit. It is the first and the best of what we have.

I like to think of it this way. I much prefer praying in the morning and asking God for help and strength for the day, rather than waiting until the evening after I've had my failures! Being proactive in my relationship with God and my time in prayer strengthens me to face my responsibilities. Wouldn't we rather be strengthened early to make good choices than to wait until the evening and seek forgiveness after our mistakes of the day? I call this being proactive rather than reactive. I believe this is what God has in mind as He encourages us through His Word to be proactive, seeking Him early in the morning.

The following are Scripture verses that shine the light on how wonderful the morning offering of time can be:

> "In the morning O Lord, you hear my voice; in the morning I lay my requests before you and wait in expectation." Psalm 5:3
> "But I cry to you for help, Lord; in the morning my prayer comes before you." Psalm 88:13

"Let the morning bring me word of your unfailing love, for I have put my trust in you. Show me the way I should go, for to you I lift up my soul."   Psalm 143:8

"Lord, be gracious to us; we long for you. Be our strength every morning, our salvation in time of distress."   Isaiah 33:2

"He wakens me morning by morning, wakens my ear to listen like one being taught."   Isaiah 50:4

"…for His compassions never fail. They are new every morning; great is your faithfulness." Lamentations 3:23

If we know that God's mercies and compassion are new and fresh every morning in the midst of our busy lives, why wouldn't we want to seek God early in the morning?   If life doesn't permit early morning time with God, we can still start our day with prayer and praise, turning our day over to God and recognizing He is in control.

I've heard people say, "I'm too busy to spend time with God." Time can always be rearranged to accommodate what is important to us. If a person learns that he has cancer, he doesn't say, "I don't have time for treatment." He doesn't say, "I'll take care of it later." No, he makes time for what is necessary and important for his health.

There have been days or seasons when I've missed this early morning time with God. But as I get ready for work, I always make sure I have allotted time to get dressed and put my makeup on. I would never go to work without dressing nice and fixing my hair and makeup.   One day I realized what happened to my priorities.   I was making sure my outward appearance was ready for my day without making sure that my inward spiritual life was fed, healthy, and ready to take on the day's responsibilities.   What we spend our time on reflects our priorities and what is important to us.

I sometimes find it hard to sit and be quiet and slow my "engine" down. Even when I am working, I prioritize easily and function more efficiently when a lot is happening and many demands are placed on me. Being quiet and still before the Lord is something that doesn't come naturally to me; I have to discipline myself to do this.

Time is an asset. The day offers 24 hours that belong to us and that we must decide how to steward. Regret comes in when we make bad choices with this precious commodity. Deeper regret comes as life forges on and we realize how much time we have lost that we'll never recover. Once it's gone, it is gone forever! Every day that passes leaves us with less and less time to steward.

Honoring the Lord with the firstfruits of our worship, money, and time helps keep our lives in balance. I don't wait until all of my bills have been paid and then, if there is money left over, tithe to my church. No, I write the tithing check first and use the leftovers to pay my bills. It substantiates the Lord's place in my life. This is what might be called, "putting my money where my mouth is!" I say Jesus is first in my life. That means I don't give Him what is left over after all of my needs, wants, and obligations have been met.

When our time is filled with busyness and our money is spent first on our needs, God may get pushed further and further down the list of priorities.

CHOOSING TO NURTURE OUR RELATIONSHIP WITH GOD

If a husband and wife begin to experience a breakdown in their relationship, it can most likely be traced to diminished time spent together nurturing the companionship, friendship, and intimacy between them. The nature of a relationship is that it must be nurtured in order to grow. It doesn't grow and develop all by itself. If we do not spend time with the Lord, we will begin to feel empty and lost. We may try to fill our emptiness with other things that don't satiate us. Soon, our relationship with Him grows cold. Then, when circumstances get bad enough, we turn to Him again and pray, talk, ask, and beg. We sometimes do all the talking! God will respond and interact with us as we quiet our hearts and listen as we read Scripture and pray. The pain in our hearts is soothed when we read verses such as Isaiah 49:23, "…those who hope in me will not be disappointed."

Pain and problems in my life have continuously forced me to spend time with the Lord in prayer. I have learned that in good times and bad, prayer and quiet time with the Lord must be a priority in my life... every day! God has blessed me so much in these times, revealing deeper things in His Word, answering my prayers, and showing me His faithfulness.

When I read and study the Bible, I am amazed by how God uses His Word to address exactly what I am struggling with in my life. I learn more about the ways of God. I begin to see things from His perspective on my circumstances. I believe that if we approach Scripture with a submissive and open heart, God will speak to us through His Word. I now consider my alone time with Him as the best part of my day. I cherish it and look forward to it. It sets the foundation for my day.

CREATING AN APPETITE FOR SPIRITUAL THINGS

You might say, "But I don't have the desire or inclination to spend quiet time with the Lord. I can't help it, my mind won't settle down into quietness." When life is good and our needs and wants are satisfied, our appetite for spiritual things can be minimal. The benefit of quiet time with God doesn't seem to outweigh the good things going on around us. People are funny – and predictable. When life is hard or there is a calamity, our appetite for the Lord increases. Maybe you simply need to create or develop an appetite for spiritual things. How do you "create" an appetite for something? By eating of it little by little until you begin to develop a hunger for it.

Years ago I wanted to begin to watch my weight. So, rather than continue to eat fast food hamburgers, I began to eat salads. It wasn't easy at first because I craved the food that I was accustomed to eating. Then, as I continued to eat salads, they began to taste better. I slowly began to develop an appetite for salads and vegetables. I have *learned* to like healthy food. I didn't have to learn how to like unhealthy food; I've always liked salty snacks, cheese, and chocolate. I didn't have to train my taste buds to enjoy those things. But knowing that eating healthier is better for my body, I have learned to enjoy vegetables and fiber and other healthy foods.

If you want to create a spiritual appetite for learning more of the Word of God, begin to eat of it daily. Isaiah 55:2 says, "Why spend money on what is not bread, and your labor on what does not satisfy? Listen, listen to me, and eat what is good, and you will delight in the richest of fare."

What does it mean to "eat" of the Word of God? "Eat" is a very descriptive word. I believe it means to do the following:

Read a passage of Scripture.
Chew on it. Meditate on it, chew, think about it, chew on it, process it, chew again.
Swallow it. Take it in. Let it settle into your mind and heart. Pray about it.
Digest it. Apply it to your life. As it becomes a part of your life, submit to what it teaches.

As you eat of God's Word, then you begin to notice something interesting. You are hungry for more! You feel hunger pangs that only His Word will satisfy.

When you are hungry again, eat again. In fact, you can eat before you get hungry. The point is, the more you eat, the bigger your appetite will become.

When you read Scripture and feel a lack of understanding, pray that the Holy Spirit will help you to understand. Spiritual things are only discerned by the Holy Spirit. The Holy Spirit teaches us and leads us into all truth. But we need to seek God with all of our hearts. We can't seek Him and keep our busy agenda. No, we seek Him and are submissive to what He has to say. Jeremiah 29:13 says, "You will seek me and find me when you seek me with all your heart."

BE STILL
Psalm 46:10 says, "Be still and know that I am God." Yet our society praises high energy and rewards constant activity. We may believe that

if we sit still and are quiet, we are being unproductive and lazy. With all of the demands on our time, we may feel guilty or restless when taking time out to pray and *be still* before the Lord.

The Bible teaches that quiet time with the Lord is the best way to renew our spirit. When we are renewed and energized spiritually, we actually have more strength with which to manage our responsibilities. Isaiah 40:31 says, "...but those who hope in the Lord will renew their strength; they will soar on wings like eagles; they will run and not grow weary, they will walk and not be faint." We are spiritually renewed, not through activity and works, rather through quietness and rest in God's presence. God strengthens us, gives us wisdom, and prepares us to do what we need to do each day. When we are strong spiritually, we can better handle the challenges we face. We will also be wiser in knowing which activities to eliminate as we prioritize our time. When we are strong spiritually and filled with the Holy Spirit, our lives will become more effective for the Lord.

GOD CALLS US TO BE FRUITFUL

We think if we are busy, we are being effective, productive, and fruitful. There is a difference between being busy and being fruitful. God does not call us to be busy; He calls us to be fruitful. Busyness can cause much regret but fruitfulness will never cause regret. Below are synonyms for "busy" and "fruitful." Which will we choose?

BUSY (not God's will)	FRUITFUL (God's will)
Toiling	Useful
Unavailable	Worthwhile
Overloaded	Beneficial
Buried	Bearing fruit
Engrossed	Rewarding
Hustling	Successful
Occupied	Well-spent
Meaningless activity	Abundant growth
Swamped	Producing good results
Anxious	Peaceful

It's no wonder that we are filled with regret when we are overloaded with busyness. Many people have regret, knowing that although they are wearing the badge of busyness, they are not living fruitful lives.

How do we bear fruit? We bear fruit in a similar manner to how a tree bears its fruit. Jesus explains in John chapter 15 that He is the vine and we are the branches. Just as a fruit-bearing branch dies if it is not connected to the vine, we will not bear fruit if we are not connected to Jesus, the true vine. Verse 5 says, "I am the vine; you are the branches. If a man remains in me and I in him, he will bear much fruit, *apart from me you can do nothing.*" (Emphasis added.)

Can a branch on an apple tree create and produce its own apples? No matter how much the branch struggles and tries, it cannot bear fruit on its own. When it is connected to the root of the tree, the life within the root flows through the tree to the branch. By simply being connected to the source, the branch begins to bear the fruit that it was created to bear. When we are connected to God, His life flows through us and we bear good fruit. The fruit is the result of the root!

Bearing fruit and doing what we are called to do will eliminate much regret. When we look back on our lives and see evidence of fruitfulness, rather than busyness, that painful feeling of regret won't fill our hearts. We won't look back and say, "I wish I could undo the busyness that kept me from fulfilling my life purpose."

CHAPTER 24

Working on Our Words

"The tongue has the power of life and death...."

PROVERBS 18:21

UNCHANGEABLE WORDS

WORDS, WORDS, UNCHANGEABLE WORDS. THIS is one area that we all have in common when it comes to regret. I don't know of anyone who doesn't have some regret for the words that they have let rise out of their heart and roll off of their tongue. In fact, if a person never says anything wrong, the Bible says he is perfect and able to control his whole body. (James 3:2) I know many nice people but I can say with certainty that I know of no one who is perfect in all of his or her words.

Though my desire is for you and me to be free from the bondage of deep regret, I do hope that a few pangs of regret regularly prick our consciences for carelessly spoken words. Too many people have been so hardened in their speech that they rarely experience regret in the way they speak to others.

James 3:2-12 says:

"We all stumble in many ways. Anyone who is never at fault in what they say is perfect, able to keep their whole body in check. When we put bits into the mouths of horses to make them obey us, we can turn the whole animal. Or take ships as an example. Although they are so large and are driven by strong winds, they are steered by a very small rudder wherever the pilot wants to go.

Likewise, the tongue is a small part of the body, but it makes great boasts. Consider what a great forest is set on fire by a small spark. The tongue also is a fire, a world of evil among the parts of the body. It corrupts the whole person, sets the whole course of his life on fire, and is itself set on fire by hell.

All kinds of animals, birds, reptiles and sea creatures are being tamed and have been tamed by mankind, but no man can tame the tongue. It is a restless evil, full of deadly poison.

With the tongue we praise our Lord and Father, and with it we curse men, who have been made in God's likeness. Out of the same mouth come praise and cursing. My brothers, this should not be. Can both fresh water and salt water flow from the same spring? My brothers, can a fig tree bear olives, or a grapevine bear figs? Neither can a salt spring produce fresh water."

The spark of one word

Because the words we speak are invisible, it is easy to be careless and believe they don't carry weight. We don't fully understand their effect on people. We think we can change our words, take them back, or apologize if necessary. Words don't seem to exhibit their power until the damage is done. Words have the ability to influence feelings, situations, people, homes, churches, companies, and nations. The passage in James compares the tongue to the bit in a horse's mouth. The bit can control and turn the whole animal. It goes on to say that a small rudder is used to steer a huge ship and a little spark can start a forest on fire.

A fire can warm or it can burn

Consider the following scenario:

The owner of a company is stressed because the economy has negatively affected his business and he is losing money. He meets with his sales manager and says, "You aren't working hard enough. If you don't figure out a way to increase sales, I'll fire you!" The sales manager thinks to himself, "I have been working hard and doing my best, it's not my fault that the whole market is down." He calls a meeting with a member of his sales team and says, "Did you make those calls to the list of companies I gave you? If you don't finish that today, your job is on the line!" The salesman responds to his boss, "You gave me a week to complete this call list and now you want it all done today?" The salesman goes home that evening and says to his wife, "Can't you keep the kids quiet, I have work to do." His wife says to herself, "I work and have had a stressful day too, can't he help with the kids tonight?" She goes to her child's room and says, "You better clean your room and get your homework done; no TV tonight." The child says to herself, "Mom said I could watch my TV show after my homework is done, it's not fair!" The child goes to bed angry and hurt.

This is a picture of a forest fire that was set off by the spark of a few words. The chain reaction caused stress in the lives of many people.

Words can destroy a reputation

Consider the following scenario:

A manager is threatened by a good employee that he supervises. He fears that the employee may want to grow into a management role and possibly take his place. He increasingly grows to dislike the employee. During a meeting with the president, he makes a few negative comments about the employee's performance and trustworthiness. The president can't seem to get the comments out of his mind as he considers the company's organization and promotions. He has an uncomfortable feeling and chooses to promote someone else instead. During his reorganization of positions, he terminates the employee based on what was discussed in the meeting with the manager.

One comment grew bigger as it swept through the lives of the people involved. In the end, a reputation was ruined and a life was permanently changed by someone else's words.

UNAVOIDABLE JUDGMENT

In Matthew 12:36-37 Jesus says, "But I tell you that men will have to give account on the day of judgment for every careless **word** they have spoken. For by your **words** you will be acquitted, and by your **words** you will be condemned." (Emphasis added.)

Before examining the subject of words, I used to wonder how God could judge every word spoken. It's just a word! How am I going to give an account for every word I speak? After studying how words create forest fires of devastation, then it hit me. We will each give an account not only for our words but the *chain of events* that we created. God holds us responsible for the negative, cruel, and careless words that start forest fires of pain in the lives of others.

The owner of the company in the first scenario will not only give an account for what he said, but he carries the weight of the affect he had on others through the subsequent chain of events. The manager in the second scenario affected the career and livelihood of the employee by speaking falsely about him. His words and the results will be exposed on the Day of Judgment.

This is what gossip has the power to do. Words of gossip are like matches that start little fires that grow and spread. Gossip, lies, and malicious talk about an individual can influence the opinions of others regarding that person. Words can build a person up or tear a person down. How many lives have been negatively affected by careless gossip? God will call to accountability those who gossip.

WORDS HAVE POWER AND INFLUENCE

POWER...

My husband and I are intrigued by World War II. We watch many documentaries, movies, and series about the war. Did you know Hitler used words to sway his people not only to follow but to subscribe to his Nazi doctrine? He delivered powerful speeches that addressed the fears and desires of the people. They attributed his maniacal statements to political zeal and declared their loyalty. Hitler rallied his followers with words as he made promises to make the country great again. Words are powerful enough to change the course of history!

Influence…
I attended a support group during my first divorce. One of the women commented that her mother had said so many negative things about her father during her parents' divorce that she lost respect for her dad. It affected her relationship with him and she didn't want to spend time with him. It even influenced her attitude toward men in general as she grew older and began dating. She wished her mother would not have spread her anger to her children. The woman's mother did not realize how influential her words were and the impact they would have on her daughter's life.

"The tongue has the power of life and death…." Proverbs 18:21

The power of words. Think of how you can stir yourself to anger with wrong words. You are also able to become calm and bring yourself to right feelings with right words. We tend to live by what we say. For example, when I go to work in the morning, I can choose what I say to myself as I drive:

A. "Why do I have to work today? I dread another day of work."

OR

B. "Lord, thank you for my job. Help me to honor You in all I do today. Let me be a blessing to others."

Imagine the feelings that rise up if I complain. I will begin to feel negative and unappreciative. My energy level will be down and I may tend to drag through the day. I'll view my job responsibilities as meaningless tasks and wish for the day to be over.

Now imagine how I might feel if I start the day speaking right words. I give myself a healthy perspective, I'm thankful and I see my duties as a way to honor the Lord throughout the day. I'm more apt to be cheerful to others and encourage them with my words.

Wow, that's a lot of power with just a few words as the day begins!

POSITIVE WORDS STRENGTHEN US

During moments or seasons of regret, we can encourage ourselves with the truth of the Word of God. We might refer to this as "pulling ourselves up by the bootstraps." David wrote many Psalms while he was suffering. He was honest about his feelings and complaints as he poured them out to the Lord. Encouraging ourselves doesn't mean denial of the pain, but it does mean that after we face the pain, we lift ourselves up with Scripture. Listen to David's honesty about the reality he was experiencing:

> "Hear my cry for mercy as I call to you for help...." Psalm 28:2
> "My soul is in anguish. How long, O Lord, how long?" Psalm 6:3
> "O Lord, how many are my foes! How many rise up against me!" Psalm 3:1
> "Save me, O God, for the waters have come up to my neck. I sink in the miry depths, where there is no foothold. I have come into the deep waters; the floods engulf me." Psalm 69:1-2
> Now listen to how David lifts himself up using words based on what he knew about God:
> "For great is your love, higher than the heavens; your faithfulness reaches to the skies. Be exalted, O God, above the heavens, and let your glory be over all the earth." Psalm 108:4-5
> "The Lord is my light and my salvation – whom shall I fear? The Lord is the stronghold of my life – of whom shall I be afraid?" Psalm 27:1

> "The Lord is my strength and my shield; my heart trusts in him and I am helped. My heart leaps for joy and I will give thanks to him in song." Psalm 28:7
>
> "You are forgiving and good, O Lord, abounding in love to all who call to you." Psalm 86:5

Even as I read the verses about God's love and faithfulness, good feelings are rising up inside of me and I feel encouraged. It is amazing how words affect our feelings and emotions. Isaiah 51:9 says, "Clothe yourself with strength." We can clothe ourselves with strength by the words we say about the truth of God. When we speak the truths of the Bible, God uses His Word to strengthen us.

Equally, we can strip ourselves of strength and hope by the negative words we use. If David would have limited his words to negativity and complaints, he would have lost hope. Because he was willing to recognize God's faithfulness and say what he believed, he was strengthened during his tough experiences.

OBSTACLES TO THE PROMISED LAND

When God was about to lead the Israelites into the land He had promised to give them (Numbers chapter 13), there were two reports from the twelve spies who went to explore the land. Of the group of men that went into the land, only Joshua and Caleb brought a good report. In verse 30 they said, "We should go up and take possession of the land, for we can certainly do it." The rest of the group said exactly the opposite in verse 31, "We can't attack those people, they are stronger than we are." The ten spies then went around to all the Israelites and spread a bad report about the land they had explored. The power of the negative words was enough to destroy the faith of the entire Israelite community.

Because of their unbelief, God did not allow the Israelites to enter the Promised Land. It would take a lot of confidence in God to possess the land and the people refused to walk in faith. Forty years later, when that generation had died, God led a new generation into Canaan (the Promised Land). Only two people from the original group, Joshua and Caleb, were permitted to enter the land.

Are we missing out on God's blessings because of unbelief? If we were to list the reasons for our unbelief, I believe that negative words, pessimistic talk, complaining, and grumbling will be somewhere on the list for each of us.

The source of our words

Negative words are the fruit of unbelief. Doubt, fear, and unbelief are reflected in the words we speak. We can tell a lot about a person by how he or she talks. The Bible tells us in Matthew 15:18 that the words that come out of a person's mouth flow from the heart. Luke 6:45 tells us, "…out of the overflow of the heart the mouth speaks."

James chapter 3 (as we saw earlier) prompts us to consider, "Can both fresh water and salt water flow from the same spring? My brothers and sisters, can a fig tree bear olives, or a grapevine bear figs? Neither can a salt spring produce fresh water." He explains that it is impossible to physically produce something other than what is in the root of the tree or the source of the water. Likewise, it is absurd to think that nice words will come from a heart that contains hate and ugliness. Our words are going to correspond to what is inside of our hearts.

We cannot go to church and praise God and then talk about someone behind his or her back after we leave the service. We should not be inconsistent in our beliefs and words. James 1:26 says, "If anyone considers himself religious and yet does not keep a tight rein on his tongue, he deceives himself, and his religion is worthless."

The Holy Spirit's control

The passage in James also says that no man can tame the tongue. So where does that leave us? Is this an impossible tool/weapon in each of us that can't be controlled?   The key words in that phrase are "no man." It's true, we cannot control this powerful and influential small bit in our mouths. But the Holy Spirit can!

The rudder on a ship is no good unless there is a captain at the helm. When the Bible says that no man can tame the tongue, it doesn't mean that it can't be done. It means that we must hand over the controls to the One who can tame the tongue. The only One who can is the Holy Spirit.

1 Peter 3:10 says, "Whoever would love life and see good days must keep his tongue from evil and his lips from deceitful speech."   How much regret can be avoided in our lives if we give the Holy Spirit control of our tongue?

CHAPTER 25

Anatomy of a Good Choice

Wake up!

Have you ever attended a church service where the sermon really touched your heart and brought you closer to the Lord? Then you talk with someone else who listened to the same sermon and he or she seems hardened to the Word. The person may comment that he or she didn't get anything out of it. The Word of God reveals what is in the heart. The soil of an open heart drinks in the living water of the Word. An unbelieving or prideful heart resists and the seeds of the Word bounce off the hard soil. What is inside of you is really determined by how you respond to the Word of God. Does it resonate with you or does it harden you? I've heard it said that the same sun that melts ice also hardens clay. It may be time to wake up and examine your heart. Are you open to submitting to God or are you still bent on continuing life in your own way? Do you want to learn how to make better choices?

Learning to make better choices is a process that we all must go through. I don't know of anyone who consistently makes excellent choices. Some people make better choices than others. We all are at different places in the learning process. The problem is when an individual does not recognize that he or she needs to change and instead continues making bad choices using the same pattern or mindset. Hopefully this book will serve as a wake-up call for those struggling with past choices and wondering how they can change.

BAD COMES NATURALLY — GOOD IS HARD WORK

Good choices are harder to make than bad choices. It is much more natural for us to follow our desires and seek immediate comfort and happiness. Since we can't see the future, it can be difficult to envision how our decisions will affect our lives later on. Good choices require self-discipline, discernment, wisdom, and sometimes, plain old courage!

Generally, bad things will just happen if there is nothing to oppose or change them. Bad things just happen naturally. We don't even have to choose to have bad things happen, they seem to come our way simply by virtue of living everyday life.

Good things such as health, success, happiness, joy, prosperity, wisdom, character, intelligence, and talent don't just happen without effort. We only have a chance at obtaining and maintaining these things if we live intentionally. On purpose we must resist temptation, resist making a bad choice, resist being negative, and resist being lazy. On purpose we must choose to be positive, patient, wise, prayerful, discerning, healthy, diligent, and hardworking.

THOUGHT PATTERNS

We may not instinctively be positive, patient, wise, and discerning. For some people, impulsiveness, negativity, and pessimism come naturally. Can we help what we think about? How do our thought patterns become so skewed that we make unbelievably bad choices?

Sometimes I look back and wonder how my thought patterns led me to make the choices I made. I wonder what sequence of wrong thoughts made me assess a situation totally differently than I would today if I were faced with the same set of circumstances. Possibly, I'm more mature, I've learned from my mistakes, or gained valuable experience. I've grown up, therefore my choices are better. Those insights contain an element of truth, but I don't think maturity necessarily makes us smarter. I don't believe mistakes guarantee that we'll do it right the next time, given the same situation. Smart choices are not a natural result of experiencing consequences of bad choices. I have made some poor choices as a mature Christian and as a person who has relatively good common sense. We must recognize that bad choices stem from wrong thinking somewhere in the depths of our complex minds.

RENEWING OUR MINDS... INTENTIONALLY

"I can't help how I think." But the Bible teaches that we *can* help how we think. In fact, the Bible is the source for alternative thoughts that we can choose to think. I call it "intentional" thinking. We seem to always have tapes playing in our heads of thoughts that come from many different sources: our past, what we've learned, tradition, what others have poured into us, our experiences, etc. We may not even know our thought patterns are wrong until our bad experiences or results of our thought patterns cause us to suffer.

Years ago I learned through much pain that I thought wrongly about relationships. For example, I thought it was normal to be in an unhealthy relationship. I thought it was OK to love someone who didn't love me back. I thought living in emotional pain was normal. I thought it was fine not to call the other person to accountability. I thought God wanted me to suffer. I thought God didn't love me. I thought if I prayed hard enough God would give me what I asked for. Those tapes (or CD's for younger readers) played in my head and I believed they were true. I acted on them as if they were true. Even when I listened to a very wise counselor and began to learn healthier ways of thinking, I still didn't know how to change the old tapes that had played for years in my head. During this struggle, my common sense told me that in order to get rid of wrong thoughts, I would have to record over them. I needed to tape new thoughts! The Bible calls this "renewing our minds." I learned that the only way to renew my mind and learn better ways of thinking was to do it intentionally. It was not going to happen naturally or on its own. I would have to be purposeful about it.

How do we purify our "rotten" thoughts? The answer is very simple. We pour enough good thoughts into the pool of bad thoughts until the bad is diluted with the good. The bad is replaced with something else, good healthy ways of thinking. The bad is dulled and weakened by something better and stronger.

The Bible tells us in Colossians 3:2, "…set your hearts on things above…." Hebrews 3:1 tells us to "fix" our thoughts on Jesus. Paul says in Romans 12:2 that we are to be transformed by the renewing of our mind. So in order to set our minds, fix our thoughts, and renew our minds, we need to be intentional. We need to train ourselves to think right.

Choosing to think right

OK, let's get practical. How can we be more intentional about how we think? How can we change our thoughts? It sounds great to say we should replace bad thought patterns with healthy ones, but in real daily life – how do we do that? First of all, we must make a decision to begin to do what we need to do. Most actions that we take begin with a decision. So we turn and set our face in a new direction. It begins every morning when we wake up. That's when our habits kick in and we begin our day just like every day. Instead of doing what we do daily, waking up and falling immediately into our bad thought patterns, we intentionally choose to think differently. For example, someone wakes up and begins to face the day by thinking, "I hate my job, life is terrible, I don't want to get up…." The person can choose instead to think about the things listed in Philippians 4:8, "Finally brothers, whatever is true, whatever is noble, whatever is right, whatever is pure, whatever is lovely, whatever is admirable – if anything is excellent or praiseworthy – think about such things." Paul tells his readers to think on noble and excellent things. The person instead chooses to say the following: "Lord, thank you for my job. Help me today as I spend the day working. Fill me with your strength and help me to do your will today."

A while back I had an old car and I became very ready to replace it. I couldn't afford to buy a new car at that time so I was forced to continue to drive my old car. There were many times that I felt like complaining to myself with thoughts such as, "This car is ugly! I wish I had a new car. I'm so embarrassed to drive this car. When am I going to get rid of this car?" When those thoughts began to enter my mind, I would catch myself immediately and turn my mind in a different direction. I would purposely begin praying and thanking God for my car. I would think (on purpose), "I am so lucky to have this car! I am so thankful that my car runs well. I know that I'll be able to get a new car when the time is right." I forced myself to think these thoughts rather than complain. I did finally purchase another car that made me thrilled. I am so glad that I did not allow myself to become a bitter, complaining person but was thankful instead. It all boiled down to making an intentional choice, redirecting my natural thoughts and developing a pattern of thinking that would be beneficial to me. I am "training" myself to think positively rather than to think negatively. I am minimizing future regret by developing within myself a thankful heart rather than nurturing a grumbling, complaining attitude.

This is just a small example of how we can choose to steer our thoughts away from the natural direction they want to go. Our positive thoughts create better attitudes and condition our hearts to be kinder and more thankful. On a larger scale, our attitude about our past choices produces thoughts that create happiness and satisfaction or unhappiness and regret. We can't stay in the mire of regret if we are thinking right. Right thinking can steer our lives in a whole new direction.

The Bible teaches that God does not honor a grumbling, complaining, murmuring person. He wants us to have our eyes open to all the blessings around us and be thankful, even in the midst of difficult circumstances. With a thankful heart, we show God that we trust Him to help us and take care of our situation. God cares more about who we are becoming than what we are complaining about.

God will renew our minds through the power of His Word. When we study and meditate on Scripture and begin to align our thoughts and actions to God's Word, our minds begin to change. When our thoughts change and become better, we make better choices.

The investment view of life

When I began researching and studying more about regret and choices, I began to see how "unintentional" I had been in many of the choices of my past. I was overcome with the realization that I never really "decided" to do many of the important things that I had done. I took turns in life without going through a decision-making process. During my dating years, if the opportunity presented itself to date a certain man and I wanted to go out with him, I would. If I didn't want to go out with him, I wouldn't. I don't remember ever evaluating what it would *mean* to my life if I dated this man. I lived for what I wanted or believed was right at that time. I thought my options were "yes, I'll do this" or "no, I don't want to do this." I never considered that there was a third option, "What's *ahead* for me if I do or don't do this?" or "Is this the *best* thing for my life?" I didn't realize that with each decision I was actually making an investment in my future. One date, one step didn't seem like a big deal. Looking back, I see how each step, however small, was actually an investment in something bigger. I operated with a short view rather than a long view of life.

Another name for the long view could be the "investment view" of life. If we have some money to invest in the stock market, we will probably be very careful which stock we choose. One important concern would be NOT to lose the money we have invested. Our ultimate goal would be to earn a good return on our investment. We would research the stock and make sure that we check the stock history, consider the economy and world market, study the industry for trends, and then make a final choice. We (hopefully) would not buy the stock just because we felt good about it that day. We also (hopefully) would not disregard the stock just because we felt that it would be better not to invest in it. We would base our decision on research and a little bit of good, old-fashioned common sense. With the stock market we know we have an option called, "if I choose to do this, what can I expect?"

Why don't we exercise that option in other decisions? Why do so many of us simply do what is in front of us without going through a decision-making process? Whether we realize it or not, each small decision we make is an investment in our future. We are investing with one date, one crime, one purchase, one mean word, one encouraging word, one hour helping, and one hour wasted. Tomorrow we will live out the result of today's choices.

Evaluate how you make decisions – big picture vs. small picture

Please take the quiz after reading the following paragraph:

You are in a room on the second floor of a house. Although there is a faint smell of smoke, there is no sign of fire in the room you are in. You believe there might be a fire somewhere in the house but there is no fire in the room upstairs so you aren't sure. The room is comfortable and appears as usual except for the faint smell of smoke.

Will you…

a. *Flee the house*
b. *Stay where you are until the fire and smoke reach the room and finally convince you that the house is burning*

This appears to be a simple quiz with an obvious answer. But I would like to propose that if the scenario above were a different life situation, some of us might get the answer wrong. It is the difference between making a decision based on the big picture vs. the small picture. Many of life's regrets are a result of making a decision based on the comfort of the small room in the burning house. We ignore the smell of smoke and stay put unless and until we are convinced that there's no hope, the house is burning down.

A woman is in a relationship with a man, she is in a comfortable room with only a faint smell of smoke. But if she examines the overall picture, she sees that the house is going down and she needs to get out. The problem comes in when the woman begins to justify staying because of the comfort of the room. She ignores the bigger picture for the immediate but temporary comfort.

Practical decision-making

Much regret could be prevented if we applied practical common sense to big decisions that we face. In spite of the fact that many of my life's decisions were made on an emotional level, I actually made several major decisions in my life using a very practical method. For decisions such as buying or selling a house, taking a job or starting a business, I have used the pro/con worksheet. This method helped me to set aside the emotions that blurred the process so that I could see the facts clearly.

I recommend laying out all of the pertinent factors affecting the decision on a piece of paper or on the computer screen. It is so helpful to see the facts, in black and white, in front of us where we can't deny or gloss over them. This is a great way to gather the information that we will need to consider. No feelings, no emotions, just facts! After I have the list completed, I circle the items on the list that rise to the top of importance. For example, when I was ready to purchase a home I was deciding between two options. I created a sheet of paper for each home. I began to list all of the pros and cons. I circled the facts that were important such as location, school district, and price. I was amazed at how the answer was right in front of me as I saw the facts thoroughly listed.

Typically when making these lists, I also go a step further. On the con side of the list, I place a big star next to any "deal breakers." A deal breaker is a factor that you know you can't live with. For example, if you are evaluating a dating relationship and the con side states that the person has a "bad temper," that might get a star if that is something you feel breaks off all possibilities for the future of the relationship. Years ago I created the pro/con list for a dating relationship and circled all of the facts that were of concern to me. Then I starred the "deal breakers," the things that I knew in my heart I could not live with. There were 13 circles (on the con side) and six stars! Of course, I could have spared myself some heartache if I would have created my pro/con list at the beginning of the relationship, before regret surfaced. I realized that my emotions had blurred my ability to identify the deal breakers until I saw them listed on paper.

Although this may not be a foolproof method of making a big decision, it certainly is a practical way to see what the wise choice would be. I have found that making the wisest choice in a situation is the choice God would have me make!

Covering our choices with prayer

We need to be diligent in covering all of our decisions with prayer. When we pray, we invite God into our decisions. Prayer helps us become submissive to God's will and tempers our strong desires. Many times when we are faced with a fork in the road, deep inside we have a desire for one of the roads. Prayer helps us be willing to follow God even if He leads us down a more difficult path.

Sometimes we are faced with multiple options. We don't know which way to go unless we pray for God's will to prevail and for discernment to see the way. When I pray for God's will and wisdom to do what He wants, I am much more confident as I assess my options. Sometimes God is gracious and closes or opens a door, making the decision clear. But for those times when things are not quite as clear, I stay close to God through prayer and studying His Word. Psalm 119:105 says, "Your word is a lamp to my feet and a light for my path." God always gives us enough light to shine over our steps so that we can see where we are going. He may not shine the light on the entire path to our future, but we can see what the next step should be. God gives us the light we need for each step in the right direction.

A future with less regret

Last week I finally got a new pair of glasses. A year ago I went to the eye doctor and he gave me a prescription for distance vision. At that time, I chose not to buy new glasses, deciding instead to hold off and wait until it was absolutely necessary. I don't like wearing glasses and have always felt constrained by the feel of the plastic frame on my face. So after experiencing daily headaches and pushing off the inevitable as long as I could, I returned to the eye doctor for an examination. After the eye test, he said firmly, "You are going to have to face it, give in and wear glasses for distance vision." So I replied, "I guess I have to surrender, finally." I gave in and ordered a pair of glasses. Immediately after putting on the new glasses, everything was clear and crisp! I've been wearing them for five days and everywhere I look things are focused and I don't have to squint anymore. It wasn't until I put the glasses on that I learned just how out of focus things were. The glasses are my new best friend. I had no idea how much my eyes were straining during the day. And, best of all, I haven't had a headache since I started using the new glasses. Now, when I put them on, I feel a sense of freedom that I didn't have before.

Do I like wearing the plastic frames on my face? Not really, but I love being able to see clearly everywhere I turn. I am enjoying feeling good without the daily headache looming over me. I now realize how blurry everything used to be around me.

I ASK MYSELF THE FOLLOWING QUESTIONS:
Am I willing to give up the freedom of not wearing glasses for the ability to see clearly?

Which is really more constraining, wearing or not wearing the glasses?

Where is my true freedom, in seeing things clearly or in getting daily headaches?

Why am I compelled to allow pain to dictate my choice?

YOU MAY COME UP WITH QUESTIONS OF YOUR OWN:
Which is true freedom, the freedom to eat what you want or the constraint of watching the calories?

Do you prefer to be free from diabetes or eat all the sugar you want?

Is the freedom to smoke better than being free of lung cancer?

Is the freedom to have sex with whomever you please better than being free from a sexually transmitted disease?

Is the freedom to have an abortion more valuable than being free of the guilt?

You are free to avoid God, or do you prefer the freedom of being His child?

Are you willing to choose the constraint of self-discipline for a better life?

THE TRUTH WILL SET US FREE

There are two types of freedom. One is the freedom to do whatever we please in the moment we are pleased to do it. No one can stop us and we don't like rules that tell us we can't do it. Great! God gave us freedom. But we are not free from the consequences of those choices to do whatever it is we want to do. Unfortunately, bad choices bring pain and consequences.

The other type of freedom is what comes when we do exercise restraint, effectively following the "rules." We experience a different kind of freedom. We are free from the consequences and the guilt and shame that come with making a bad choice. We don't experience the sick feeling of regret that envelops us when we wish we would have done things differently while we had the chance. Which type of freedom is really true freedom?

Jesus said, "If you hold to my teaching, you are really my disciples. Then you will know the truth and the truth will set you free." (John 8:31)

We value our freedom. We will not give it up without a fight. Many people will never give up their freedom to indulge their flesh and live whatever way they want regardless of what the Bible teaches. Some people eventually surrender to the Lord because the pain of doing things their own way has brought them to their knees. Eventually we come to understand that in giving up our freedom to live our own way we are gaining the freedom that Jesus provides. True freedom is living in relationship with the Lord, without guilt, shame, or regret.

If only we could get so comfortable with our freedom in Christ that we disdain the voice of the world suggesting that true freedom is in doing whatever we want to do. The world shouts, "Don't read the Bible, don't put your glasses on! You don't want anyone telling you what to do. You are free! You won't enjoy the constraints that Christianity requires."

I don't think we know how blurry and unfocused our lives actually are until we look through the clear, crisp lens of Scripture. Mistakes, pain, and regret bring on a fog and we think we see clearly but we have no idea what we're missing. It's not until the pain pushes its way into our lives that we finally say, "I wonder if a new pair of glasses would help?"

When good choices cause regret

Making good choices doesn't provide a guarantee that we will not experience pain at some point in our journey. It is much more probable that life will go better for us when we make good, wise choices, but it is not a guarantee that regret will not surface.

Those of us who are alive and living on planet earth are like boats trying to navigate in one body of water. Other people's choices may create waves that cause our boat to start heading in a direction we don't want to go or even cause our boat to rock so much that it threatens to capsize.

There may be many choices we have made in our lives that we wish would have provided different results. Even if we make consistently good and healthy choices, we are still at the mercy of the actions of others. Thus, regret threatens to seep into our lives even when we believe we chose well.

The innate problem with all choices is that we can't see or predict the future. If we could, we would choose according to what the future is revealing or warning against. No, we are all given a certain amount of information with which to make our choices, so we must do the best we can and seek God's guidance.

The problem of regret that surfaces from making good choices is very unique. We know we made a good choice yet suffering was the result. This causes a certain measure of fear as we face the reality that our lives are not completely in our control. If I can make a good choice and life doesn't reward me, then what else can I do?

I was driving down the freeway and noticed on the opposite side going in the other direction the traffic appeared to be backed up for a long distance. Something caused an accident and there were two cars on the side of the road along with police cars and an ambulance. I don't know what split-second decision took place that caused the accident. Maybe the driver of one car tried to change lanes and didn't see the other car in the next lane and they collided. What amazed me was how one small decision by one driver was now affecting the lives of hundreds of other drivers on the freeway behind him. One of the people in the traffic jam might have missed an appointment and another driver might have missed a dinner that was planned. Another might have missed an airplane and vacation plans were disrupted.

Even when we come to the point of making good and healthy choices, feeling like life is really under control, someone else makes a choice that can turn our world upside down.

Good choices change us

Our choices and our response to the choices that other people make will shape, develop, and change us. Do we want to become bitter, angry, and resentful? Or do we want to become more understanding, forgiving, and patient? Our attitude, thoughts, and actions influence the type of people we are becoming, whether we are dealing with regret from our own bad choices or choices others have made that affect us. We can choose to be intentional in our thinking, changing our natural thought patterns. On purpose we can strive toward becoming better by renewing our minds with the Word of God.

Whether or not we are rewarded for our good choices, we still must answer the question, "Do I want to become the person God created me to be?"

CHAPTER 26

The Best Answer for Regret

"For the Son of Man came to seek and to save what was lost."

Luke 19:10

180 DEGREES

GOD INTERVENED IN MY LIFE through the intercessory prayer of my mother. When she saw the road I was on during my college years, she prayed that I would have a Christian roommate. Just weeks before I graduated, a student knocked on my door and asked if she could live with me. I invited her in and agreed to let her move in for the remainder of the semester. Soon after Kim moved in, she opened the Bible and asked if we could read a passage and talk about it. She challenged me with Scripture about the way I was living. She invited me to attend church with her and I began the journey back to my Christian roots. After I graduated I learned that my mother had prayed and God heard her prayer. (Intercessory prayer is powerful!)

This event in my life eventually led to the one choice that is at the top of wise decisions that I have ever made: my decision to completely and wholeheartedly turn my life over to the Lord. I remember that it came down to one simple choice, one simple week, in my young simple life. I was 25 years old and had been attending church weekly, listening and learning about the Lord. But each Friday and Saturday night, I went out with my friends to do the usual: go out to the bars and drink. Finally, I felt "stuck" and unhappy enough to force myself to call the office of the church where I was attending. I requested an appointment with the pastor for the coming week. The secretary stated that the pastor was busy and could see me the following week. I cried out desperately, "I need to see him now!" (Yes, at times I could be a little dramatic!) So she granted me an appointment with one of the associate pastors the next day.

In Pastor Dave's office, I explained how I attended church regularly and questioned him as to why I was still living the way I did while I was in college. Why was I still going out and drinking with my friends and why was I still so unhappy? Why was I feeling that life was empty and why couldn't I feel God anywhere? He answered simply, "That's easy, you have one foot in church and one foot in the world. You must make a choice. Who is Lord of your life?"

So there it was, a fork in the road. Decision-time. I remember vividly sitting in my car, just about to leave the parking lot and saying aloud matter-of-factly, "Well, if it's that simple, then I choose Jesus." I looked down at the piece of paper that Pastor Dave gave me with the address of a Bible Study group that met every Friday night. So I made a "simple" decision. I would not go out with my friends for the usual activities on the coming Friday night; rather, I would try this Bible Study. One degree off my normal path. One degree that turned into a 180-degree life change.

When I entered the home of the Bible Study, I was amazed to meet young people who actually talked about the Bible on Friday nights. They were socializing, listening to music, and having fun! There were two young men playing Christian music on their guitars (I had no idea there even was such a thing as Christian music other than a church hymnal). A new world opened up to me. I knew in my heart I would never go back to my usual Friday night activities.

Since that day 30 years ago, the Lord has changed me and I have grown in my relationship with Him. Over the years, I have regularly attended Bible Studies, listened to Christian music, prayed, fasted, and studied. I have led many study groups, read countless Christian books, learned from wise Bible teachers, written Christian articles, served on church committees, and have clung to Jesus as most important in my life.

"Why then…," you may ask, "…did you make so many mistakes? Why didn't things go more smoothly for you? Why didn't life turn out the way you had hoped? How did your path get riddled with so many thorns, rocks, and potholes?"

A short answer: the loooooong sanctification process

My husband and I were sitting in church recently and there was a man and his son sitting a few pews ahead. During the entire service the little boy ran up and down the pews, grabbing pencils and other items. The father did not discipline his son and it didn't seem to really bother him that the boy was running around. After the service, my husband asked me, "What would make a man not discipline his son?" Without hesitation I answered almost flippantly, "It's proof that just because you're a Christian doesn't mean you're smart!"

I believe that quick answer was just sitting on the edge of my tongue, ready to come out at the most convenient opportunity. I had been writing on the subject of regret and it occurred to me that my book may stir up some Christian critics. I could almost hear their comments, "Christians don't need a book on regret, they shouldn't regret anything. Christians trust the Lord, they don't have regrets. Don't focus on regret, forget the past." I would respond the same way to those comments, "Just because you're a Christian doesn't mean you're smart!"

Many people who turn to the Lord for salvation are men and women who are hurting. They have tried resolving the issues of life in their own strength with no good results. Finally willing to surrender their own wills, they submit to God on His terms. They are people with problems and they need healing. Many physical, emotional, and social factors influence our personalities and emotional makeup.

Patterns, habits, traditions, experience, environment, DNA, and many other contributing elements weave together to form a complex tapestry of thoughts, beliefs, and ways of choosing. Many people may have thought, as I did, that by becoming a Believer, problems would disappear. God would make life easier and lead me down happy paths. Why doesn't this philosophy seem to work?

When repentance takes place in a human heart and the Holy Spirit comes to indwell the Believer, He begins the process of sanctification. God uses the process, along with a sharp set of pruning shears, to teach us, change us, and develop us into being what He desires us to be. We are taught through His Word to seek wisdom, knowledge, and many counselors. While we are growing and learning, we are still bound for mistakes that threaten to plant seeds of regret in our lives.

I stand by the statement that rolled so quickly off my tongue. Just because we are Christians doesn't make us suddenly wise in every aspect of life, preventing us from doing foolish things. We are saved, not necessarily smart! Because we are not naturally smart and wise, the Bible encourages us to seek wisdom above all things. Here are a few exhortations from Proverbs:

> "Blessed is the man who finds wisdom, the man who gains understanding...." Proverbs 3:13
> "Get wisdom, get understanding; do not forget my words or swerve from them." Proverbs 4:5
> "Wisdom is supreme; therefore get wisdom. Though it cost you all you have, get understanding." Proverbs 4:7
> "How much better to get wisdom than gold, to choose understanding rather than silver!" Proverbs 16:16

There are many other verses that teach us to love wisdom, seek wisdom, and pray for wisdom. It is not an automatic gift that fills our mind on the day we are saved. No, it is a result of the sanctification process, growth, prayer, and seeking wisdom.

LEARNING TO BE A STEWARD

I've come a long way from that day when I made that 180-degree choice. Through the help of the Holy Spirit, in-depth study of the Bible, and listening to wise pastors, I have learned how to strain forward rather than looking back to the past. I have learned how to seek wisdom regarding my life situations. God's pruning shears have been sharp and painful in my life but I seek to submit to my loving Father.

There is one passage in the Bible that compels me to continue to evaluate my life and take responsibility for my choices. The passage is a parable told by Jesus and is found in Matthew 25:14-30. It is the parable about stewardship of what God has given us.

We have all heard variations of this parable, sometimes even with a human twist. The twisted version might sound something like, "just do it, go for it, go for the gusto, make the most out of life, grab every opportunity, you only live once, live it up!" But in this parable, Jesus teaches us clearly that what we have is entrusted to us by God and that we are responsible to *Him* for what we do with it. In other words, while we are alive on earth we own nothing but are temporary stewards of what actually belongs to God.

In teaching about the Kingdom of God, Jesus tells the story of a man who entrusted his property to three of his servants. The first thing we notice in the parable is that the master gave the three individuals a different amount, according to each servant's ability. The master entrusted his property to the hands of each servant. The one who received five talents of money invested wisely and doubled the amount. The second man invested the two talents he received and also doubled the amount. The third man dug a hole in the ground and buried his master's money. When the master returned, the first two men were eager to see him and report the good news that they had increased what the master had entrusted to them. Indeed, the master was so happy due to the increase and the wise investment of the two servants that he promised to place even more under each of their care.

The third servant was not eager to see his master. He began his report by blaming the master, claiming he was a hard man and accusing him of wrongdoing. He then admitted that he was afraid and, therefore, hid the money in the ground. When he returned the property, the master called him wicked and lazy. He basically said, "If you really believe what you just said about me, why wouldn't you have at least deposited the money in the bank to earn interest?" In other words, "Why didn't you try to do even that little bit to please me rather than nothing at all?" This third servant was considered worthless and thrown outside into the darkness.

The same thing was required of each servant regardless of how much he had under his care. Each was charged with taking wise care of the master's property. Faithfulness in the use of his talents was required of each servant. Laziness and indifference to the master's property was the basis for condemnation of the third servant. We also see that the master's response and reward system was the same for each servant, regardless of how much he had to manage. If he managed the property well, the master gave him more. If he hid the property in fear and did nothing at all, the master took away even the little that the servant had.

This parable is a clear reminder that all we have belongs to the Lord. When we leave this earth, we take none of it with us. Our gifts, talents, abilities, belongings, families, and property all belong to the Lord and we are simply (temporary) stewards. When I dwell on these words, I inevitably feel humbled and repentant at the selfish or careless way I've handled what belongs to God. I ask for forgiveness and long to honor Him by learning what pleases Him and glorify Him with what He has entrusted to me.

You may feel the same way when you consider this truth about stewardship. You may ask, "Where is the good news?" **The good news is in God's mercy!** As long as we have life in us and time left on this earth, there is an opportunity to be a good steward with whatever we have in our hands at the moment. This is good news for anyone living with regret about how they have managed their lives up to this point. God does not want us to look backward and live in the mire of regret. God's desire is to redeem His people, fill us with the Holy Spirit, and enable us to do His work at every point in our lives.

LOSING WHAT WAS ENTRUSTED TO US

What if someone has arrived at the point in life where he or she has lost everything? What if a person has lost all the property that he once managed or wasted his gifts, talents, and abilities throughout a lifetime of foolish living? Is there any hope in this situation? God's Word teaches that there is always hope for the Believer who seeks the Lord.

One of my favorite stories in the Bible is found in 2 Kings 4:1-7. This is not a parable, but a true story about the widow of a man who worked with Elisha the prophet. The woman sought out Elisha and told him that her husband had died. One of his creditors was going to come and take away her two sons as slaves in order to repay the debt. First her husband died and now she was faced with losing the rest of her family.

The widow approached Elisha because she felt that she had no hope at all. She could not see how she could remedy this dire situation herself. She needed a miracle, so she went to the one person who she had seen do many miracles. Elisha didn't ask her how she ended up in this mess. He didn't ask her to explain how her husband got into debt. Instead, he asked her to think of what she might have in her house. You can almost hear her desperation as she explains that she has nothing at all in the house, then mentions the little bit of oil that she has left. Elisha told her to go around and ask all of her neighbors for empty jars. He encouraged her to collect as many jars as possible. He instructed her to pour the oil into each jar and to fill all of them.

I have studied this passage many times over the years and each time I marvel at the loving way God deals with his people. Why wouldn't Elisha just send the widow home and give her the miracle of a pile of money in the corner of her house? Because God wanted to increase her faith and involve her in the process of recovery. (This is a great principle that is true for all of us.) In other words, God wanted the widow to actively participate in His plan for her healing and increase her faith in Him during the process. He doesn't just feel sorry for people and give them whatever it takes to make them feel better.

God wants changed people. He wants Believers who have faith in Him. If we don't understand this about God, we'll have a pity party, feel sorry for ourselves, and wonder why God doesn't come immediately to our rescue.

When God involves us in His plan, the level of our faith directly impacts the greatness of the outcome. Elisha gave this widow an opportunity to exercise her faith and have an impact on the process of healing. If it were me, I am ashamed to say that I probably would have questioned Elisha a little more. I might have asked why I should collect multiple empty jars when I only have a little bit of oil. I might have complained and reminded Elisha of the seriousness of the matter. But the widow didn't question Elisha at all, she simply obeyed and let her faith take over. She even got her sons involved in her journey of faith and obedience. They went to all of their neighbors and collected as many jars as they could. She began pouring oil into each jar and one by one, they were filling up. What a miracle!

God took the little bit of oil and increased it so that it filled all of her empty jars. Her faith never ran out. Even when all of the jars were full, she still told her son to bring her more jars. He replied that there were no more jars left. Then the oil stopped flowing. God's supply went as far as her faith and obedience. Even then, with a houseful of jars of oil, she didn't presume anything but sought God's will by visiting again with Elisha. She reported to him what God had done and he gave her further instructions. Elisha told her to sell the oil and pay the debts. Then he said that she and her sons could live on what was left. God gave her a purpose, a business, and a job to do! She could choose to sit home and do nothing with the resources God had given her, or she could wake up every day and actively participate in God's plan. God used practical means, along with a wonderful miracle, to engage the widow, increase her faith, and redeem her situation. By obedience to God through Elisha's instructions, she received a chance to be a steward over what God had provided her.

If you are in a hopeless situation, God does not want you to live in regret, looking back and dwelling on how you got there. The first thing to evaluate is not how much you don't have but what it is that you do have. What you have at this point in your life is likely what God will choose to work with. You may say that your circumstances are worse than the widow's situation because you don't have anything. You may be in prison and have no belongings. You may be in a hospital bed and have no ability to actually "do" anything. You may be elderly and your talents, energy, and resources have ebbed away.

Did you notice that what the widow had in her house was oil? I believe that God wanted this true story included in His Word as a physical example of a deeper spiritual truth. Throughout Scripture, oil represents the Holy Spirit. As Believers, we have the Holy Spirit dwelling inside of us. Therefore, if you are a Believer, you cannot truthfully say that you have nothing at all. If you have no possessions or abilities (most of us have some of each), as a Christian, you have the oil of the Spirit residing on the inside.

"Well, what can I do with the Holy Spirit?" The answer I have for you is the same as the answer I would have given the widow if she would have come to me saying all she had was a little bit of oil and creditors were bearing down on her. I would answer, "I don't know!" I would add though, "I'm sure God will come up with something!" I don't know what the answer is for your particular situation. What I do know is that you need to seek the Lord with all of your heart and He will guide you.

God can use each of us no matter where we are in life, even those who are behind bars or in a nursing home. We are still stewards of what is currently being entrusted to us in our small world, whether it is possessions or just a few drops of oil. A little oil can go a long way depending on the measure of our faith. A prisoner seeking to be a good steward of the little bit he has in his care can pray for the prisoner in the cell next to him. What a gift to that prisoner next door who does not have even a little bit of oil. An elderly woman who can't move unless someone places her in a wheelchair can be a witness to the nurse. She can be a light in a place that may be very dark to others. Yes, a few drops of oil can fill as many jars as we can gather.

It's time to follow

If you feel that you do not have the Holy Spirit residing inside of you, that you have not made a commitment to the Lord Jesus and that you are not yet a Believer, now is the time to make that decision. Some of you may be thinking, "I'll commit after I get my act together. I'll give myself to the Lord after I clean up the mess I've made of my life. I'll get better and then I'll follow Christ." Jesus says just the opposite. He tells us to follow Him and then we'll get better! The call of Jesus is simple and straightforward. In fact, it is two words only: **Follow Me.**

In Matthew 9:9, Jesus passed by a tax collector named Matthew sitting in his tax collector booth and said to him, "Follow me." He and His disciples had dinner at Matthew's house along with many other tax collectors and sinners. Tax collectors of that day were not highly regarded. As a matter of fact, they were hated. They were Jews who were contracted by the Roman government to collect taxes among their people. They were to pay Rome the tax and they could keep whatever else they charged for themselves. They had a reputation for stealing and extortion.

When Jesus was having dinner with the tax collectors, the Pharisees criticized Him and questioned why He would eat with tax collectors and sinners. Jesus responded by stating that it is not the healthy who need a doctor but the sick. He said that He came not to call the righteous but to call sinners. Jesus did not wait for Matthew to change before He called him to follow. He called Matthew to follow Him and Matthew responded by eagerly listening and learning what Jesus had to teach him. Matthew eventually became one of the twelve disciples of Jesus. How did he become a disciple? By following Jesus!

The call to follow is a call to Jesus – not to a set of rules or a denomination. It's a relationship, a personal attachment. When Jesus told Matthew to follow Him, He was inviting him into a relationship. That's what Christianity is all about. It's about a relationship with Jesus. He is the best answer for regret!

PART 4

Living Your Life Purpose

CHAPTER 27

God's Purpose

Did I miss Main Street?

I've heard it said many times, "God has a plan for your life." When I was a new Christian, I found comfort and hope in those words. I wanted to believe that God had a specific plan for me, who I would marry, where I would live, and what career I would pursue. I spent much of my time trying to determine God's plan for me. It was very important to me to follow the Lord and pray about every decision, especially big decisions. I tried to sift my thought processes through my understanding of the Bible and the "wisdom" I had in my twenties. Needless to say, both were somewhat limited.

When I met with a pastor at my young age while struggling through my first divorce, he was very matter-of-fact and stated that I had "missed Main Street." I was devastated. After all of my searching and desiring to do God's will, how could I be on the wrong street? I reasoned that if that were true, then I was in the wrong house, wrong city, wrong state, wrong friends, wrong life! I believed I had to redirect, somehow get on the "right" path, get back on track, and find my way to that narrow strip of roadway called God's Plan for My Life.

It was a strange feeling to consider on one hand that I could be traveling on the wrong road, yet on the other hand I was experiencing all of the blessings God had placed in my life while I was on that road. God had blessed me with a wonderful daughter, a loving family of in-laws, great friends, a wise counselor, a beautiful house, new experiences, and most of all, free time to attend Bible Studies and grow in my walk with the Lord. In spite of the fact that I was struggling through a divorce, I did not feel regret for my marriage or the life that flourished from it. I married the man I loved and I didn't believe that a failed relationship meant it never should have happened.

THE PRINCIPLES OF THE PROMISE OF ROMANS 8:28

I dug into God's Word and began to study Romans 8:28, which says, "And we know that in all things God works for the good of those who love him, who have been called according to his purpose."

"All things" means "all things." Bad choices, bad habits, a bad economy, sickness, pain, and accidents fall under the category of "all things." I thank God that all things include sin, failures, and mistakes.

God works together all things into the dimensions of our lives, including circumstances and relationships. He essentially weaves sin, choices, and circumstances into the fabric of our lives, like a master weaver carefully creating a masterpiece out of the multitude and variety of threads. Some threads match, some contrast, some are frayed, and some are smooth. But rather than allow the weaving of the fabric of life to follow its natural course and create a messy, frayed, mix of threads, God intertwines each strand carefully to design a beautiful tapestry that only the expert weaver could produce.

"For the good" means it will become valuable, positive, pleasing, or favorable. "Good" even sometimes means, excellent, marvelous, or great. When God weaves those raunchy fibers in with the beautiful threads, the end result is going to be something for which we will be thankful.

"Those who love him" is our part. This entire verse is a conditional promise from God's Word. It is not an automatic principle that works in every life regardless of the individual's belief or understanding of the Lord. This promise is for those who *love* the Lord. We don't just say we love Him with words but we show it by abiding with Him. We show our love for Him by following His teachings, growing in intimacy with Him through prayer, studying His Word, and serving Him.

The final phrase of the verse is God's part, "who have been called according to his purpose." I love God (seek and abide with Him) and I am called to fulfill His purpose on earth. Wow – God has a purpose for me! A purpose is so much bigger, greater, and more important than a plan! The purpose is the goal, the vision, the target. A plan is important but the purpose is the *reason* for the plan. The purpose is the desired result, the plan is the way to get there. The plan can be adjusted as factors change and new things develop. But the vision stays the same. So, what God is telling us with this treasure-filled verse is that He has a plan for each of us and He can use all of the circumstances and choices of our lives to accomplish His purpose. God can achieve His purpose in spite of our problems, sin, and mistakes. We seek to know the plan; God is focused on the purpose. We want to hit the mark of the details and figure out the plan, but we should be focused on God's purpose, which is greater than all of our mistakes and life problems.

Plan	Purpose
Tactical details	Big picture
Path toward the mission	Mission
Roadmap	Goal
Can be adjusted if necessary	Vision
Focused on tasks	Desired result

Young people should embrace Romans 8:28 as they experience disappointments in their lives. Later they will be able to look back and see evidence that God has indeed worked all things together for their good. Placing hope in the truth of this verse can help a person be positive about his or her current life situation. Rather than live in depression and regret because life isn't bringing them what they desire, young people can be secure knowing that God will use their life situation for their ultimate good.

My sister, Linda, was single for many years. She longed to be married, have children, and a home of her own. The way she explains it, she could have easily fallen into a deep depression and sense of regret for the lost years and broken dreams. She could have ended up on medication for depression. She also could have become bitter and hopeless for the rest of her life.

She still says today that Romans 8:28 is her favorite verse in the Bible. It provided her hope that God had a plan and a purpose for her. She says that the verse is the "key to life!" Linda is now married with two wonderful stepchildren. She wouldn't trade her family for anything in the world. She looks back on her 20+ years of singleness as a time of great growth in her life both professionally and spiritually. Yes, God used her singleness, the thing that caused her many years of loneliness, to draw her close to Him and teach her to depend on Him.

God's ultimate purpose for our lives

God created us for His glory (Isaiah 43:7) and His purpose is to make us more like Christ. God can, and will, use everything in our lives to accomplish His ultimate purpose for us. As we become more like Christ, we will love, obey, serve, and live out the individual plan that He has for each one of us. He wants us to grow in relationship with Him and be a good steward of the gifts, talents, and abilities that He gave us, following the guidance of the Holy Spirit.

If each of us had a Mission Statement, it should reflect this great truth. Our personal Mission Statement should read something like this:

To follow Jesus, serve where I am called, and be a faithful steward of all God has entrusted to me; through the guidance of the Holy Spirit I consistently pursue a life of obedience and fulfillment of His will with the ultimate purpose of glorifying God in every way.

I have come to realize that while I'm busy trying to figure everything out, God is busy with His vision of making me more like Christ. While I'm focusing on the roadmap, God is calling me to a relationship with Him.

GOD'S PURPOSE DOESN'T GET LOST IN THE DETOURS

Do you feel that you have lost your purpose in life because of the mistakes you have made and the detours you have taken? God's purpose for each of us can be accomplished at any point in our journey. When we let go of the fog of regrets, we are able to see and understand more clearly what God's purpose is for our lives. As long as we are willing to follow Him, we can be on the road to accomplish His great purpose for our lives. In other words, His purpose is the same, no matter what the detours are on the road we are traveling. I find that truly amazing!

What if I wouldn't have made mistakes that led to regret? If I would have made different choices, I believe my calling would remain the same: to help others by sharing what God has done for me. The subject matter of my books might have been different, but my calling would have been the same.

If someone would have asked me when I was in my twenties what type of person I would like to become, I would have answered the following: I would like to be hardworking, kind, happy, helpful, spiritually strong, and emotionally healthy. If I were asked what I would like to do in my life, I would have responded with the following: I would like to own a business, be a mother, be a wife, write books, and serve the Lord. I would want to use my talents and abilities for something greater than a paycheck. I would desire to make a difference for the Lord in some way that counts.

Now that I am in my fifties, I can look back and assess whether my desires have truly been accomplished. I believe they have! It's been a long road with detours, potholes, and pain, but somehow God has helped me to become what He wants me to be. Am I all the way there yet? No, but I'm still heading in the right direction and seeking with all my heart to follow the One who guides my steps. Have I done all that I long to do yet? No, but I'm pressing forward to use my abilities to contribute to God's work on earth. How did God mold me into being a spiritually strong and emotionally healthy person in spite of all of my past mistakes? By miraculously working all things for good in my life and calling me according to His purpose.

Because of God's promise in Romans 8:28, I can still live out the call on my life, in spite of my past choices, or quite possibly, because of my past choices. God is so good to allow broken, sinful people to be vessels of His power and goodness. He not only permits the brokenness in our lives, but uses it to reach others and help heal their brokenness. Will you allow God to use your pain to minister to others and give them hope? God has a unique plan for your life, in spite of your mess! Your part is to follow the Lord and be willing to look past your circumstances. If you do, God will not let your pain go to waste.

Is it possible to miss God's plan, purpose, and will?

Romans 8:28 is the glimmer of hope for those whose detours have taken them miles away from God's good and perfect will for their lives. The fact that God promises to bring good out of our mistakes is a wonderful gift that takes the sting out of regret.

Is it possible to miss out on God's plan for your life? I'm sorry to say, the answer is: Absolutely. Millions of people miss out every day on the plan and purpose for each of their lives. We have free will, remember?

Because of our free will and ability to make choices, it is quite possible and very common for people to miss out on the following:

- Being a faithful steward of the blessings in my life, home, family, money, job
- Using the gifts, talents, and abilities that God has given uniquely to me
- Developing a close relationship with God through Jesus Christ
- Serving in the way that God desired and planned that I would serve Him on earth
- Learning about God through studying the Bible
- Overcoming life's problems through faith and trust in God
- Accomplishing something for God that would cause Him to say "Well done good and faithful servant"

- Helping others find hope for their lives by teaching them about Jesus
- Sharing with people in need so that I can make their lives better
- Receiving from God the blessings that He desires for my life
- Worshipping God and thanking Him for all He has done for me
- Giving financially to churches and missionaries who work to fulfill Jesus' commission to make disciples and take the Gospel into all the nations
- Doing what I was created to do, living out the specific calling on my life

The list could go on and on about what we miss out on if we choose to ignore a relationship with God.

Never too late

God's ultimate purpose for you and me is to become like Jesus. Is it ever too late to become like Jesus? Does God ever throw up His hands and say, "Forget this guy, he is too far gone!"

You may miss out on many blessings when your life is filled with bad choices. But we are all included in "whoever" in these verses:

> "All those the Father gives to me will come to me, and **whoever** comes to me I will never drive away."   John 6:37
> "The world and its desires pass away, but the man who **[whoever]** does the will of God lives forever."   1 John 2:17
> "**Whoever** believes in Him shall not perish but have eternal life."   John 3:16
> "Then Jesus declared, I am the bread of life. He who **[whoever]** comes to me will never go hungry, and he who **[whoever]** believes in me will never be thirsty."   John 6:35
> "I am the light of the world. **Whoever** follows me will never walk in darkness, but will have the light of life."   John 8:12

"Whoever" sounds great until we read:

> "If anyone would come after me, he must deny himself and take up his cross daily and follow me. For **whoever** wants to save his life will lose it, but **whoever** loses his life for me will save it." Luke 9:23-24

There are two facts to consider for those who want to start today to live out God's purpose for his or her life:
It's never too late, God is waiting for you.
    You must follow Him, give up your life in exchange for the life God has for you.

What you receive in return:
For the rest of your days on earth, God will guide you into His purpose for your life.
    Eternal life, where God's work of making you more like Christ is ultimately and fully accomplished.

Does Main Street exist?

It wasn't until much later in my life that I realized that the pastor who told me that I "missed Main Street" was wrong. I have learned that Main Street is a myth rather than a missed reality. My "Main Street" was simply an outline of my ideal life plan, filled with wispy dreams that blew away like feathers with the strong winds of bad choices. God, in His mercy, has a purpose for me that is unshaken by mistakes and regret. His plan for me has unfolded daily in my close walk with Him. His faithfulness is like an oak tree, unmoved by winds and storms.

CHAPTER 28

God's Will

DOES GOD HAVE A SPECIFIC WILL FOR ME?

The Bible teaches that God is in control and does have a distinct plan for each of His children. Paul tells us in Romans chapter 12 that we are all different and have unique functions in the body of Christ. He compares the body of Christ to a human body, made of up of many members, each having its own function within the body. We each have different gifts and God will use them to accomplish His work on earth if we submit to His Lordship and individual will for our lives.

If you are skeptical that the Creator of the universe knows you personally and has a unique plan for your life, meditate on the Scripture verses below:

> "…and he determined the times set for them and the exact places where they should live. God did this so that men would seek him and perhaps reach out for him and find him, though he is not far from each one of us." Acts 17:26-27
>
> "All the days ordained for me were written in your book before one of them came to be." Psalm 139:16
>
> "For I know the plans I have for you, declares the Lord, plans to prosper you and not to harm you, plans to give you hope and a future." Jeremiah 29:11
>
> "In his heart a man plans his course but the Lord establishes his steps." Proverbs 16:9

"I know, O Lord, that a man's life is not his own; it is not for man to direct his steps." Jeremiah 10:23

God entrusted each of us with gifts, talents, abilities, and opportunities. God calls us to use the gifts He has given us to work toward accomplishing His purpose in this world. Our free will creates interference. At times we use our gifts to honor God and promote His Kingdom and at times we waste what He has given us on our own selfish desires.

God wants to reveal His will to us. He does not want us to flounder through life in the dark, not understanding what He expects of us. That is why He provides His instruction book, the Bible, to teach us. He also gives us the gift of the Holy Spirit to guide us. And we have His gift of prayer so that we can be in direct communication with Him any time.

GOD'S WILL IS REVEALED IN HIS WORD

The Holy Spirit lives within Believers, prompting, guiding, and leading us to do God's will. Philippians 2:13 says, "...for it is God who works in you to will and to act according to his good purpose." Daily obedience is the key to following God's plan for our lives.

I have asked these questions and I hear many people ask the following:

"What is God's will for me?"

"How do I find God's will?"

"How do I know if my decision is God's will?"

"How can I be sure of God's will?"

The surprising thing is that many people are not persistent in digging into God's Word where much of His will is revealed and written for us. I believe that avoiding the study of God's Word is due to a lack of faith in who God is and how He has chosen to communicate to us. If we really believed that God has revealed Himself to mankind through His Word, we would read it. If we really trusted what Scripture says about itself, that it is

God-breathed and inspired by the Holy Spirit, we would take it seriously. We would want to know what God has to say if we truly desired to nurture intimacy in our relationship with Him.

Imagine one of your family members serving in the military overseas. If you were only allowed written communication, you would write letters and you would be thrilled to receive letters. When letters arrived at your home, you would not stack them on a shelf unopened and say, "What nice letters, I wonder what David has to say?" No, you would read and re-read each letter, hungering for intimacy with the person you love who is temporarily physically distant from you.

GOD'S WORD IS A LIGHT TO OUR PATH

There are aspects of God's specific will for us that He reveals only as we walk closely with Him. When we do study Scripture and begin to follow what we learn and understand to be God's will, He promises to shine more light on our path. God will not give us more light until we obey the light we have already been given. Psalm 119:105 says, "Your word is a lamp to my feet and a light for my path." If we walk outside in the dark, carrying a lantern, we need the light to shine on our feet, not on the path way up ahead. We need to see what is immediately in front of us so that we don't stumble or trip. God's Word is a lamp for our feet, each step of the way. And God will give us more light for the next step as we obey the light we already have. God grants us deeper understanding as we are faithful to what we do understand. The principle in Scripture is this: If we are faithful in little things, God will bless us with more. If we are obedient to what God has already revealed, He will take the veil off of our hearts and reveal more of Himself and His plan to us.

Here are a few verses regarding God's will that shed light on our path:

- It is God's will that we should be sanctified. 1 Thessalonians 4:3
- We are to be joyful, pray continually, and give thanks in all circumstances. 1 Thessalonians 5:18

- It is God's will that we be transformed by the renewing of our minds. Romans 12:2
- We are to keep His commands and live righteously. Psalm 119:10, Ephesians 4:24
- God calls us to be a witness for Christ. Acts 1:8
- God wants us to glorify Him and bring honor to Him in all we do. Psalm 86:12
- God desires that we come to the knowledge of His truth. Colossians 1:9
- We are to serve others and be good stewards of our gifts and abilities. 1 Peter 4:10

God's specific plan for your life

God created each of us with unique gifts, according to His grace. God has a will, a purpose, and plan for each person who walks with Him. Listed in the previous section are verses that express God's will for every Believer. This section focuses on God's individual plan for you and for me. In addition to guiding our steps according to His overall will for Believers, the Holy Spirit lays on each of our hearts a calling, an individual purpose that we are able to sense strongly when we walk closely with the Lord. If someone says, "I have a passion to be a doctor. I can't explain it, I have always been interested in medicine and want to be a doctor." I would conclude that it's a strong possibility that the Lord is calling that person to become a doctor. But this is only one piece of the puzzle in determining God's specific will for your life. Desire, passion, talent, and ability can be good indicators of God's leading.

Sometimes God calls us to a specific assignment and we feel the burden on our heart to accomplish it. When Moses was called to lead the Israelites out of Egypt, he was afraid and didn't feel that he was capable of doing it. So how did Moses know that he was supposed to lead the Israelites out of Egypt? Because God spoke directly to him, calling Moses to accomplish His will. God doesn't speak out loud to us in the same way because we now have His written Word. But I believe that He still speaks loud and clear through His Word and the Holy Spirit in calling individuals to specific tasks.

Moses was the best candidate for the job of leading the Israelites out of slavery in Egypt. Consider how God had prepared him for this assignment: Moses grew up in Pharaoh's household, fled Egypt, and then spent 40 years shepherding a flock of sheep in the wilderness. Moses eventually was called by God to shepherd His flock through the wilderness for 40 years.

Sometimes when we are in a desert, God is actually using that hard time as a training ground for His plan for us. I spent many years dealing with singleness, broken relationships, and regret. Now, as I write on the subject of regret, I am using all of my experience in the "field" to reach out and pull others from the mire of regret. I wasn't aware at the time that I was actually in boot camp training!

So God has a will for me… how do I find it?

We want a roadmap; God wants a relationship. Wouldn't it be nice to have a blueprint, a map, a list of details for us to follow to know we are in God's perfect will? There is no such roadmap. If God provided a map, we would follow it without seeking the relationship that God wants us to have with Him. Even without an easy-to-read roadmap, the Bible does reveal many things that are God's will for us. If we want to know God's will for us individually, we must understand *how* He reveals His will to His people. Here are principles that help us understand how God directs us into His specific plan for our lives:

1. Prayer is our intimate connection to God. Seeking God's will begins with prayer and must be covered continually with prayer.
2. God's will is revealed in His Word. God won't ask you to do something that is contrary to His Word.
3. God speaks through spiritual counselors and mentors. Mature spiritual counselors have wisdom that can help us make good decisions.

4. God speaks through opportunities. As we explore opportunities, God will direct us.
5. God directs us through circumstances. God uses our circumstances in many ways to lead us. He opens and closes doors to help guide us.
6. God uses our desires, talents, and abilities. They are gifts from Him to help direct us to our role in the body of Christ.
7. The Holy Spirit leads us with promptings in our hearts. He lives within us and impresses things upon our hearts that make us say, "I know that I know that I know."
8. God gives us His peace. We have an inner peace and assurance that a decision is God's will.

Roadblocks to finding God's will

If we stubbornly cling to our desires, we are probably not open to seeking God's will. We already know what we want; therefore, our hearts are closed to what God has to say. If that is the case, we must take a step back in our decision-making process and be open to learning what God's will is on the matter. Unfortunately, we can be stubborn! Our stubbornness and selfishness cause roadblocks to finding God's will.

On the other hand, we may be so open and pliable that we can be influenced and pressured by other people. If we are seeking God's will, we need to be careful when listening to opinions of others, especially if they are not praying about our specific situation. Taking counsel from other people should be a deliberate choice on our part, choosing wise Christians who are as interested in God's will for our lives as we are. Seeking guidance and counsel from wise, mature Believers is Scriptural. What we don't want is to be tossed about by the waves of peer pressure.

Sin also can keep us from being able to discern the will of God for our lives. If we are harboring a sinful lifestyle or a known specific sin in our lives, God may not take us forward until we are willing to repent. When we want God to guide our path, yet feel stuck and can't see the way forward, we need to clear the path of the rubble of sin that keeps tripping us on our journey. Is it possible that God can't lead us on the right path if we are insistent on traveling down the wrong path?

Learning God's Word is crucial to being able to be guided into His will. The less we know what the Bible has to say, the more we will rely on our own understanding and reasoning. We can measure our thoughts and desires against God's Word as we seek His will in our circumstances.

Patience in seeking God's will

It's so easy to become impatient when we want to know God's will. I have learned that while I'm waiting on answers and guidance from God, He is working in so many ways that relate to my situation. Maybe He is changing a person, working in circumstances, or preparing a new path in order to bring about His will in my life. Because there are so many unseen factors, trusting God gives me the patience to wait until His will is revealed to me. I have come to realize that if His will isn't clear, it may be because I am exactly where He wants me today, doing just what I am being called to do in this moment. I keep searching, praying, and maintaining readiness to move ahead when the Spirit leads.

Searching through the mystery of God's will

God's will, purpose, and plan are complex, sometimes clear and sometimes filled with mystery. But we shouldn't be discouraged or disheartened just because it's mysterious. It's the mystery that keeps us searching and following Him closely! It's the mystery that forces us to continually pray and diligently seek the Lord.

Just to simplify it, let's distinguish God's purpose, will, and plan:

God's purpose for me: To become more like Christ and glorify God in all I do.

God's will for me: To be a good steward of the gifts, talents, and abilities that He gave me, grow spiritually in my relationship with Him, follow the guidance of the Holy Spirit, and serve Him as I am led and as I am able.

God's specific calling or plan for my life: God's individual assignment, plan, or task for me is revealed as I walk closely with Him and study His Word, being led by the Spirit and trusting His guidance. God's calling on the Apostle Paul's life was to preach God's Word to the Gentiles. God's plan for me at this point in my life (I believe) is to share with others what God has taught me.   God's assignment for you is a task He may be laying on your heart right now. As you follow Him, He will open the door of opportunity for you to accomplish it!

CHAPTER 29

Raw Material Crafted into Instruments

RAW MATERIAL DOESN'T SOUND VERY good, does it? If we were to define it we might say it is useless material that may have the potential to become something helpful, productive, or fruitful. Sometimes raw material is ugly and doesn't look at all like the finished product. Raw material, in the hands of an expert craftsman, can become something completely different, useful, fruitful, effective, and profitable.

Isaiah 64:8 says, "Yet you, Lord, are our Father. We are the clay, you are the potter; we are all the work of your hand." We are raw material in God's hands and if we submit to Him, He will change us into what He wants us to be. In fact, God specializes in remaking us, reworking the raw material of our talents, abilities, and personality into instruments that can be used for His purpose and glory.

Jesus changed Peter's name from Simon to "Stone" or "Rock." Can you imagine? Peter had some good raw material for Jesus to work with but he was hardly a rock when Jesus changed his name. Jesus saw the raw material in Peter and began working in his life. Peter was a burly fisherman who was impetuous and outspoken and bold. When Jesus was finished training Peter and using his mistakes and experiences to refine him, Peter had changed into a rock! He became submissive, humble, and courageous. Most of all, Peter became the leader of the Christian Church in the first 12 chapters of Acts. There are now churches, cathedrals, and cities named after Peter, not to mention countless baby boys!

Is this the same Peter who walked on the water but began to sink due to lack of faith? The same Peter to whom Jesus said, "Get thee behind me Satan!" And finally, the same Peter who actually denied the Lord three times on the very night Jesus needed him the most?

Jesus took the unbridled boldness of Peter and turned it into Godly courage that filled Peter when he preached. Acts 2:37 says that after hearing Peter preach, the people were "cut to the heart." Peter faced the Sanhedrin in Acts 5:29 after they had ordered him not to preach and Peter boldly proclaimed that he chose to obey God rather than men.

Peter went on to write two Epistles in the Bible called 1st and 2nd Peter. He writes, "Humble yourselves, therefore, under the mighty hand of God, that he might lift you up in due time." (1 Peter 5:6) Peter was humbled and now teaches us to be humble. Peter teaches us to be "clear-minded and self-controlled" in 1 Peter 4:7. He learned through consequences of his impulsiveness to be self-controlled. In 2nd Peter 3:18 he says, "Grow in the grace and knowledge of our Lord and Savior Jesus Christ." He tells us to grow because he had to grow. We would not have these exhortations from Peter's life if he had not learned these lessons firsthand through his own mistakes.

God takes the raw material of our character, personalities, and talents and molds us into something better. He teaches us with His Word and refines us through our experiences. Do you think Peter was filled with regret after denying the Lord Jesus three times? Yes, he was, especially when the rooster crowed and he remembered the words Jesus had spoken to him earlier that evening. Regret forced him to go outside where he "wept bitterly." (I'm sure I would be filled with regret if the mistakes of my life were going to be recorded in the Bible for millions of people to read over the course of many centuries!)

There is no hint of regret after the resurrection when Jesus asked Peter three times, "Do you love me?" Peter confirmed his love for the Lord and Jesus said, "Follow me." Peter truly turned away from his regret and lived out God's purpose for his life. Regret was washed away with the forgiveness that he received. Jesus then commissioned Peter to go forward and feed His sheep. Peter obeyed and never turned back to his past again.

I imagine that Peter felt completely fulfilled, knowing that his personality and abilities were being used to accomplish a greater purpose and for the glory of the God he loved. He must have felt so loved by God because he was forgiven, changed, and given purposeful work to do.

Yes, regret adds some ugliness to our raw material, but God still sees what is inside of us that He can make into a beautiful, finished product! Our hearts are fulfilled when we allow God to take our raw material and change us into what He intends for us to be.

CHAPTER 30

The God of Second Chances

*"…he who began a good work in you will
carry it on to completion…."*

PHILIPPIANS 1:6

THANK GOD FOR SECOND CHANCES! God doesn't only give second chances – let's just say He gives chances – multiple chances! In my life, God has given me many chances to get things right. He doesn't just give a first chance and then a second chance as a back-up. No, God gives us chance after chance, while we live on earth, to press on in the area we are seeking victory.

Let's review some examples of those who received second chances from God:

Moses – He fled Egypt after committing murder while attempting to save the Hebrew people. God gave Moses another chance and called him to lead the Israelites out of Egyptian bondage.

Samson – After failing in his calling as judge of Israel, Samson lost his power and had his eyes plucked out by his enemies. He pleaded with the Lord to be with him and give him back his strength one more time. God listened and strengthened Samson to go on to a great victory over the enemies.

Peter – After cursing and denying the Lord three times, Jesus forgave Peter and enabled him to go on to be a great preacher and servant.

John Mark – After deserting the Apostle Paul, God gave Mark (also known as John Mark) a second chance to accompany the missionary, serve in the ministry, and write the Gospel of Mark.

Second chances for you and me

Years ago the teacher of my Sunday morning class was teaching on God's principle of second chances. I had been feeling somewhat hopeless about my future. I felt that I had missed my chance and had no idea how I was going to find the right road to begin to accomplish something for the Lord. I had always wanted to write and teach about God but when I got divorced once and then twice, I felt that I had lost my credibility. Who would listen to a failure teach about the things of God?

My teacher revealed something that I hadn't known about her. She got married as a young girl back in the late 1940's. The marriage fell apart shortly thereafter and she was divorced during a time when divorce was not common. She eventually remarried and raised a family. I had only known her as someone who had been married for over 40 years and who was a wonderful Bible teacher. After telling her story, she exclaimed, "Thank God He is a God of second chances!" That phrase lit a fire of hope within me. *Do you mean when you fail or miss out on your calling, dream, or purpose, God will actually give you another chance?*

God isn't finished with me yet

I have heard some preachers take the principle of second chances and turn it into a doctrine that promises another chance with health, wealth, and many other things. I think we need to be wise and understand that a principle is not the same as a promise. A principle is a general, fundamental truth. A promise is a declaration, intention, or commitment to fulfill something specific. The principle is this: God is a God of second chances. History proves that God has provided second chances to many of His people. God's character is one of granting chances to change and chances to become better. God isn't finished with us as long as we live on this side of Heaven!

He may not promise that your health will be turned around, your marriage will be restored, or that you will be released from prison. The second chance God wants to provide may not be another chance to make a different choice in the exact same matter in which we failed. **God's second chance is His open door to follow His will going forward with Him in the way that He leads.**

Isn't that the best second chance possible?

CHAPTER 31

Destiny

*"There is no greater discovery than seeing
God as the author of your destiny."*

RAVI ZACHARIAS

WE HEAR A LOT ABOUT destiny today. In fact, some teachers and motivational speakers make it sound like our destiny is under our control. They say that if we believe, press hard enough, and are determined to fight for our dreams, then we will be successful and reach our destiny.

But the actual definition of destiny is something quite different. The true meaning of the verb "to be destined" means to be set apart for a particular purpose, to be foreordained or predetermined, as by divine decree. The understanding is that destiny has been appointed beforehand, decided by God. It is wrapped up with God's will and purpose for each of our lives.

Reaching our destiny is fulfilling God's specific role or assignment that He is calling us to do. It is broader than doing God's will on a daily basis; it is the fulfillment of a specific calling. I think of destiny as a "destination." I seek God's specific will for my life and I purposefully obey what I already know to be His will as revealed in Scripture. As I do that, I believe I will fulfill the destiny that God created me to accomplish. Destiny is the result of following God's plan!

If it's true that destiny is chosen and determined by the God who created each of us, then we cannot make our destiny happen on our own. As we strive to learn and accomplish God's specific will for us every day, God's mysterious, invisible hand leads us to our unique assignment. King David was a shepherd boy that was destined to be king over Israel. Queen Esther was a humble Jewish girl who was destined to be Queen of Persia and be used by God to help save her people from annihilation.

Destiny is something that can't happen without God's powerful, unseen hand moving in the circumstances to lead us to our task. If it's not up to me, then what is my part?

- Follow the Lord daily with all my heart
- Pray about everything
- Make decisions that are in line with His will
- Nurture and strengthen the gifts, talents, and abilities that God has given me
- Do the best I can in all that is in front of me to do
- Watch for opportunities
- Keep my faith strong
- Repent of all known sin in my life
- Place all of my trust and hope in God
- Persevere as I press forward

We will not reach the destiny that God has designed for us unless we walk with God, abide in Him, and submit to His leading. God is the author of our destiny! He is the one who must lead us into His plan.

MISSING OUR DESTINY

There are clear examples in Scripture of people who missed out or lost their destiny because of sin and disobedience. King Saul, the first king of Israel, was chosen by God to reign over His people. Saul didn't choose himself and the Israelites didn't choose him. He was appointed by God to lead the Israelites and deliver them from the Philistines. Saul began to live out his destiny but eventually compromised and fell into disobedience. He could not and would not fulfill his destiny because of his disobedience. There are others in the Bible who had a destiny intended for them by God but because of selfishness and sin, missed out on the fulfillment of it.

What about our mistakes? Will we miss our destiny if we have made bad choices? Does repentance guarantee that we'll reach our destiny? The answer is in God's hands, but I believe we have a much greater chance of reaching our destiny if we submit to God, honor Him, and walk intimately with Him. There are examples in Scripture of individuals (King David, Jacob, Peter) who sinned greatly and yet fulfilled their destiny.

Why do some who have made mistakes miss out and some see the fulfillment of their destiny? The key is the state of our heart toward God. If you study the story of King Saul, he did not repent. He was sorry, that is clear. But he was sorry that he got caught in disobedience. He did not have a repentant heart. King David, on the other hand, had a heart for the Lord. When he recognized his sin, he turned back quickly and completely to God.

OUR TRUE DESTINY

As Christians, our ultimate destiny is to live with the Lord for all of eternity. We can't confuse our attempts to do wonderful things for God on earth with our ultimate, true destiny, which is to become more like Jesus and live with Him forever in Heaven. Too many people work so hard to make their dreams come true and strive hard after their "destiny." How many of those people miss God while they are working to make their dreams become a reality? Ultimately, God wants to accomplish one important thing in us as we live and work toward our earthly destiny. **God wants each of us to become more like Jesus.** All the destinies of all of God's people fall under this overarching goal.

Unfortunately, there are many people who believe that God exists to serve us and make us happy, successful, and fulfilled. They tend to "use" God as a means to their ends. When we have an attitude of "using" God as a means to accomplish our destiny, our focus is on ourselves and what God can do for us rather than maintaining our focus on God and what we can do for Him.

We all want the dreams in our hearts to become reality. The truth is, God does want to bless us – but we are to keep our eyes on Jesus, not place our desire for success above Him. Jesus says plainly in Matthew 6:33, "But seek first his kingdom and his righteousness and all these things will be given to you as well." We don't seek "these things" first; we seek God first, and "these things" will be given to us.

God has blessed me in ways I could have never imagined. He has guided me by His Word in spite of my failures and mistakes. But notice the subtle difference of God's Plan versus Man's Plan. Man strives to discover the secrets of finding ways to get all he can out of life. God wants us to seek Him first and He will guide us, bless us, and give us purpose.

When we understand that our true destiny is to become like Christ and spend eternity with Him in Heaven, then none of us needs to miss out on our ultimate destiny! Due to past choices or unfortunate circumstances, some may miss out on using their gifts, talents, and abilities for God's glory here on earth. But we do not have to miss the true destiny that God has for all those who trust in Him, an eternity with God in Heaven.

THE DESTINY OF JOSEPH

It's hard to study the subject of regret and destiny without using Joseph in Genesis chapters 37-50 as an example. The story of Joseph and his brothers presents many lessons on regret. Joseph's brothers hated him because he was favored by their father. They plotted to kill Joseph but decided instead to overpower him and sell him to traveling merchants. While Joseph was taken as a slave to Egypt, his brothers returned home and told their father that he had been killed by a wild animal. Imagine how Joseph must have felt that fateful day when his entire life changed. In the morning he was the favored of twelve sons, wearing a richly ornamented robe given to him by his father, and in the afternoon he was stripped of his robe and carried off in shackles to a faraway country by slave traders.

If anyone had reason to live in regret, Joseph certainly did. Regret could have filled his soul when he thought about the times he told his brothers about his dreams that he would rule over his family. Even his father rebuked him when he described his dream about the sun and moon and eleven stars bowing down to him. Each time he relayed his dreams to his brothers, they were filled with more anger until it developed into a strong enough hatred to make them want to kill their brother. Joseph received the brunt of his brothers' jealousy, bitterness, and anger. He was a victim, now heading toward a life of pain, suffering, and regret.

Unfortunately, the Scripture doesn't tell us exactly how Joseph felt, only how he acted and responded. Joseph clearly did not act out of regret. He was sold to Potiphar, one of Pharaoh's officials. The Bible tells us that "the Lord was with Joseph" and gave him success in everything he did. Joseph found favor in Potiphar's eyes and eventually was put in charge of the entire household. God blessed everything Potiphar had while it was under Joseph's care. Joseph had to learn a new language and transition into a foreign culture. He handled all of his responsibilities with integrity. I imagine he felt the presence and favor of God in all that he did. It is amazing that Joseph, in spite of his terrible suffering, *chose* to do his best in all of his responsibilities rather than be debilitated by anger and regret.

Because Joseph was handsome, his master's wife tried to proposition him. Joseph refused saying that his master trusted him with his whole house, so how could he "sin against God"? Eventually, she falsely accused Joseph of attacking her and Potiphar had Joseph put in prison. Again, Joseph's life took a 180-degree turn in one day. In the morning he was in charge of Potiphar's household and enjoying success and in the afternoon he was hauled off to prison under false accusation. But the Lord was with Joseph and granted him favor in the eyes of the prison warden. There is no record of Joseph complaining, weeping, or getting depressed. On the contrary, Joseph was put in charge of all of the prisoners and handled all of his duties successfully. We can surmise that the prison guard would not promote a negative, complaining person, rather someone he could trust to do things right. Joseph proved that even in terrible circumstances, he would not surrender to regret and depression.

During Joseph's time in prison, he was given the opportunity to interpret the dreams of two individuals who had worked for Pharaoh. God had given Joseph the ability to interpret dreams and now God brought him an opportunity to use the gift he had been given. If Joseph had been inward-focused and wallowing in regret, he would not have been sensitive to the needs of others around him. Instead, Joseph noticed that two prisoners were "dejected" and asked them why they were so sad. They explained that each had experienced very powerful dreams and didn't understand what their dreams signified. Joseph correctly interpreted them. One of the individuals was freed from prison and sent back to the palace to work for Pharaoh. Joseph asked the freed prisoner to remember him when he returned to his service as the Pharaoh's cupbearer. If the man would put in a good word for Joseph, maybe there was a possibility that he could be set free.

Two years passed and nothing happened. Again, Joseph could have been filled with remorse and anger. He helped someone and that person forgot about him completely. Yet there is no record of Joseph becoming angry or resentful. But later, Pharaoh had a dream and no one could interpret it. Finally, the cupbearer remembered Joseph and told Pharaoh about Joseph and how he had interpreted his dream correctly. That day, Pharaoh summoned for Joseph to interpret his dream. God gave Joseph the meaning of the dream and Pharaoh was so pleased that he promoted Joseph to second in command over the affairs of the entire land of Egypt! Now Joseph would have the opportunity to use all of the skills he had developed in Potiphar's house and in prison to manage something much greater.

God honors our good choices

Remember the brothers who sold Joseph into slavery? They enter back into the story in Genesis chapters 42-50. There was a great widespread famine in the land and Joseph's brothers traveled from Canaan to purchase food from Egypt. Because Joseph was second in command in Egypt and in charge of overseeing the buying and selling of food during the famine, his brothers ended up on his doorstep. The dreams that God gave Joseph when he was young were fulfilled. His family bowed down to him and Joseph would soon rule over them. When his brothers learned that Joseph was still alive and was in command over Egypt, they were filled with regret. They feared that Joseph would retaliate against them. But listen to how Joseph responded to them in Genesis 50:20, "You intended to harm me, but God intended it for good to accomplish what is now being done, the saving of many lives."

This is the attitude we should have in the face of huge disappointments. If we follow God in each step of our lives, making the choice not to live in regret, we will witness the fruition of God's activity in our lives. We will be able to say, "God intended all things for good in my life."

I don't believe Joseph would have fulfilled his destiny had he been filled with anger and regret during the hard years of his life. Instead, he was able to forgive his brothers and live out the calling on his life, in spite of the detours that his path took. In fact, it was the detours that got him to the place where God wanted him to be!

When we consider the following questions about Joseph's life, we can see many Scriptural truths come alive regarding regret, choices, destiny, and God's power:

Did Joseph have reason to experience regret?
Did God take away the free will of those involved in this story?
Would Joseph have been justified in retaliating against his brothers?
Did Joseph do the best he could in difficult life situations?
Did Joseph trust God in the detours of life?
Did the brothers succeed in thwarting God's plan for Joseph?

Was God sovereign in all of Joseph's affairs?
Did Joseph ultimately reach his destiny?
Is God sovereign in your life?
Do you believe God intends for good all that is happening in your life?
Will you trust God to accomplish His plan and purpose for your life?

CHAPTER 32

Conclusion – This Very Thing

REGRET. THE CHOICE THAT STEERED me in a new direction. The path that became filled with pain and consequences. God reached into my life and placed my regret into His mighty hand, using it as a powerful tool to prune me, change me, and make me more like Christ. He has turned my life path into a training ground, a boot camp to prepare me to help others and serve Him. The deepest longings of my heart have been fulfilled, in spite of the detours that threatened to turn my hopes and dreams into a desolate place, empty of happiness. Consequences of my choices have been turned into blessings that cause my heart to be filled with thankfulness. God has done this little by little, step by step, day by day, and year by year as I have followed Him. I am pressing forward, seeking to fulfill God's purpose for my life.

Jesus healed people, performed many miracles, and brought hope to hurting people. He taught them about the Kingdom of God. He even claimed to be equal with God. The disciples believed He was the promised Messiah. They followed Jesus and participated in His ministry for three years, watching, listening, and learning. They placed their faith in Him and believed in Him.

Just a few days earlier Jesus was welcomed into the city of Jerusalem as a king, with people laying their robes on the path where Jesus rode His donkey and waving palm branches to honor Him. But then Jesus was betrayed, arrested, and sentenced to death. It was all so unbelievable. Now there He was, hanging on the cross with a criminal on either side of Him. His head hung down with a crown of thorns that had been pressed into His brow, causing streams of blood to fall to the ground. Nails had been driven into His hands and feet. Not only was He dying, but He was dying by a shameful, cursed punishment reserved for criminals.

How could this happen? At the foot of the cross all hope was gone. As His followers looked up at Jesus suffering, they thought they were witnessing the worst thing, the end of their hope. They did not realize that what they thought was the end was really the beginning! The very thing that brought them crushing sadness and despair would soon bring them unbelievable joy and happiness. The cross that ended Jesus' life was actually the means by which God would save those who believe in Him. The cross itself would become the worldwide symbol of Christianity!

The people thought they were looking at pain and suffering but what they were really witnessing was the ultimate triumph of life over death. Jesus would rise from the grave three days later, demonstrating His power over sin and death and proving that every word He said was true. Imagine the joy that flooded the hearts of the disciples when the women reported the words of the angel at the tomb in Matthew 28:6, "He is not here; he has risen, just as he said." All hope was restored as the disciples were filled with faith again!

Isn't that just like our God? He turns pain and regret upside down. He overcomes the bad and works it into His good plan for us. He takes the impossible and makes it possible. This is God's way. Our regret feels impossible and unchangeable. But God sees it differently. The very thing we think is a problem is what God will use to free us, deliver us, and take us forward in our walk with Him.

The Israelites stood at the edge of the Red Sea, the dead end that left them face to face with their enemies. When they looked at the massive sea, they had no idea that their impossible problem would become the very solution that God would use for their deliverance. God would divide the water and open a passage through the impossibility. Not only that, He would crush their enemies with the same sea that He used to grant victory to His people.

When we consider the painful circumstances that were caused by our past choices, we can begin to view our regret through the lens of Scripture. We don't have to live in regret when we realize that God can use our suffering, pain, and mistakes to accomplish His purpose. The Master Weaver will weave our past into the fabric of our future. How can we have regret when God is ultimately in control?

INEVITABLE PAIN – INEVITABLE VICTORY

Jesus plainly said in John 16:33 that we will have trouble in this world. We should not be surprised when life throws suffering, problems, and pain as inconvenient rocks and potholes onto our path of life. After warning that we will have trouble, Jesus then said, "But take heart! I have overcome the world." Yes, we will have problems, *but* Jesus has overcome! Even if God doesn't cause our pain, He can still use it. Even if we have regret for choices that we should have never made, God can still use them for His glory. Therefore, we are able to come to the point of contentment and even happiness in the midst of our circumstances.

We must remember that God has a greater mission taking place on this earth than simply making each of us happy. His mission is to give life and healing to the poor and helpless. His mission is to grant us salvation and keep us from eternal separation from Him. It is miraculous how God uses pain and death to actually bring life and hope. That is why Paul could honestly claim that he rejoiced in his suffering… because he saw how God used it to breathe life into the Church. (Colossians 1:24) Paul even went as far as to say in the midst of being persecuted, shipwrecked, imprisoned, and beaten, "So then, death is at work in us, but life is at work in you." (2 Corinthians 4:12)

Through our pain and suffering from choices made in our lives, we can actually help push God's mission forward. What that means for you and for me is very simply this: how we handle our regret can give life and hope to someone else. When we suffer the consequences of wrong choices, rather than look inward and feel sorry for ourselves, we can look outward and focus on how God can use it to minister to others. We are, in reality, closest to God when we identify with Him through our suffering and allow Him to change us and use our suffering for His glory.

When I'm tempted to regret all of the years that I spent in struggle and loneliness, I focus on the fact that it was those years that gave me training for my life assignment today. At times, I want to look backward and change things that happened in my life, but God invites me to go forward and share what He has done for me. I've always had a desire to write a book and God has used my past to teach me what He wants me to write. Before calling me to write this book, God walked me through the regret in my life and proved to me that He is true to His Word. He works all things out for good in our lives if we walk with Him. God is faithful, even when I am not. God is faithful, even when you are not. God is faithful!

If I were given a choice to go back and change my past, would I do it? Would I accept an offer of going into my past to have the chance to make new choices? No... I would not change my past and give up the opportunity to effectively help another person who is struggling with regret. In fact, I am *grateful* for years of pain if it inspires others to hope. I have prayed for each person who picks up this book, reads it, takes it in, and works it out in his or her life. My prayer is that you experience the fulfillment of hope that turns regret into a shadow of the past.

When we fulfill the purpose for which God created us, our regret has no more power over us. Regret becomes a shadow, a powerless memory that no longer brings us pain as we see how God has used it to change us and strengthen us for His purpose.

I realize that the life situations that I regret have actually brought me healing. The things that I complain about are the very things that God is using to give me a purpose in my life. The life experiences that have caused me pain are the same things that God uses to heal, cleanse, bless me, and minister to others.

The regret that surfaces when we live out the consequences of our choices becomes the very thing that God uses powerfully in our lives. Could it be that your regret is the *very thing* that God uses as a tool in His mighty hand to accomplish His broader purpose in your life and in His world?

What a marvelous answer for regret!

Author's Note: What's next?

*"For God so loved the world that he gave his
one and only Son, that whoever believes in him
shall not perish but have eternal life."*

John 3:16

Steps toward a future free of regret

Now that you have read **Beyond Regret**, my hope is that you have a more thorough understanding of why we make mistakes, how God uses our past choices to change us, how we can prevent future regret, and the hope that God gives each of us to fulfill His purpose for our lives.   Possibly your response to reading this book is, "Yes, I understand and I have hope, but what can I do today to get started on a new path and keep my life moving forward?"

The first and most important step is to make sure you are in a right relationship with God through Jesus Christ.   Romans 10:9 says, "…if you confess with your mouth, 'Jesus is Lord,' and believe in your heart that God raised him from the dead, you will be saved."   When we truly repent and submit to His Lordship, Jesus promises to give us eternal life.

1. **Pray that God will forgive you of your sins.** You may use the following as a guide as you pray:

Dear Lord, I recognize that I am a sinner and that I need your forgiveness. Please forgive me of the sins of my past. I ask you to forgive me of all that I do that is against your will. I believe that Jesus paid the price for my sins and through Him I can come into your presence and be in right relationship with you. Please fill me with your Holy Spirit to guide me, counsel me, and lead me into righteousness. Thank you for saving me and giving me the promise of eternal life with you. In Jesus' Name, Amen

Jesus promised to send the Holy Spirit to those who belong to Him (John 14:15-17, John 16:7). The Bible tells us that when we receive the Holy Spirit, God sets His "seal of ownership" on us with a seal that can't be broken (2 Corinthians 1:22). We have the Holy Spirit living inside of us! God Himself has chosen to indwell Believers to guide, strengthen, counsel, and lead us through daily life. Because of this marvelous gift, we should choose to live in a way that doesn't grieve the Holy Spirit who seals us (Ephesians 4:30). Our changed life is evidence that the Holy Spirit is at work within us.

2. **Begin to study God's Word.** This is the way that God has chosen to reveal His truth to the world. Be nourished by His Word every day, learning more about God and seeking His will in your relationships and daily circumstances. The New International Version (NIV) is an easy-to-understand version for Bible study. Not studying the Bible is like planting seeds and not watering them. The study of God's Word is fundamental to Christian growth.
3. **Fellowship with other Believers by becoming part of a Bible-believing Church.** Small groups are also a good way to be strengthened as you learn more about your walk of faith.
4. **Pray daily!** Spend quiet time with the Lord and pray about everything that is on your heart. Listen for the Holy Spirit's guidance in your heart. Keep in close communication with God throughout the day.

5. **Choose to do things that honor the Lord, live a life that pleases Him, and resist the thoughts and activities that are contrary to His will.** Strain forward in your Christian walk, letting go of the past and what is behind. Be encouraged by what Paul says in Philippians 3:13-14, "...But this one thing I do: Forgetting what is behind and straining toward what is ahead, I press on toward the goal to win the prize for which God has called me heavenward in Christ Jesus."

As an author, I have sought to relay principles and Biblical examples of God's truth and how He works in our lives. Please seek professional help where you feel it is necessary for healing of deep personal issues such as addictions or abusive circumstances. As you work through your own personal life situations, pray for God to help you find healing for your past and the pain you may be suffering in the present. Ask Him to give you hope for a healthy future.

I pray that you will place your hope and trust in God and press forward through the power of the Holy Spirit. Be determined and intentional to live beyond regret as God leads you into His purpose for your life!

Laurie Driesen

www.ingramcontent.com/pod-product-compliance
Lightning Source LLC
Chambersburg PA
CBHW071305110426
42743CB00042B/1180